I0812994

POSTCARD HISTORY SERIES

East Contra Costa County

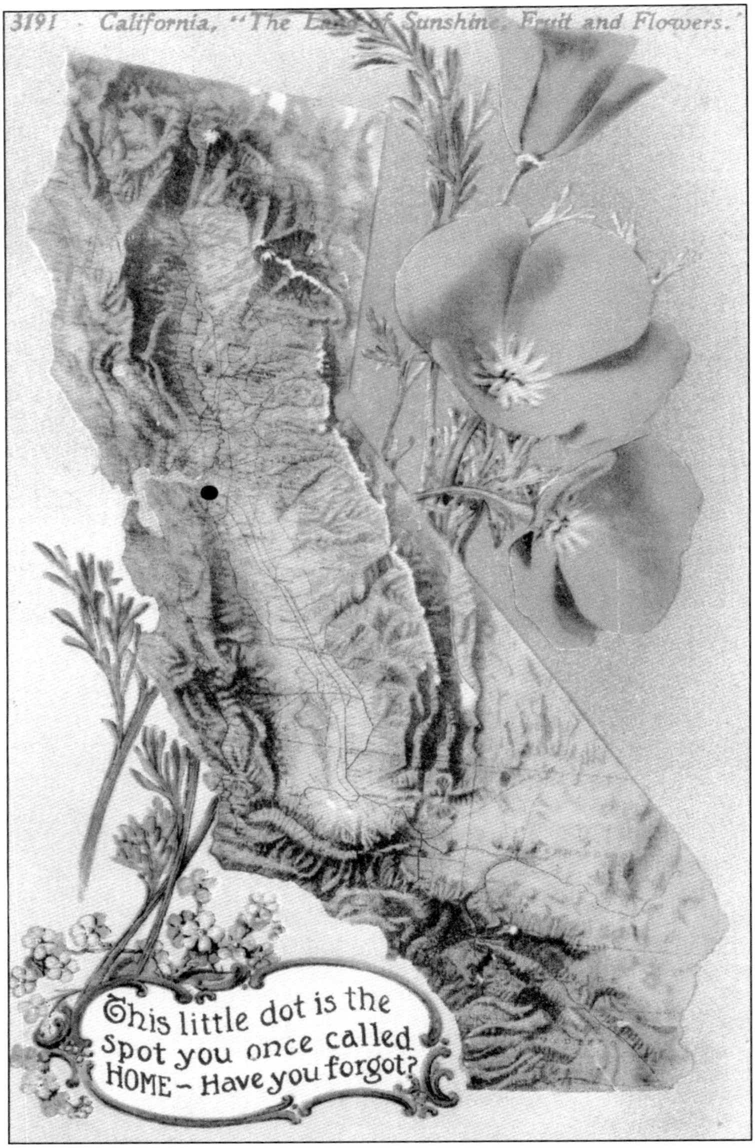

Relief postcard maps of the state of California were very popular in the early 20th century. This one features the state flower, the golden poppy, and blue forget-me-nots. Together they represent the state colors: blue and gold. The dot notes the location of east Contra Costa County.

On the Front Cover: A beautiful spring day in an almond orchard typifies the pastoral beauty of the rich Sacramento and San Joaquin River Delta. Almond, apricot, and cherry orchards in bloom are perhaps the most beautiful sights in the area. (All vintage postcard images provided for this book appear compliments of a private collector.)

On the Back Cover: The planned destination of the very first overland immigrant train to California is Dr. John Marsh's residence just west of present-day Brentwood. A sturdy group of men, one woman, and a daughter traversed the Sierra Nevada, arriving here in 1841. Marsh welcomes them to the Golden State.

POSTCARD HISTORY SERIES

East Contra Costa County

Carol A. Jensen
East Contra Costa Historical Society

ARCADIA PUBLISHING

ISBN 978-0-7385-4774-9

Published by Arcadia Publishing
Charleston, South Carolina

Printed in the United States of America

Library of Congress Control Number: 2007923837

For all general information contact Arcadia Publishing at:
Telephone 843-853-2070
Fax 843-853-0044
E-mail sales@arcadiapublishing.com
For customer service and orders:
Toll-Free 1-888-313-2665

Visit us on the Internet at www.arcadiapublishing.com

Dear R. L. J. and D. M. J.,
"Having a wonderful time. Wish you were here!"
Yours, C. A. J.

Contents

Acknowledgments		6
Introduction		7
1.	John Marsh Stone House	9
2.	Agriculture and Husbandry	17
3.	Civic Pride and Public Buildings	37
4.	Commercial Districts	53
5.	Domestic Life and Tranquility	67
6.	Country Schools and Education	81
7.	Recreation and Amusements	89
8.	Resort Life and Celebrity	105
Selected Reading		126
Index to Communities		127

ACKNOWLEDGMENTS

This book would not have been possible without Kathy Leighton and the resource room of the East Contra Costa Historical Society. The Charles Weeks Photograph and Postcard Collection was particularly invaluable. I am also indebted to the following organizations and their staff members: the Antiquarian Booksellers' Association of America, the Contra Costa History Center of Martinez, the John Marsh Historic Trust, and the Brentwood Public Library.

Warm appreciation goes to the following businesses for providing needed content: Pamela Munkelt, Country Tyme Gifts; Heidi Calvin, Not-Only-Baja; Diane Cross, the UPS Store; Union Cemetery District; the *Brentwood Press*; and Bethel Island Treasure Chest. Thanks also to Mark White, who shared his aunt Edna Hill's postcard collection and family reminiscences. Community leader John Gonzales rose to the occasion and provided two new Knightsen postcards. The Union Cemetery District Board of Directors created a new postcard honoring a member of the famous Donner Party just in time for inclusion in these pages. Many anecdotes were contributed from sources too numerous to list. I hope they are captured correctly. Thanks to all for sharing local histories. The errors and omissions in the writing are all mine.

Members of the San Francisco Bay Postcard Club (www.postcard.org) have been most generous in providing access to their personal collections. The officers of the club welcomed my inquiry and passed the research requests along to the membership. President and ephemera dealer Ed Herny and newsletter editor Lew Baer deserve particular note. My gratitude is extended particularly to club members Edmund Clausen of Oakland, Darleen Thorne of Cupertino, and Jack Hudson of Dublin. Alice van Ommeren and Ronald Chapman, both of Stockton, aided with wonderful early agriculture and farm equipment postcards. Thank you Robert Chandler for the new John Marsh house postcards. An anonymous Southern California collector provided real-photo postcards from the Brentwood district of Los Angeles. Thank you, Margaret Light, for your persistent search for an O. J. Simpson postcard from Brentwood, Los Angeles. As we say in reference to our neighbors to the south, "O. J. is from Brentwood and so am I." How confusing! Regrettably, there are no historic postcards available for the relatively new community of Discovery Bay.

Ephemera dealers are crucial to collecting. In this capacity, Ken Pragg, Ken and Dorothy Harrison, and Jeff Carr are indispensable. We rely on them to find and save "just the perfect card" for us. Thanks to Devon Weston, Arcadia Publishing acquisitions editor, for her interest in the growing communities in eastern Contra Costa County. The aid and patience of the irreplaceable Robert D. Haines Jr. cannot be overstated. Writing is impossible without an excellent and through copy editor. Marcy Protteau is a copy editor extraordinaire.

Please contact the author at the e-mail address Historian@ByronHotSprings.com if you can contribute to eastern Contra Costa County history with an oral history, family documents, letters, or ephemera.

INTRODUCTION

East Contra Costa County consists of the present communities of Brentwood, Byron, Knightsen, Oakley, Bethel Island, and Discovery Bay. All the communities are part of the Bay Area Rapid Transit District (BART) and considered part of the Greater San Francisco Bay Area. Transportation from San Francisco to Brentwood takes one and a half hours by personal automobile. Transportation by BART with transfer to bus from Bay Point easily takes over three hours. Culturally, east Contra Costa has been a community apart from the rest of the county as it emphasizes agriculture and recreational uses compared to the urban communities in the East Bay.

Historically the area included communities now remembered only by road signs, including Point of Timber, Borden Junction, Bixler, Orwood, and Marsh Landing. A series of islands reclaimed from the San Joaquin and Sacramento Delta are encompassed in "East County," including Jersey Island, Widby Island, Middleton Island, and Clifton Court. Discovery Bay is the newest community in the area threatening to consume original Byron in its suburban expansion. Byron Hot Springs, established in the 1860s, predates all the cities in the area and refuses to fade from physical or cultural memory. Plans are once more underway to restore this historic resort.

The area is changing physically, culturally, and environmentally. The delta was once the bread and fruit basket of the United States. Brentwood is now identified as the fastest growing community in the state of California according to the California Board of Realtors. Farmers are just as likely to "raise" eight houses to the acre instead of six tons of almonds to the acre. Commercial agriculture now equates with "U-pick" and boutique organic farms in the public mind. Gone are the Tilly Lewis, Heinz, and Hunts commercial fruit and vegetable cannery contracts. New suburban communities with residents employed outside the area pose new challenges to towns where employment was once exclusively seasonal agriculture or local shops.

East Contra Costa County attempts to capture a landscape fast receding from contemporary memory.

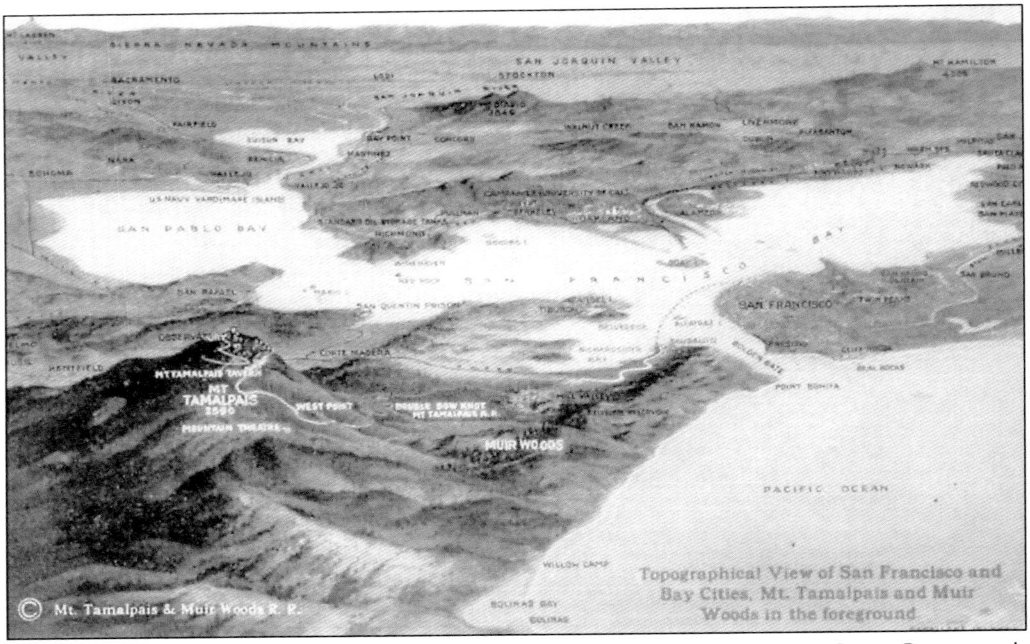

This aerial view of the Greater San Francisco Bay Area shows eastern Contra Costa County as it peaks behind Mount Diablo. Eastern Contra Costa County is located at the extreme eastern edge of the Bay Area within commuting distance to San Jose, Silicon Valley, and San Francisco.

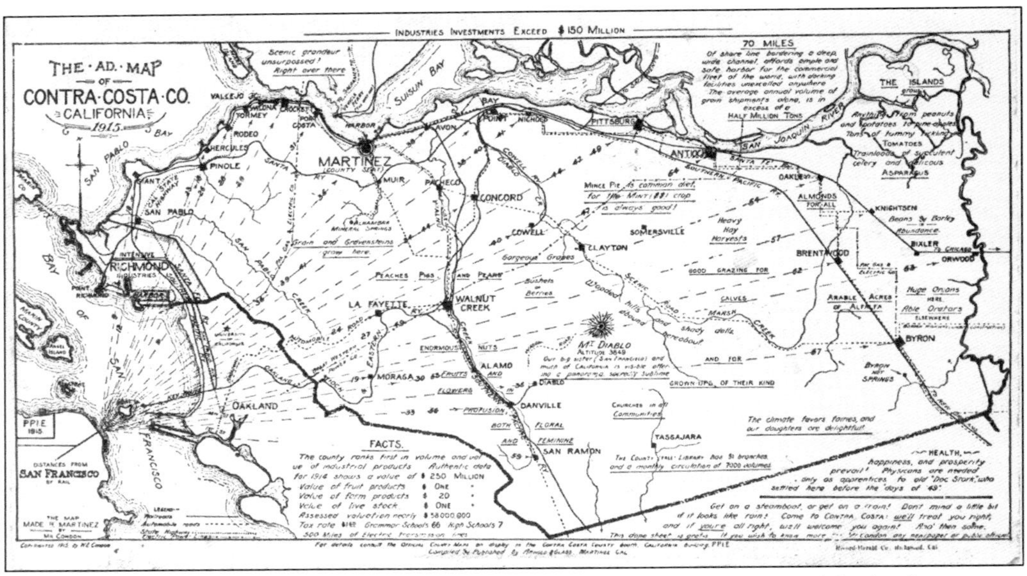

This Contra Costa advertising map notes all the current and past communities in the county, including the main agricultural products. The locations of Oakley, Knightsen, Brentwood, Byron, and Bethel Island can all be found here. Note that the communities of Bixler, Point of Timber, Eden Plain, and Borden Junction have been absorbed or just faded away over the past century.

One

John Marsh Stone House

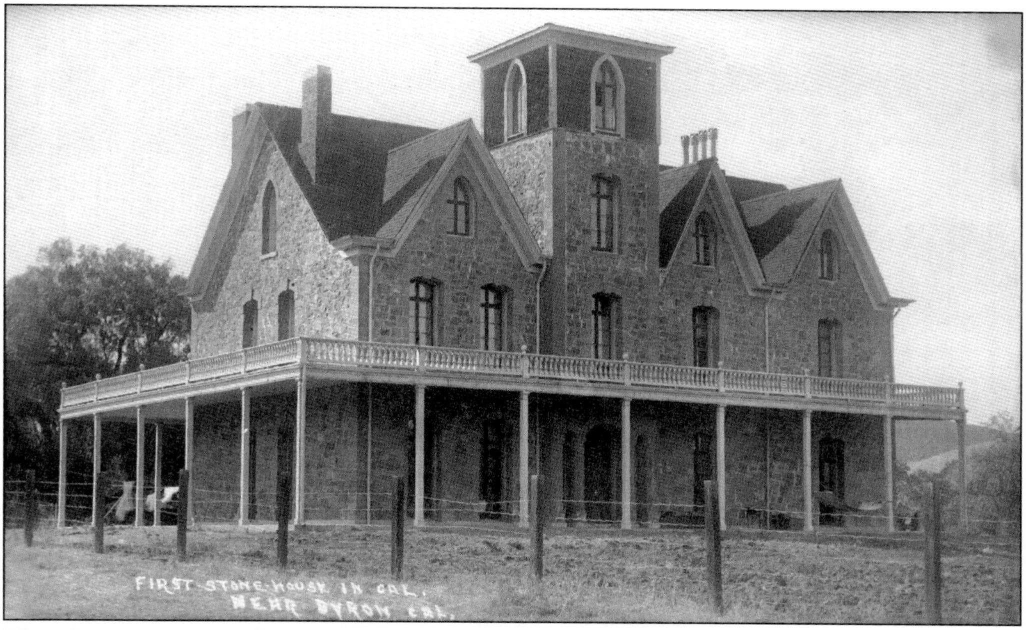

The pioneering Dr. John Marsh built this great stone house in 1856. Marsh was the first European American to settle in the California Central Valley, predating John Sutter by several years. His nearest neighbors to the east were in St. Louis, Missouri. The exterior of the house is buff-colored sandstone quarried on the site. The stones are rectangular and finely tooled. The interior and exterior walls of the house are separated by a four-inch void that would have moderated the seasonal temperatures of the area.

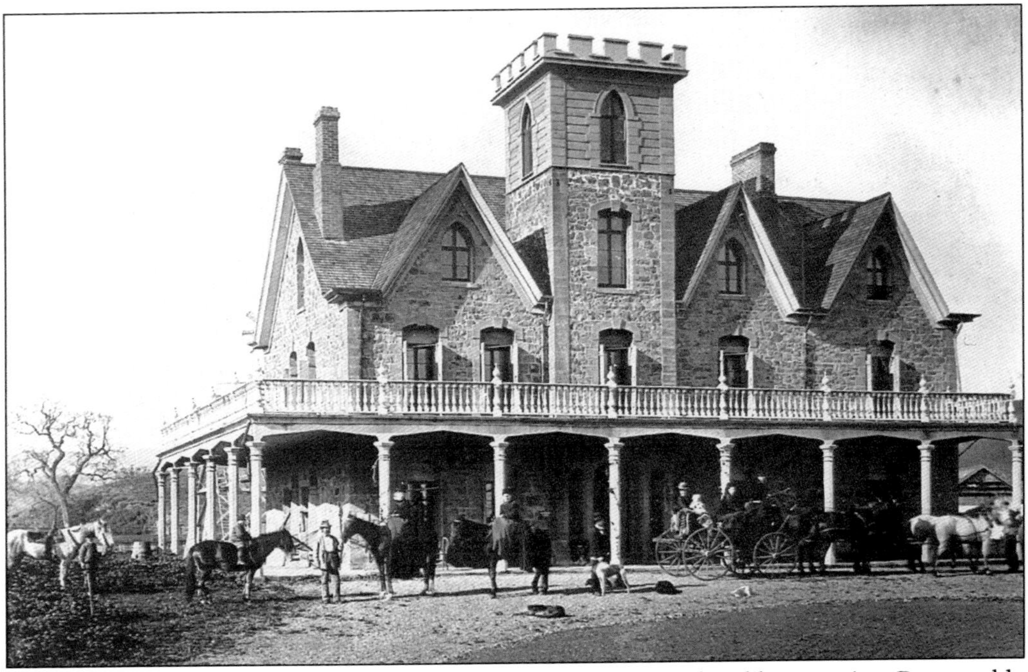

Marsh originally built the John Marsh home for him and his wife, Abby, to enjoy. Regrettably Abby died before its completion in 1856. Marsh lived in the house a few short months before he too joined his wife in death. Their son Charles inherited the home and estate.

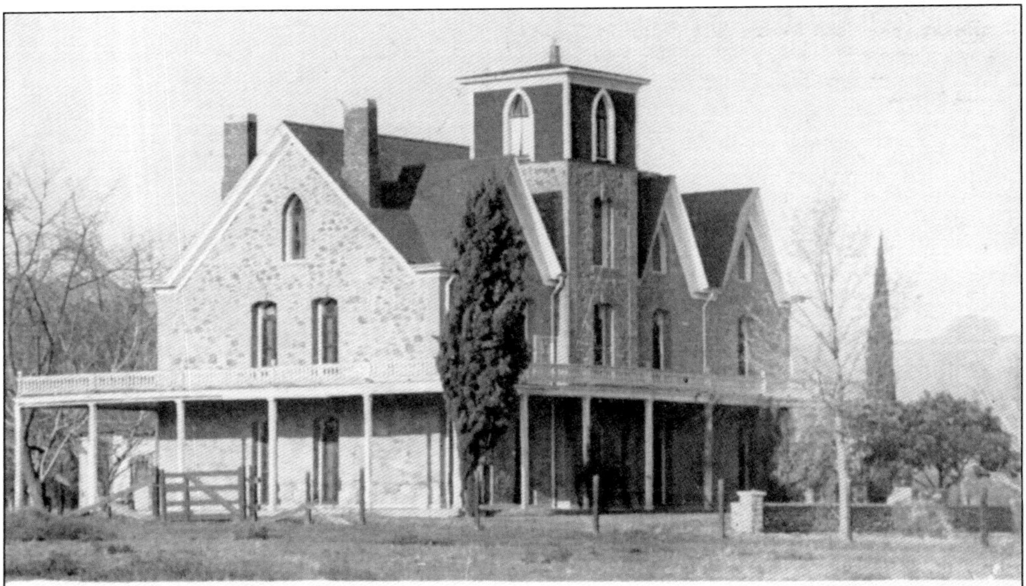

The Harvard University–educated Marsh built a stone house of seven gables after the Nathaniel Hawthorne novel of the same name. Its stone edifice reflected the status that Marsh believed he had earned after many years on the frontier and financial success.

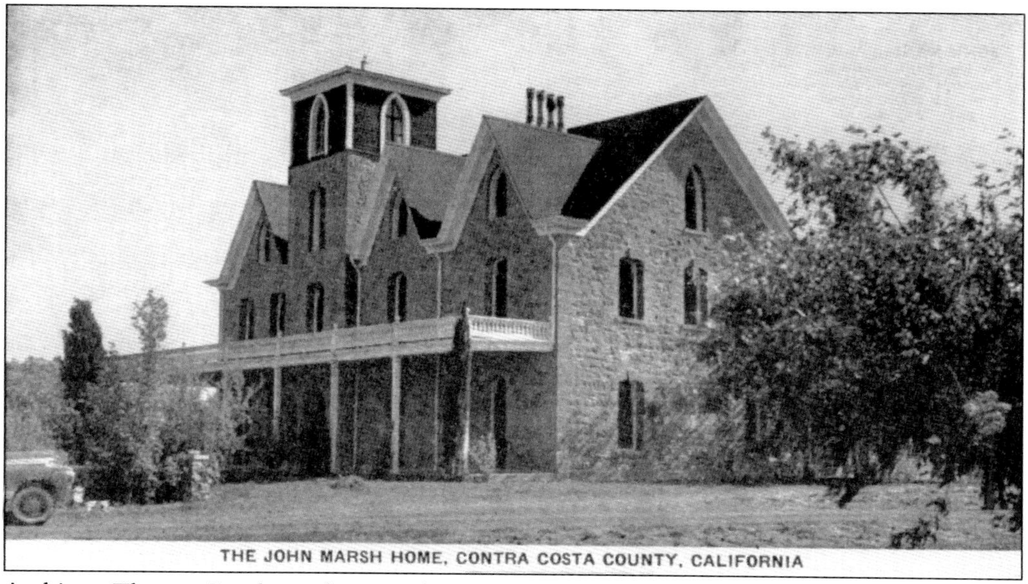

Architect Thomas Boyd, newly arrived in San Francisco, designed the house with rectangular proportions of 36 feet by 60 feet by 40 feet to the ridgeline of the roof. The interior walls of plastered brick stack up through three levels. As such, the Marsh home is the first building of its kind in California.

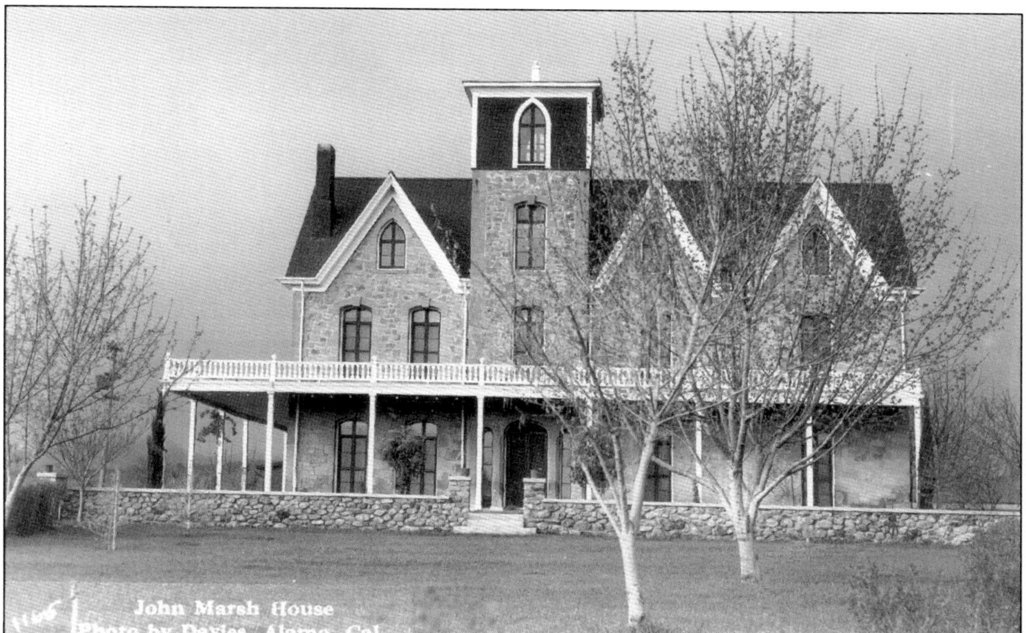

The roof of the Marsh home is very steep with four large dormers. The stones were quarried and the bricks fired at the Rancho Los Megaños. The roofing was originally hand-split tapered redwood shakes in alternating rows or "fish scales." A steep 45-degree roof ensures easy rain runoff.

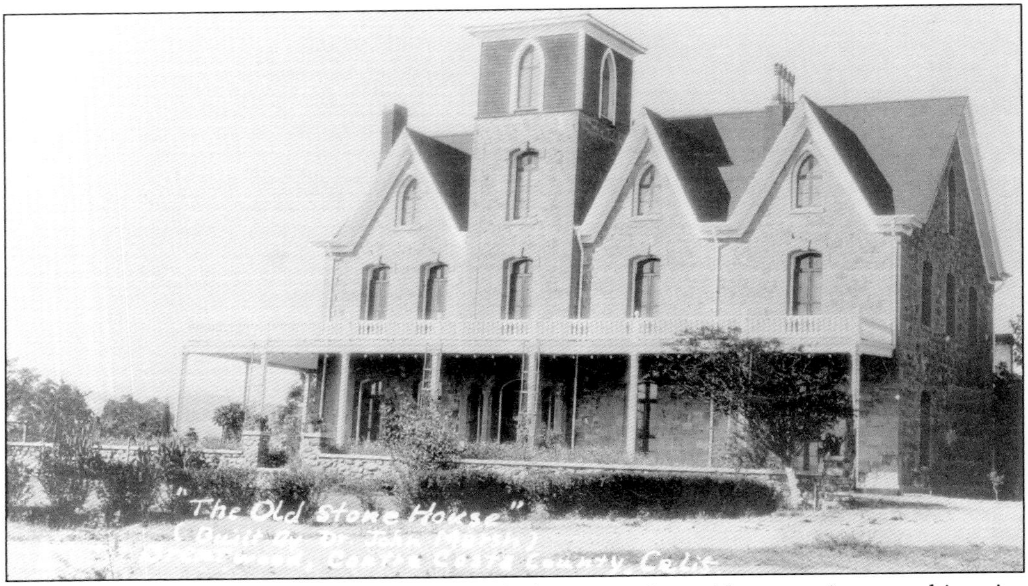

A 10-foot-wide verandah or porch encircles the house on three sides, ensuring a cool interior and pleasant outside areas during hot August nights. Two small balconies at the third level on the east and west sides add to the balance of the house.

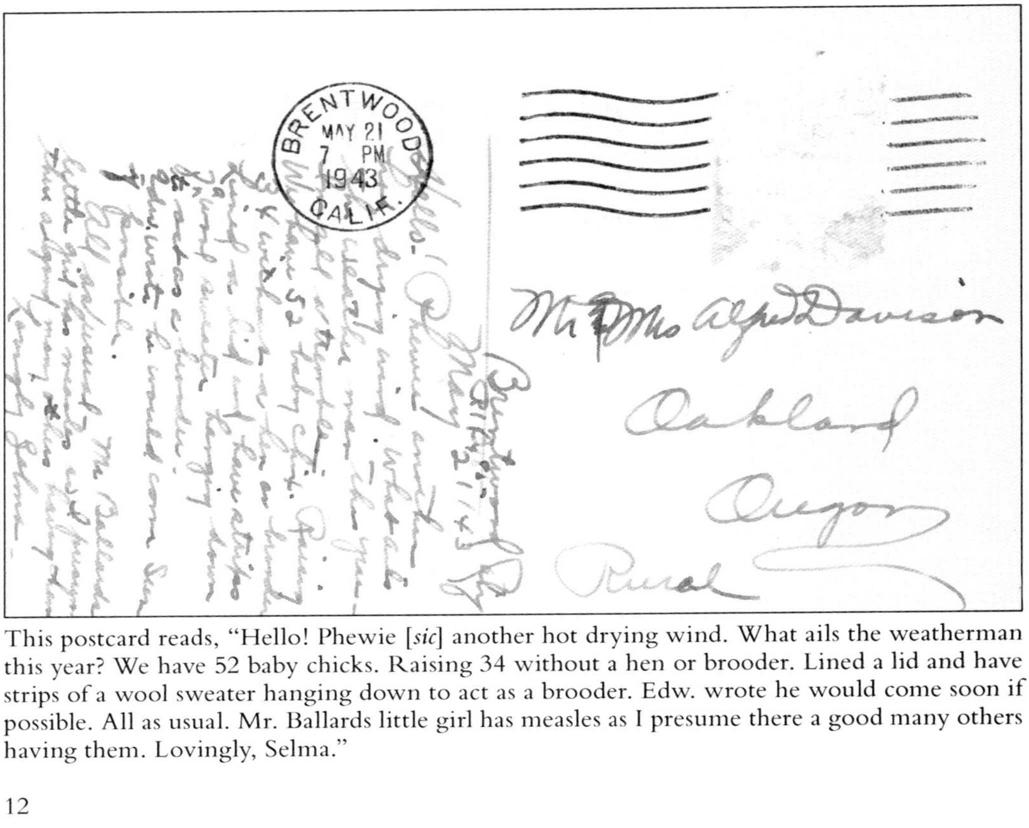

This postcard reads, "Hello! Phewie [*sic*] another hot drying wind. What ails the weatherman this year? We have 52 baby chicks. Raising 34 without a hen or brooder. Lined a lid and have strips of a wool sweater hanging down to act as a brooder. Edw. wrote he would come soon if possible. All as usual. Mr. Ballards little girl has measles as I presume there a good many others having them. Lovingly, Selma."

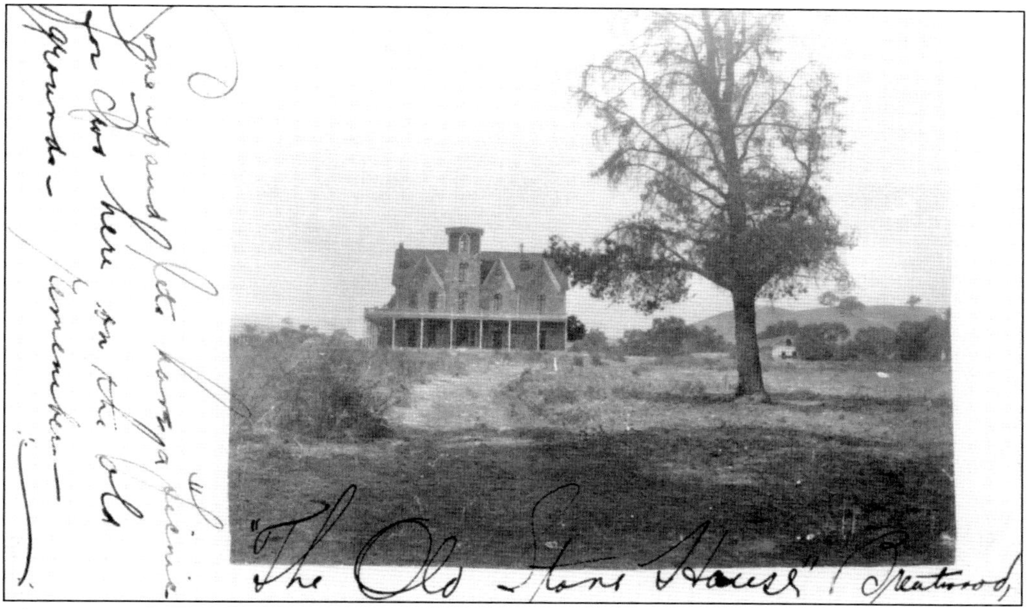

The Marsh house was a favorite picnic site fondly remembered. The original real-photo postcard of the era urges the recipient to "come up and lets have a picnic for two on the old grounds—remember—'The Old Stone House' Brentwood."

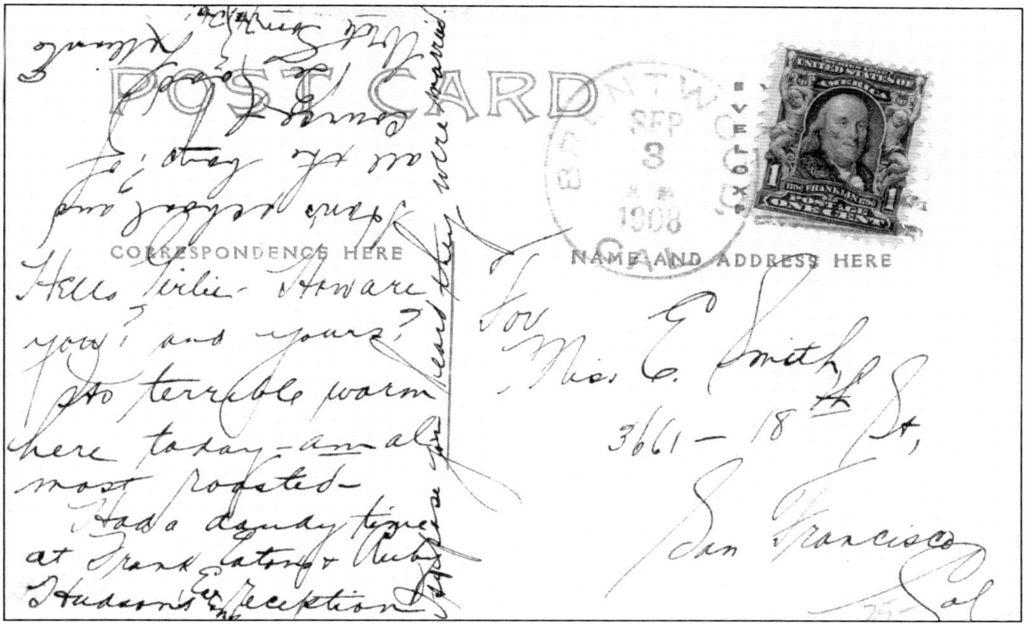

This postcard reads, "Hello Girlie—How are you? and yours? So terribly warm here today—am almost roasted. Had a dandy time at Frank Eatons and Ruby Hudson's Eatons reception. I suppose you heard that they were married. How's school and all the boys of course? Be good and write soon Ha Ha! Lillian E."

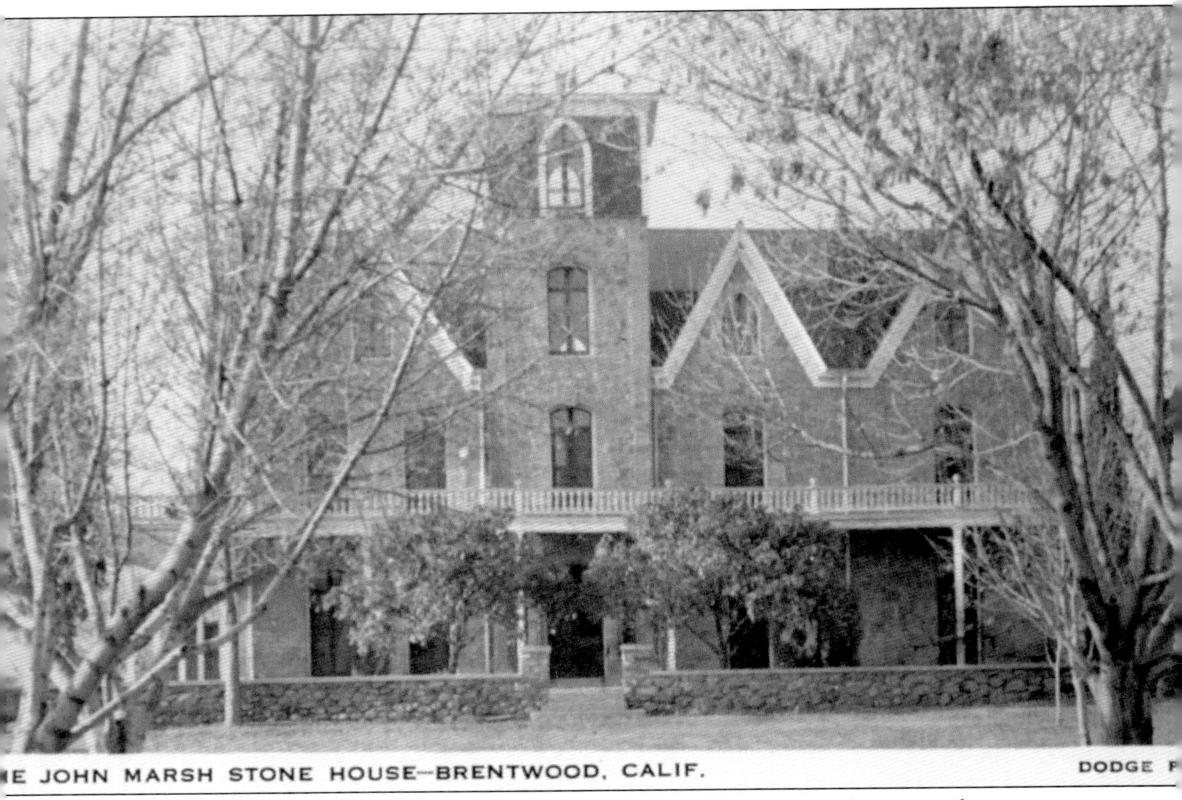

The fine home continued to be a prominent residence into the mid-1950s. The property was occupied by Balfour Guthrie Investment Company managers and subsequently turned into rooms to let. The last man to sleep in the house was Robert D. "Bob" Gromm of Bethel Island on the night of an early fund-raising "Romeria" (an early Californio festival or celebratory event) in 1972.

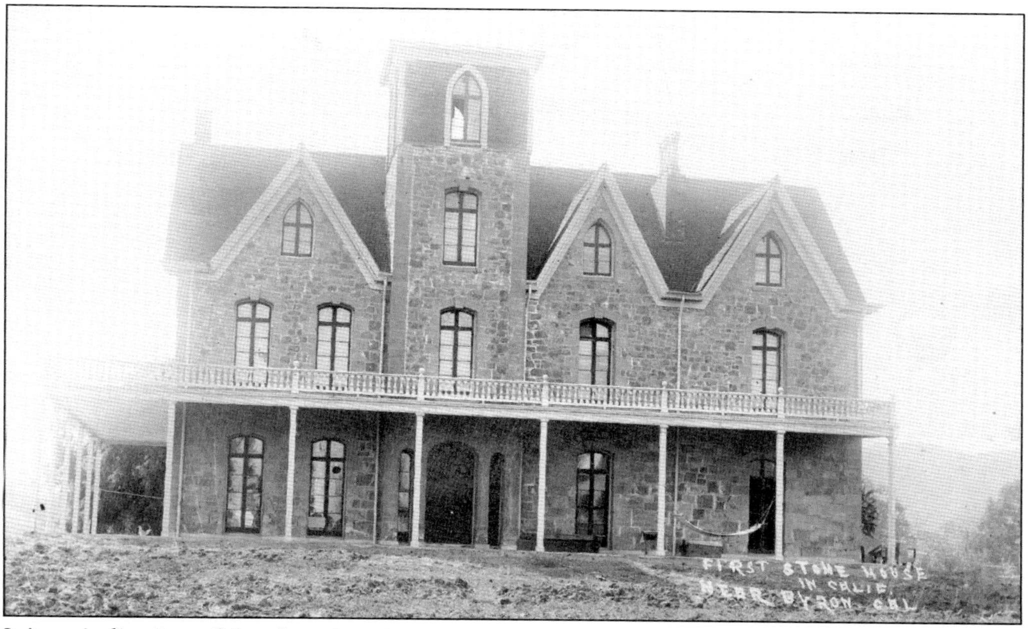

It is an indication of the changing times in eastern Contra Costa County that the Marsh home was once considered in close proximity to Byron, the largest community in the area prior to 1920. The stone house is now located on the city limit line of Brentwood, the largest town in the area.

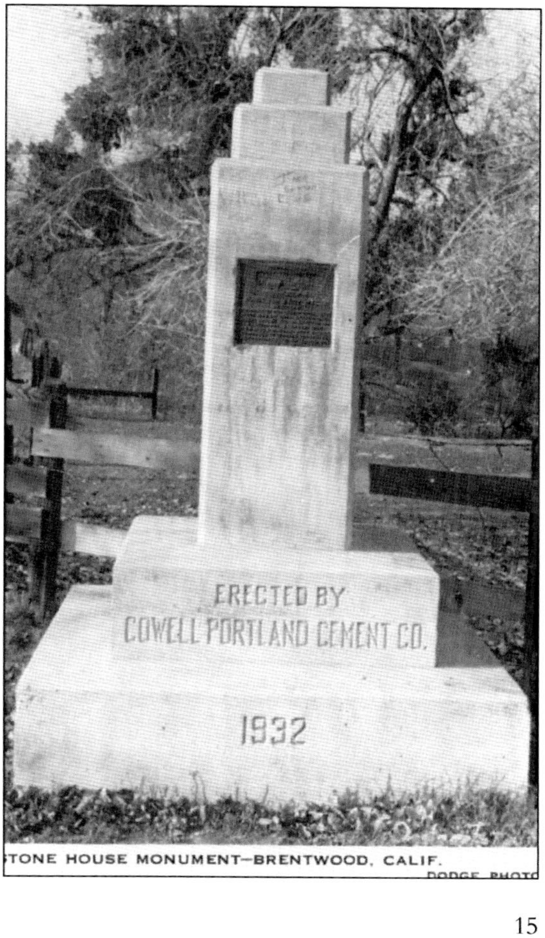

Early pioneers John and Abby Marsh are honored here by the Native Daughters of the Golden West in conjunction with the Cowell Portland Cement Company with a plaque and monument. The Native Daughters, Donner Parlor of Byron, will rededicate the monument on September 27, 2007.

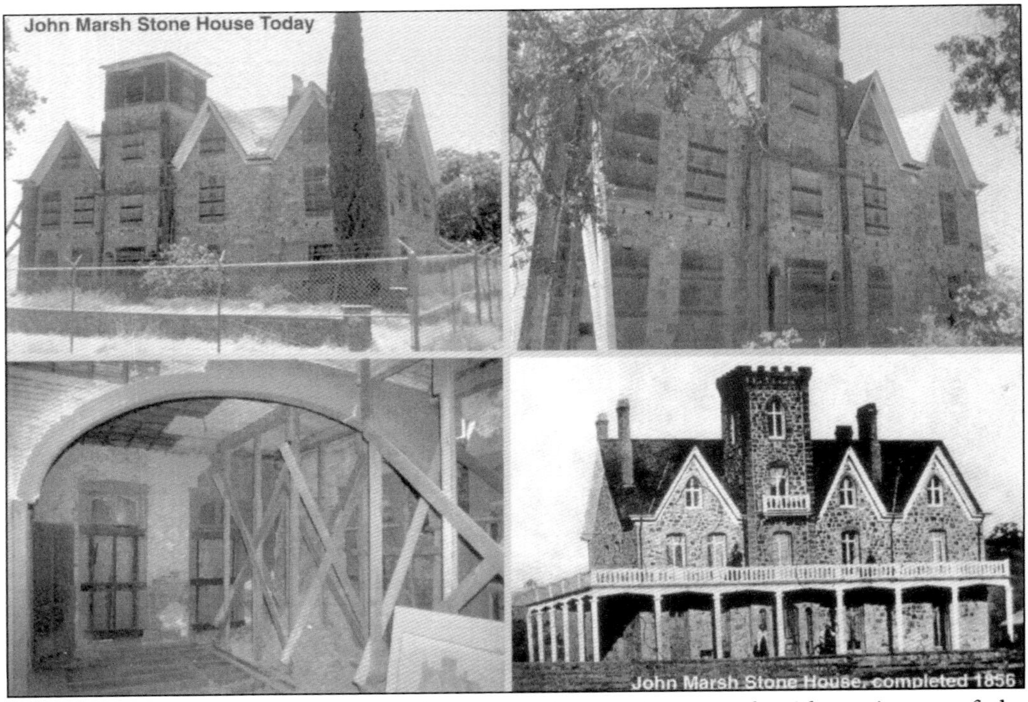

Images of John Marsh property as it exists today are juxtaposed with an image of the property taken shortly after its construction in 1856. The John Marsh Historic Trust (www.JohnMarshHouse.com) seeks to save and restore the house to its original state as part of a new John Marsh State Historic Site.

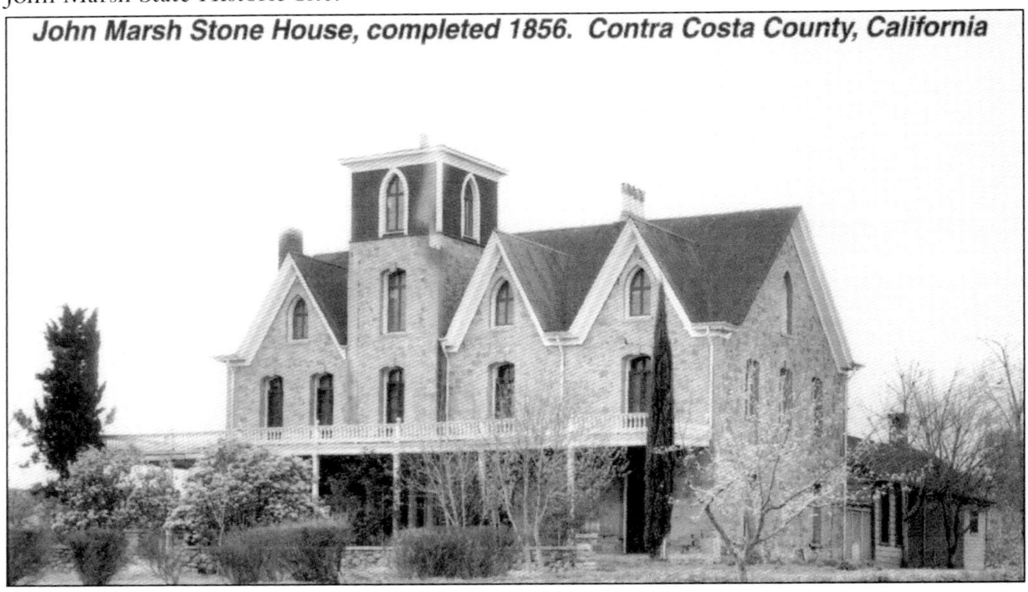

The John Marsh house, seen here in Gothic design, will be the crown jewel of the proposed 3,600-acre state historic park. The City of Brentwood, California State Parks and Recreation Department, and the John Marsh Historic Trust are working to save this historic part of California.

Two

Agriculture and Husbandry

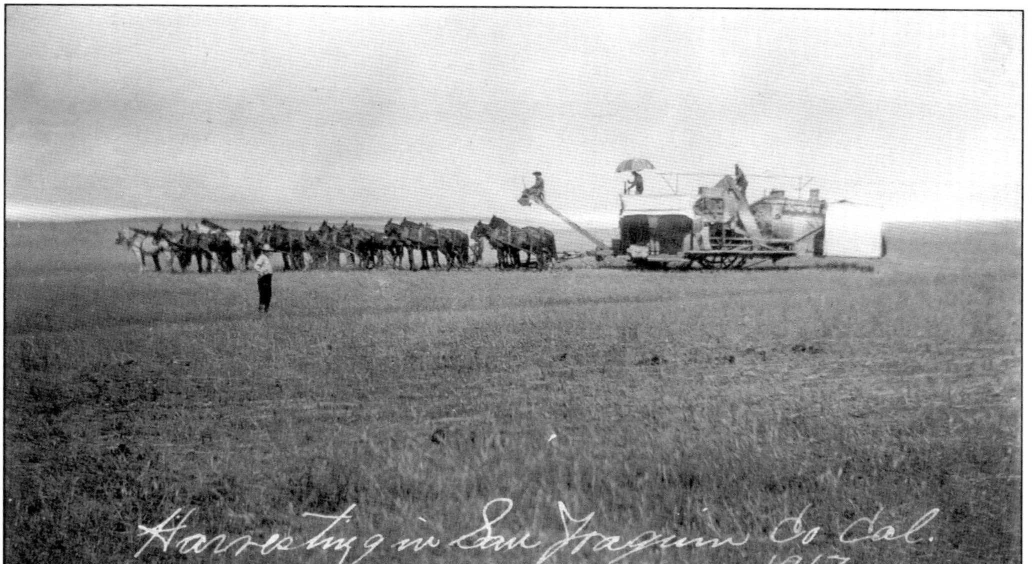

This real-photo postcard of 1917 shows large-production wheat farming in the delta. Only a few men were required to harvest thousands of acres of dry farming land in the greater San Joaquin area. Traveling photographers moved out of their studios and captured real lives in the late 19th and early 20th centuries.

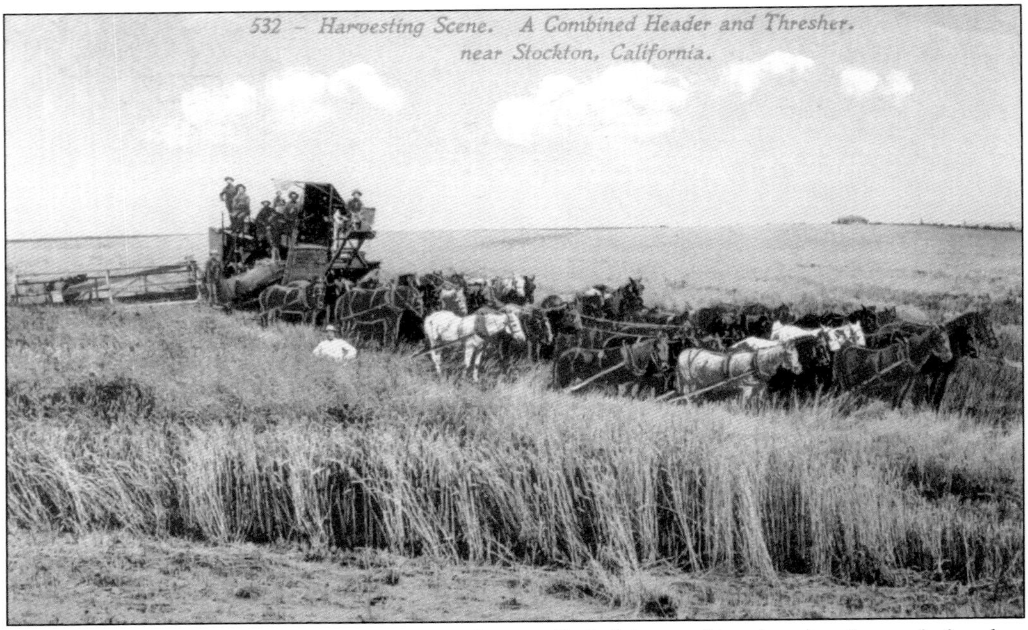

Twenty-four horses harnessed in teams of six pulled this combination header and thresher through the wheat fields. The grain stands chest high on the man in the foreground. The area between Stockton and Brentwood was the largest wheat-producing area between San Francisco and New Orleans between 1880 and 1890.

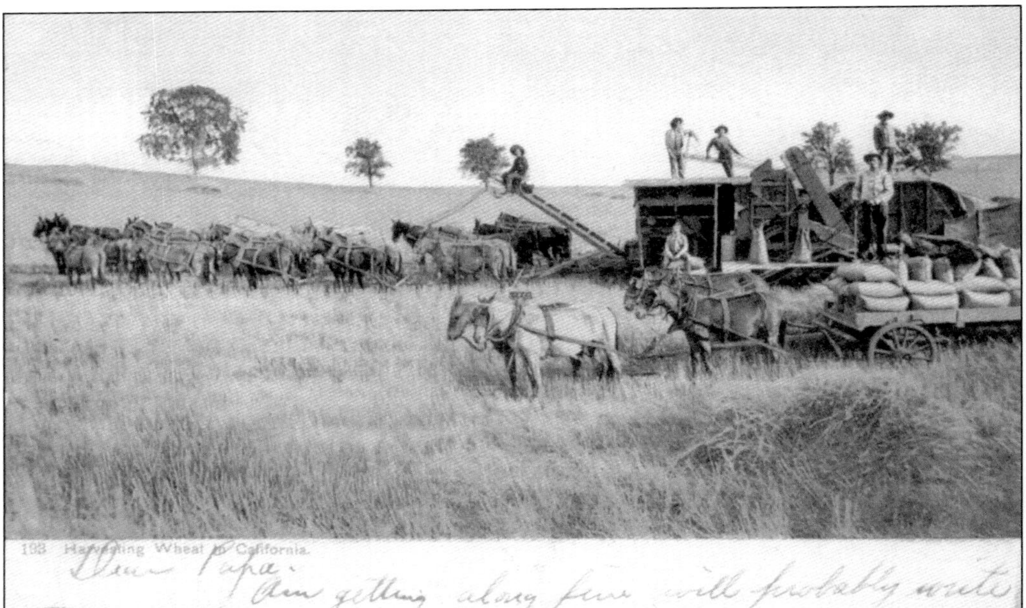

Farm skills from the Midwest translated easily to California with gainful employment for all. As this postcard reports from son to father, "Am getting along fine. Will probably write to you tomorrow. Otto."

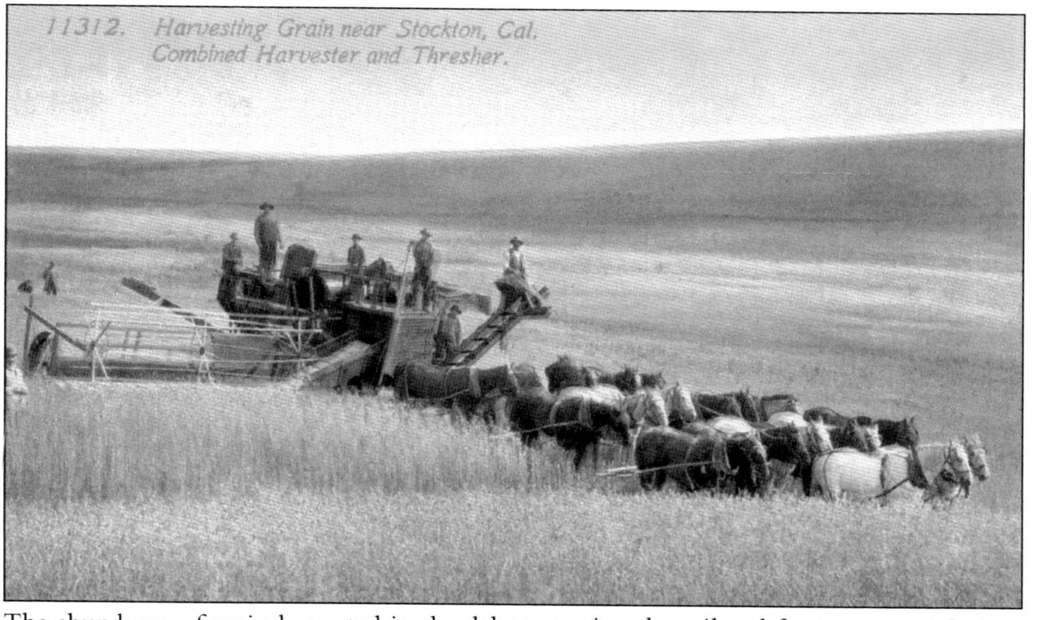

The abundance of grain harvested in the delta necessitated a railroad for transport. The San Pablo and Tulare Railroad, later absorbed into the Southern Pacific Railroad, moved grain from the Central Valley to Port Costa, Contra Costa County, for shipment aboard. Shiploads of grain went to Ireland—not to feed the population, but to brew Guinness beer.

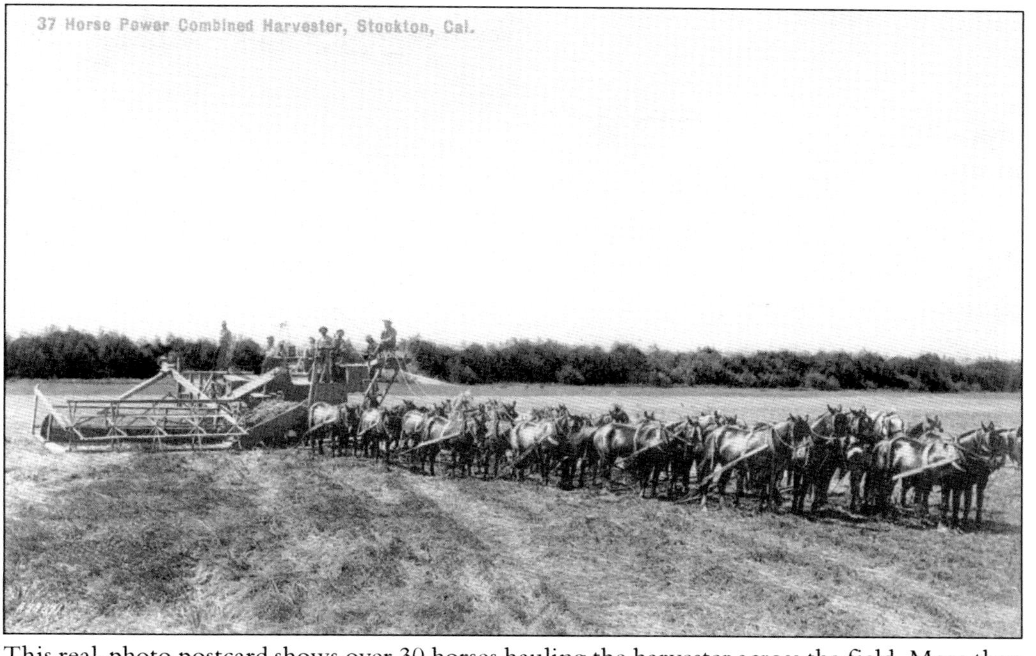

This real-photo postcard shows over 30 horses hauling the harvester across the field. More than 100 acres of grain per day could be harvested in this manner. It took more men to prepare and harness the horses than it did to process the threshing.

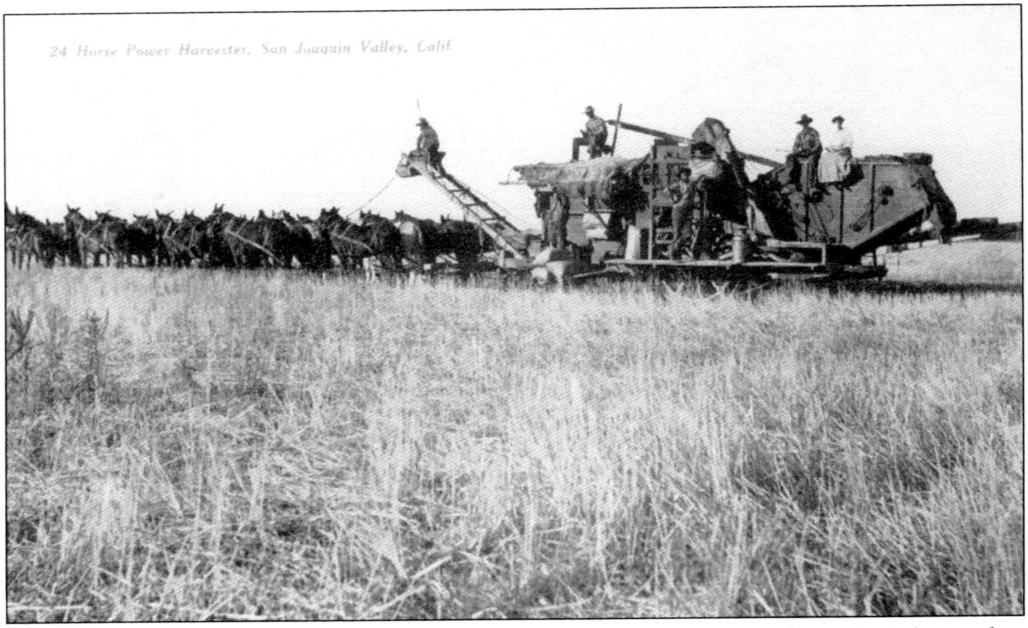

Delta lands are alluvial soils consisting primarily of fertile peat lands. The grain is heavy, but the land itself is soft. The equipment is not heavy, but pulling a harvester over peat lands is similar to driving a car with four flat tires. The equipment sinks into the ground and requires tremendous effort to roll.

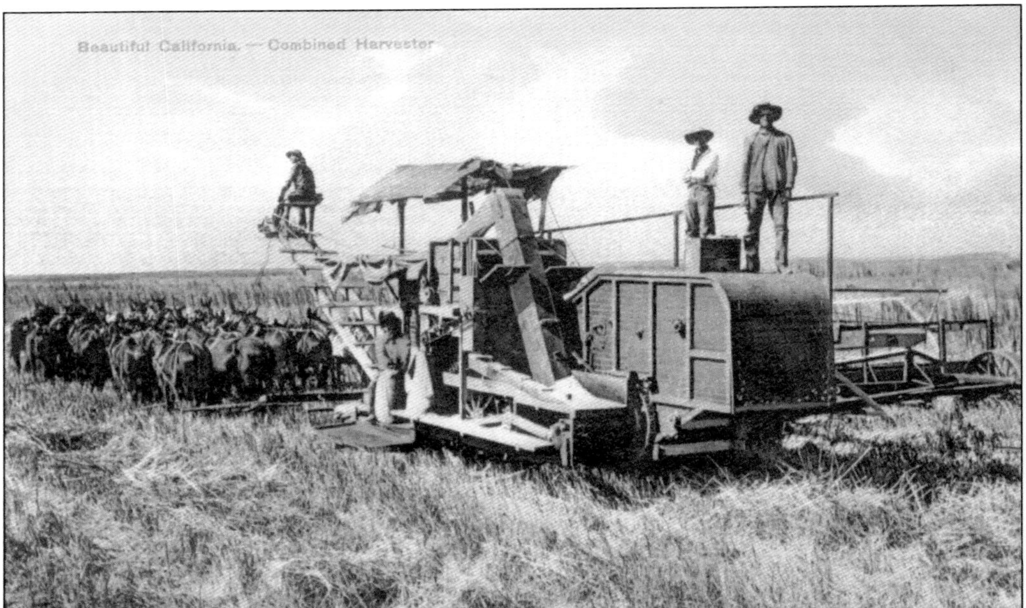

This view of a grain thresher shows the small wheels and effort required to move the machine through the field. The blades of the harvester turn with the movement of the equipment through the field. Specialized crops and large-scale farming epitomized California agriculture from the start.

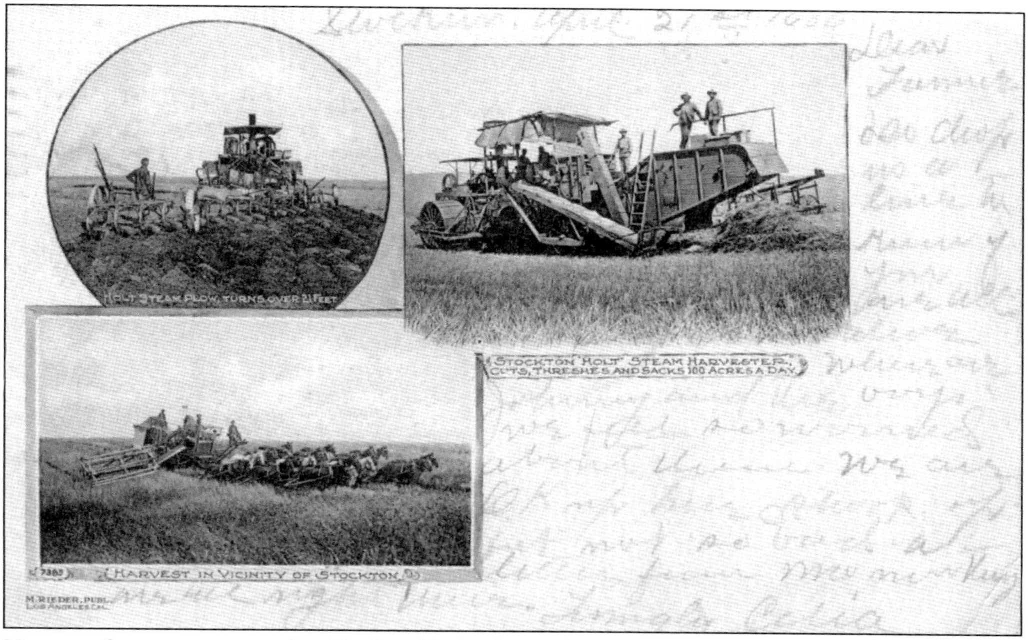

Horse and steam power exist side-by-side in this early description of Holt Brothers agriculture equipment. The 24-horse team represented in the lower left is soon replaced by steam-powered tractors and harvesters. Holt Brothers, of Stockton, were early inventors of specialized farm equipment designed for delta needs.

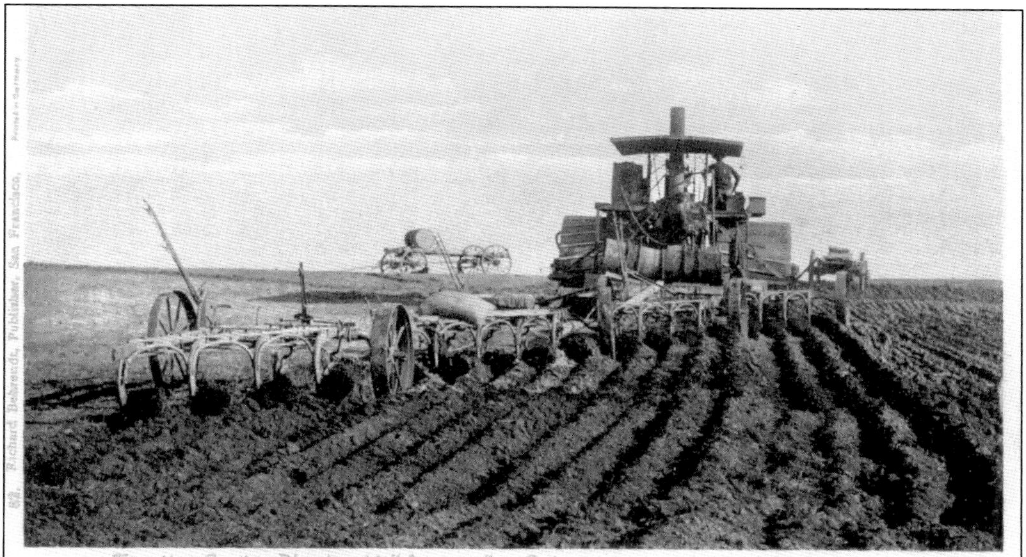

Furrows are cut 16 inches apart for miles using this early steam-driven tractor and furrow. Farming in California involved many sections of land (640 acres) dedicated to a single crop. The small-scale Tennessee farmer with 20 acres of corn and a mule would not recognize the scale of agriculture in the West.

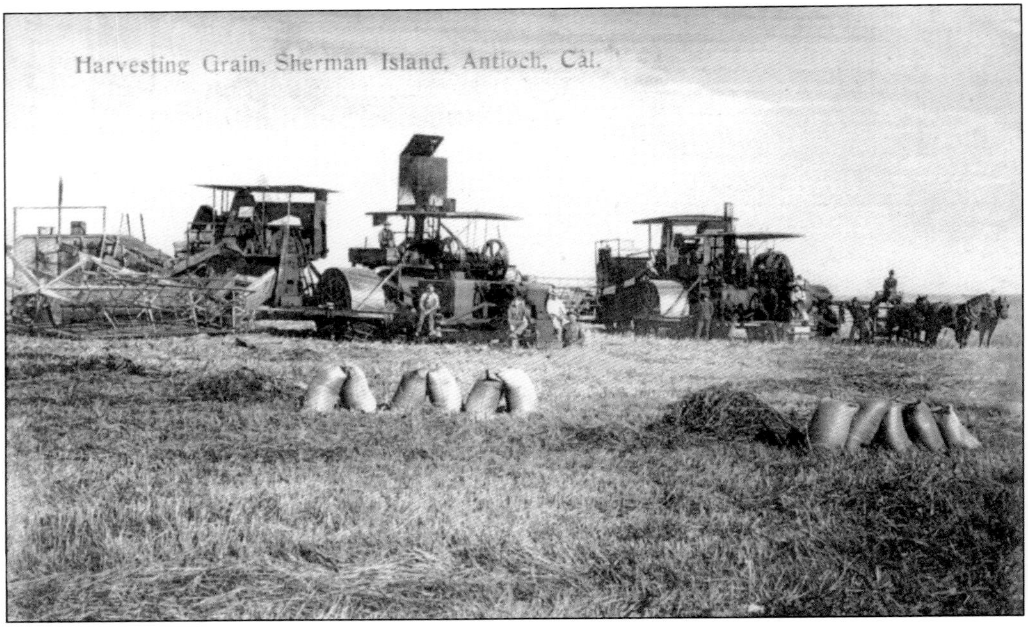

Steam tractors replaced 24-horse teams, but the equipment was heavy. These early tractors are literally steam locomotives on wheels, burning coal to boil water for steam pressure. Wide tracks are required to keep the equipment from sinking into the soft peat dirt.

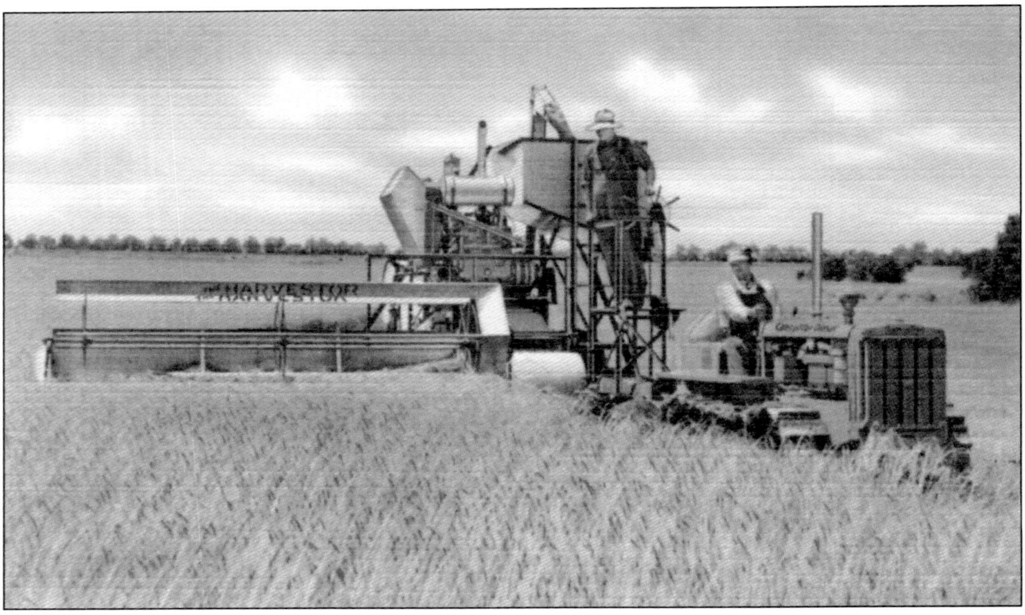

Tractor innovations continue by the Holt Brothers with the invention of the wide tracks made famous by the Caterpillar Tractor Company. Here the steam tractor is replaced by a lighter-weight, diesel-fuel-burning tractor. Two men have replaced a team of horses and thresher in this 1940 image.

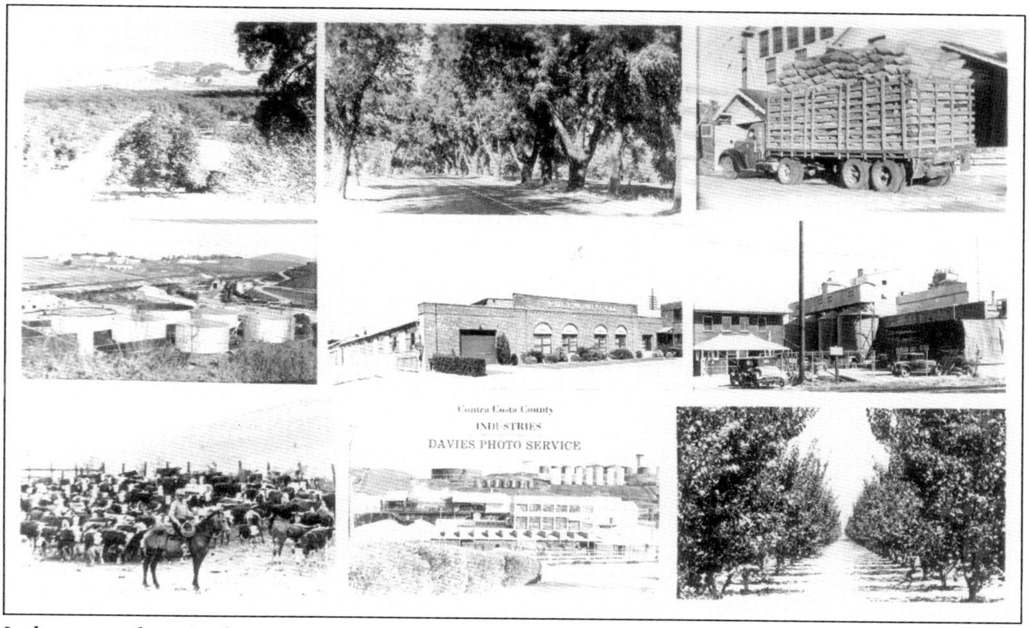

Industry and agriculture mix in this 1940s postcard promoting Contra Costa County. Oil refineries in Richmond are highlighted, along with cattle, orchards, and grain. Tree-lined, well-maintained roads are available for Sunday drives.

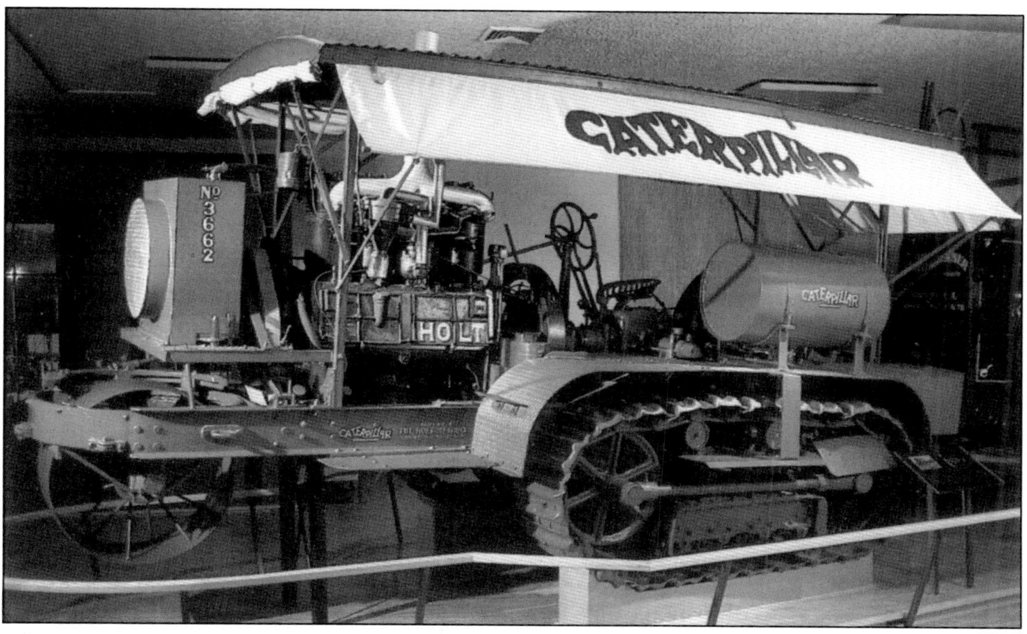

The development of the Caterpillar tractor and its distinctive tracks parallel the success of agriculture in California. This early tractor combines a light frame, air-conditioning for those hot Central Valley days, and much more horsepower than a 20-mule team could ever deliver.

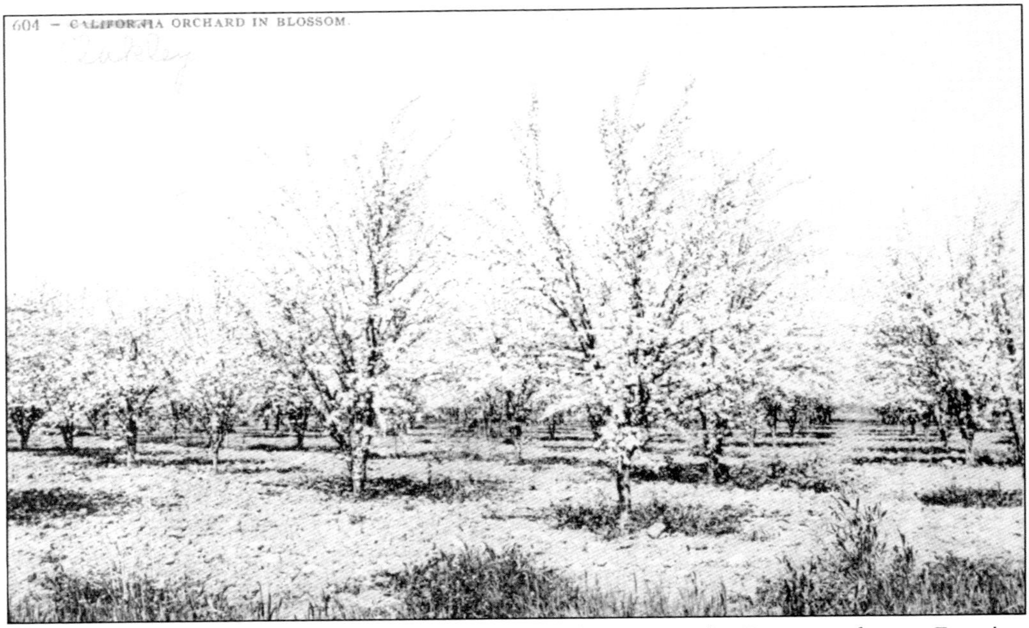

Grain and orchards have always been hallmarks of farming in the Brentwood area. Farming has never been a subsistence activity. Miners drawn to the mother lode in 1849 worked their claims and purchased beef and grain. Central Valley farmers efficiently supplied the miners with specialized produce.

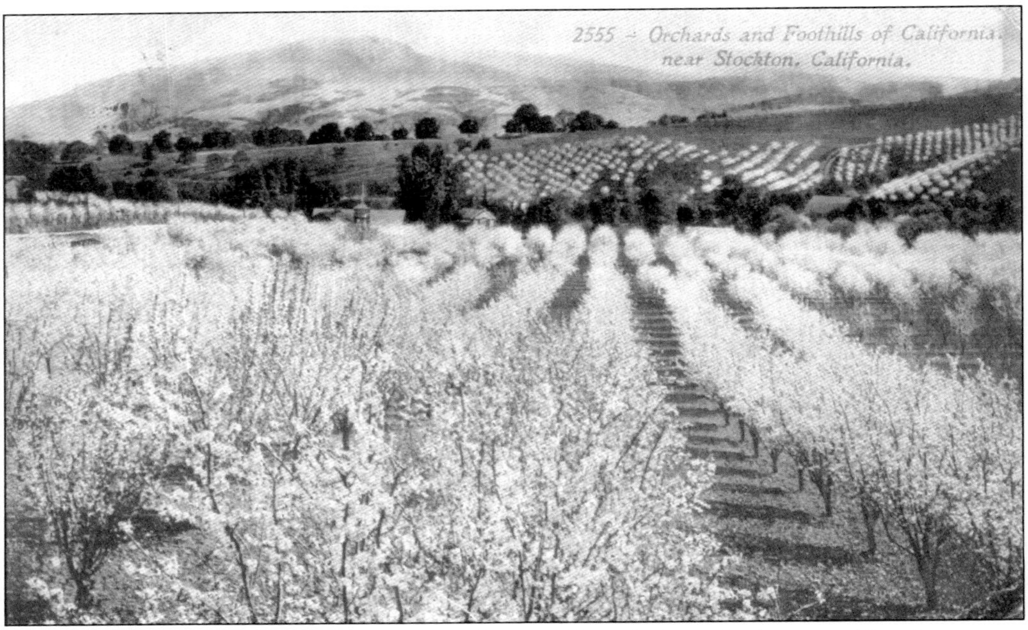

Specialized farming for export continues today as California farms feed the world and represent the largest component of the state's economy. California's almond production represents over 90 percent of the world's production and is the state's largest monetary crop.

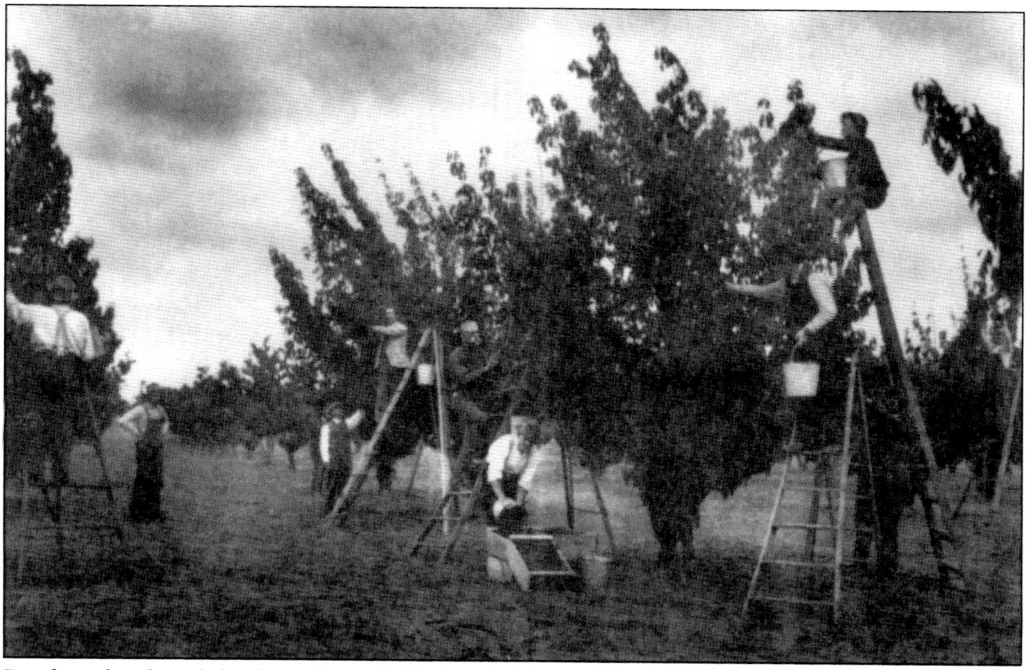

Peach orchards and the three-legged, 12-foot ladders will be familiar to "U-pick" and weekend-harvest fruit lovers. Peaches are selected here for immediate consumption, canning, and drying for an international market.

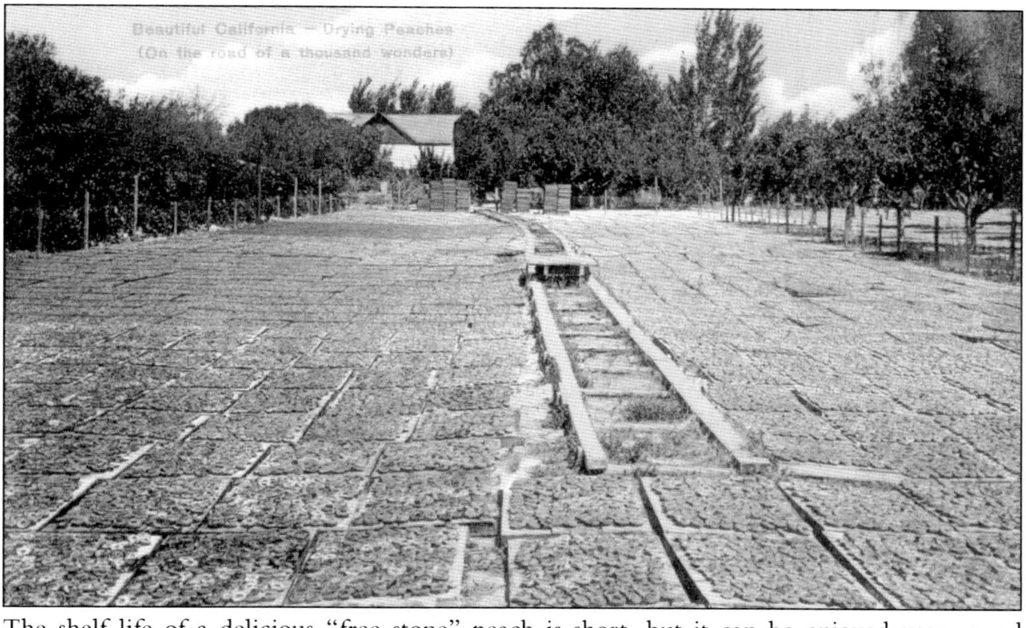

The shelf life of a delicious "free stone" peach is short, but it can be enjoyed year-round if dried. Most orchards had fruit-drying operations to supplement their fresh fruit shipping operations. The attraction and interest in fruit production is captured in this early Southern Pacific Railroad marketing image. A rail trip through east Contra Costa County was promoted as one of a "thousand wonders."

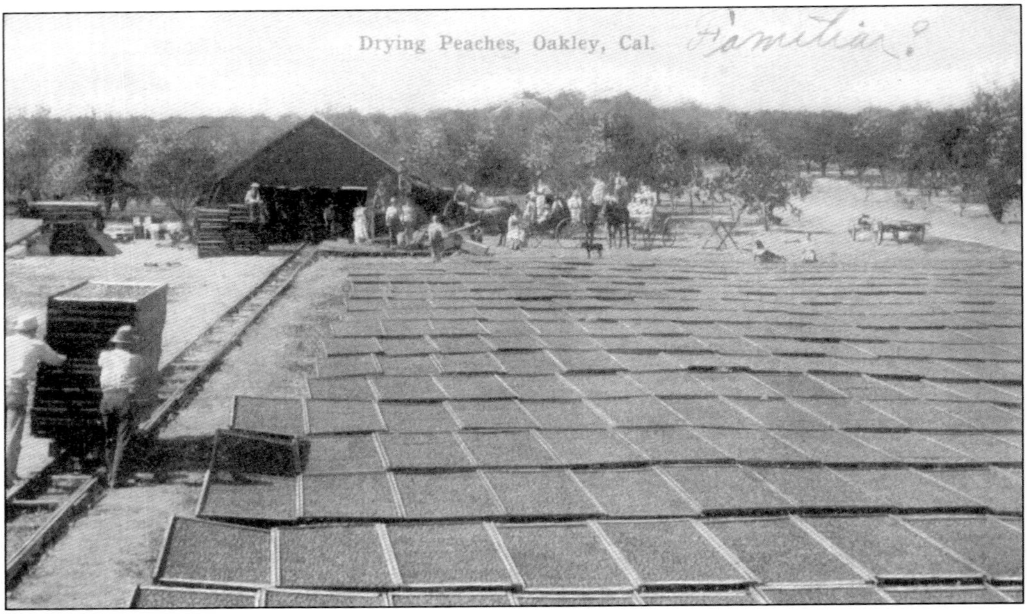

The largest fruit-drying yards in the United States were found in East County. This peach-drying operation employed hundreds of individuals, mostly women, who hand-cut each peach and placed them on a tray for drying. As late as the early 1960s, one could earn $1 a lug by "cutting cots."

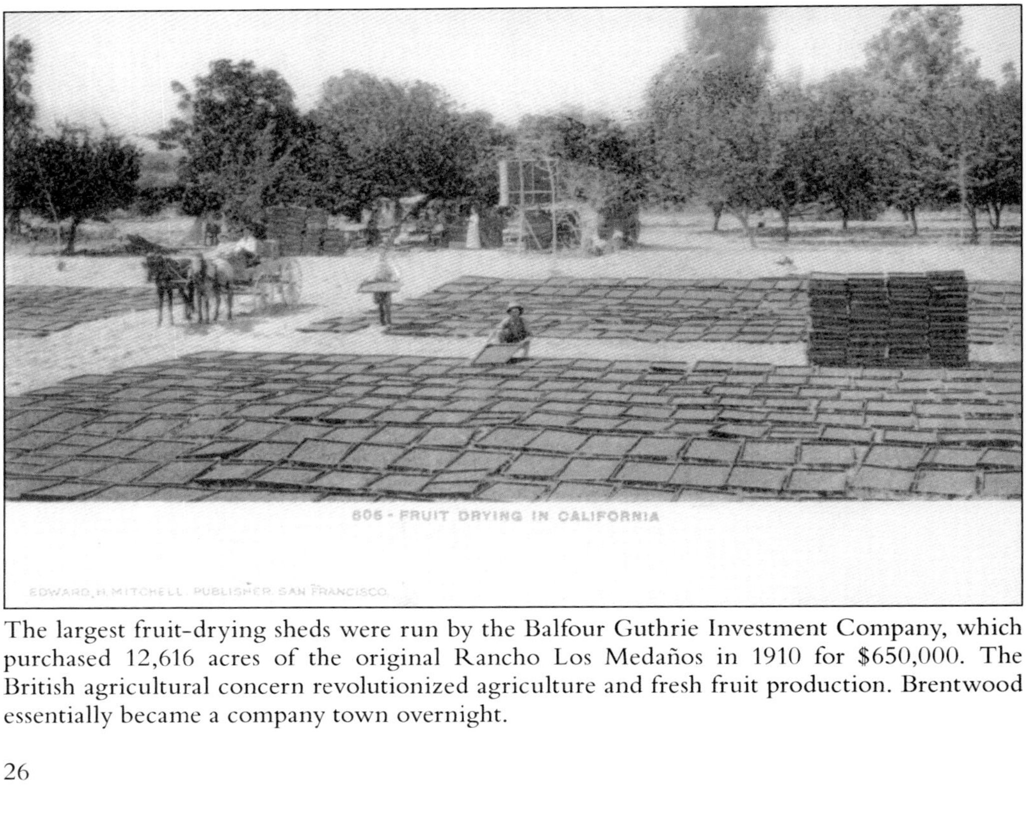

The largest fruit-drying sheds were run by the Balfour Guthrie Investment Company, which purchased 12,616 acres of the original Rancho Los Medaños in 1910 for $650,000. The British agricultural concern revolutionized agriculture and fresh fruit production. Brentwood essentially became a company town overnight.

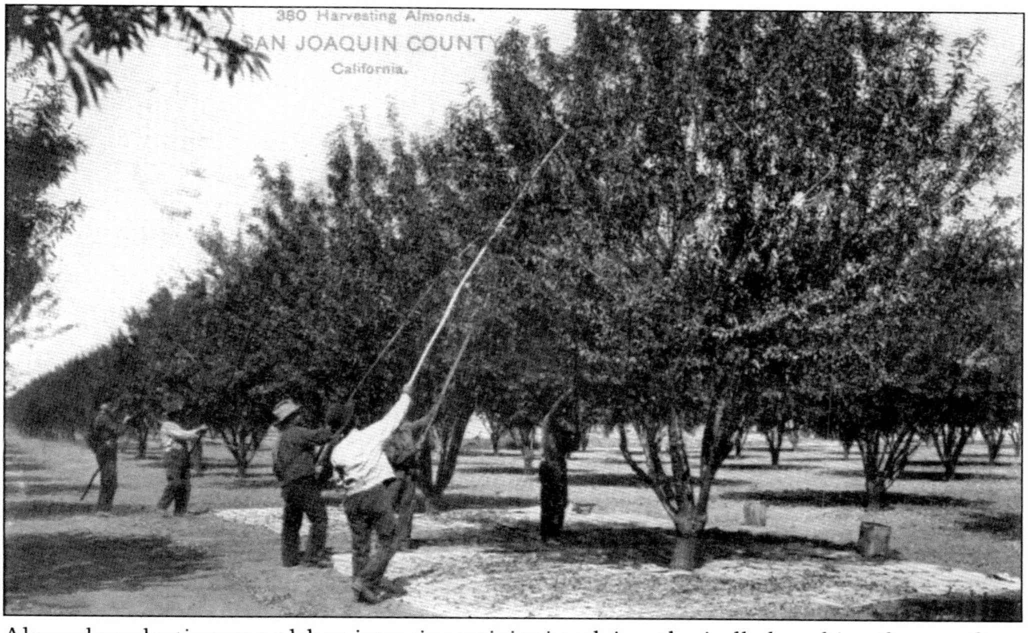

Almond production was a labor-intensive activity involving physically knocking the nuts from the trees using rubber mallets on the tree trunks or long poles on the treetops. Note the use of large canvas tarps under the trees to capture the nuts on the ground.

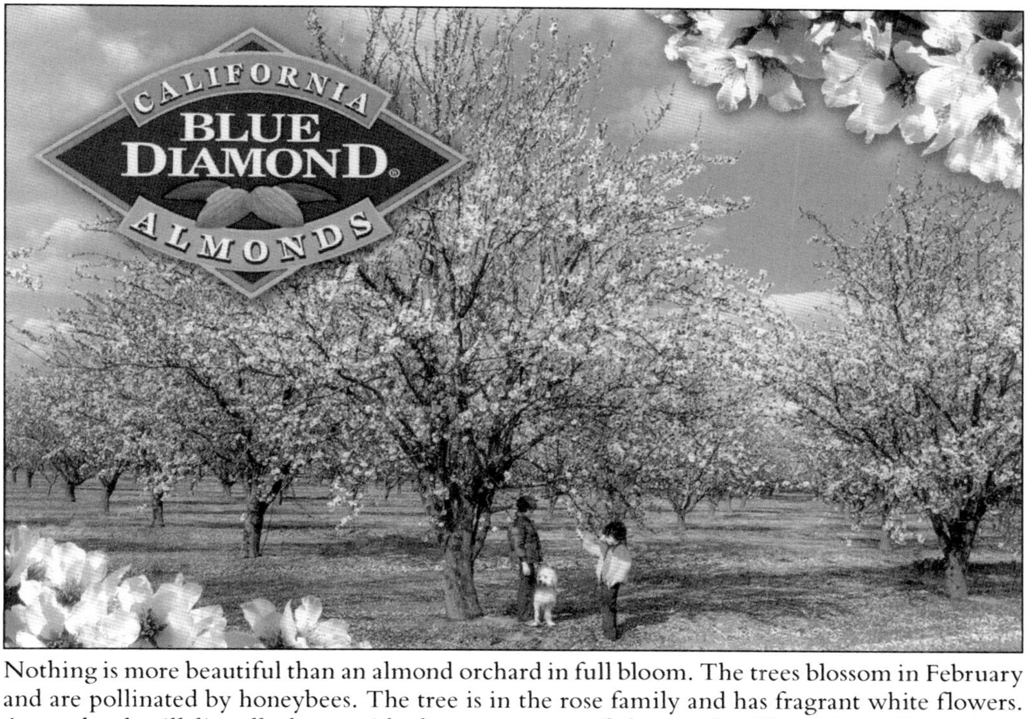

Nothing is more beautiful than an almond orchard in full bloom. The trees blossom in February and are pollinated by honeybees. The tree is in the rose family and has fragrant white flowers. An orchard will literally hum with the excitement of thousands of honeybees flying from flower to hive.

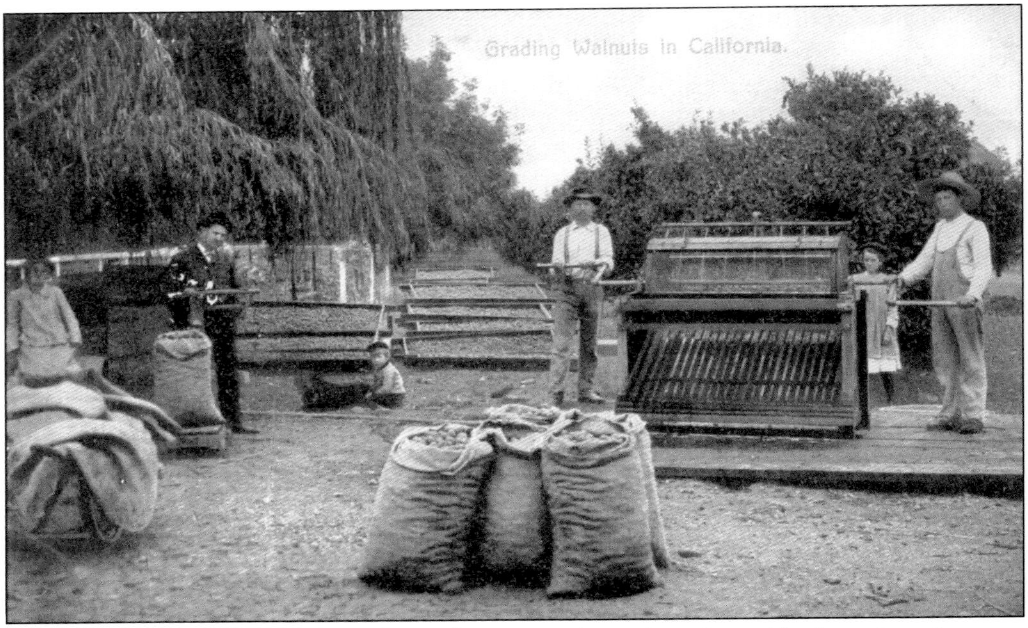

Walnuts are an important crop and are often grown in conjunction with almonds and grapes. Removing the fleshy, green hull from the hard shell encompassing the nut meat is accomplished with a sorter or grader. There is a lot of manual work involved in hand cranking the machinery. Automation lags behind. Orchards of 20 to 40 acres are relatively small scale when compared to multiple sections (640 acres) of wheat cultivation.

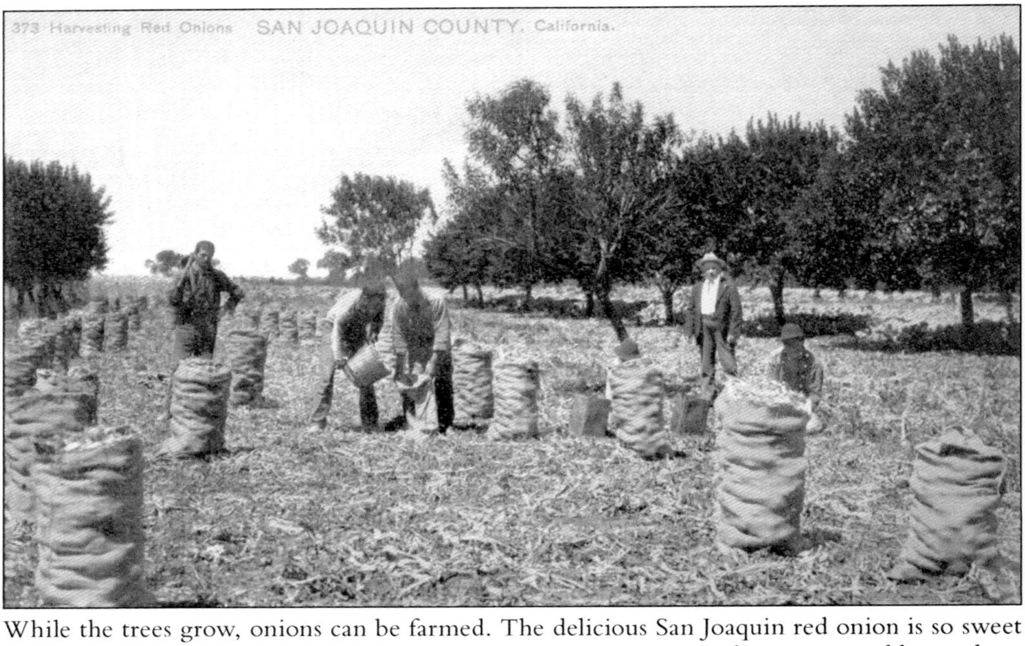

While the trees grow, onions can be farmed. The delicious San Joaquin red onion is so sweet that many people eat them like apples. Onions are easy to grow and transport and have a long shelf life. Even a small acreage could produce a cash crop while trees matured.

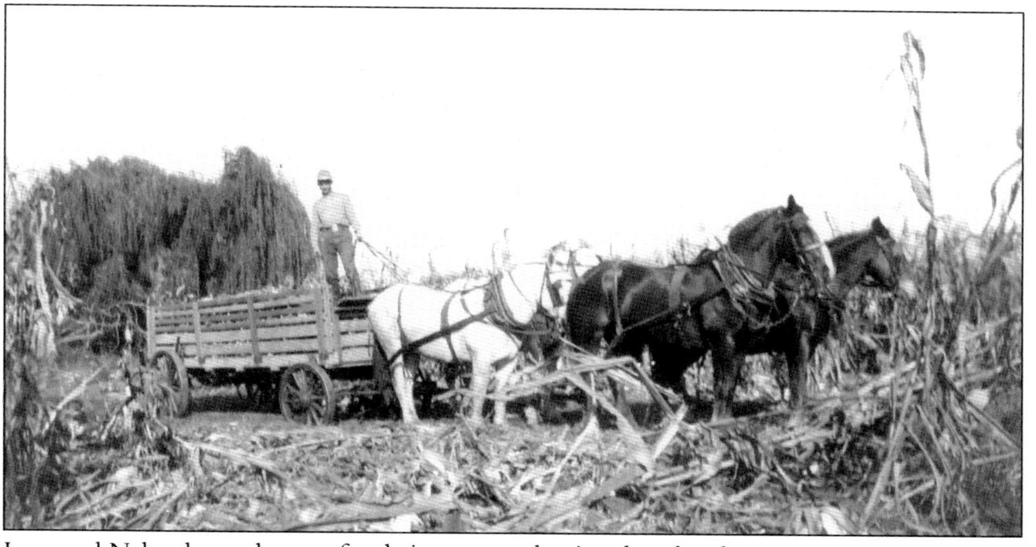

Iowa and Nebraska are known for their corn production, but they have nothing on California. Corn is a cereal grass and loves water. Where better to grow corn than soft delta loam with water in abundance? This image shows an early corn harvest.

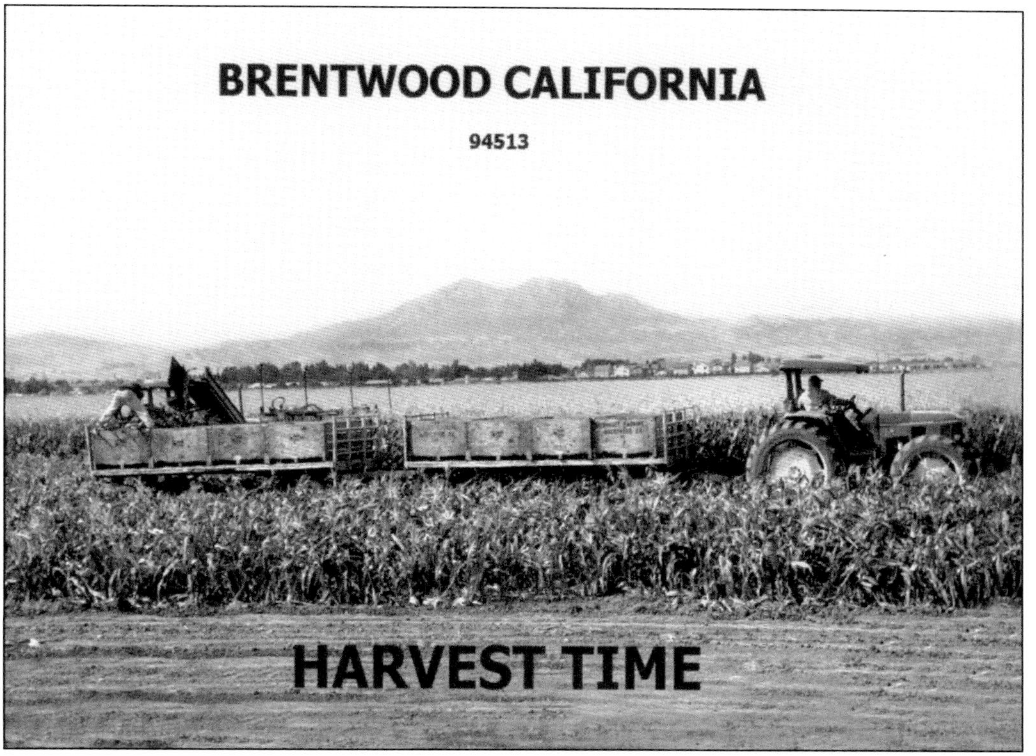

Brentwood corn is justly famous and marketed nationwide. July brings the Cornfest celebration to Brentwood (beginning in 1992) and lots of sweet yellow corn for all to enjoy. This image of a cornfield and view of Mount Diablo is taken from the east.

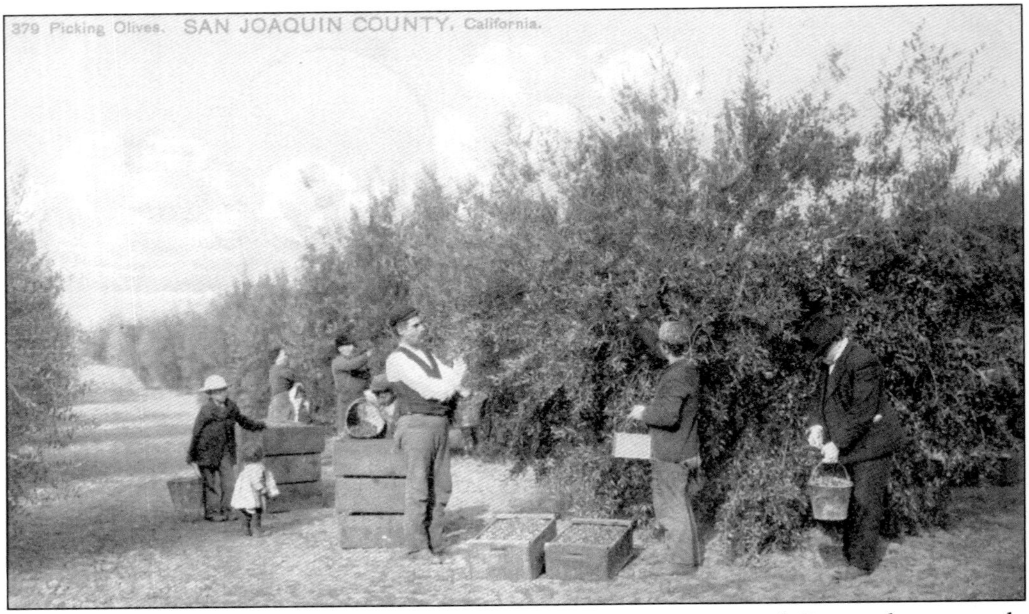

Immigrants from the Azores, Germany, Greece, Spain, France, and Portugal were early settlers of eastern Contra Costa County. With them came crops that transferred easily from the Mediterranean to California. Olive groves were established, and there was hardly a family home without an olive tree in the backyard.

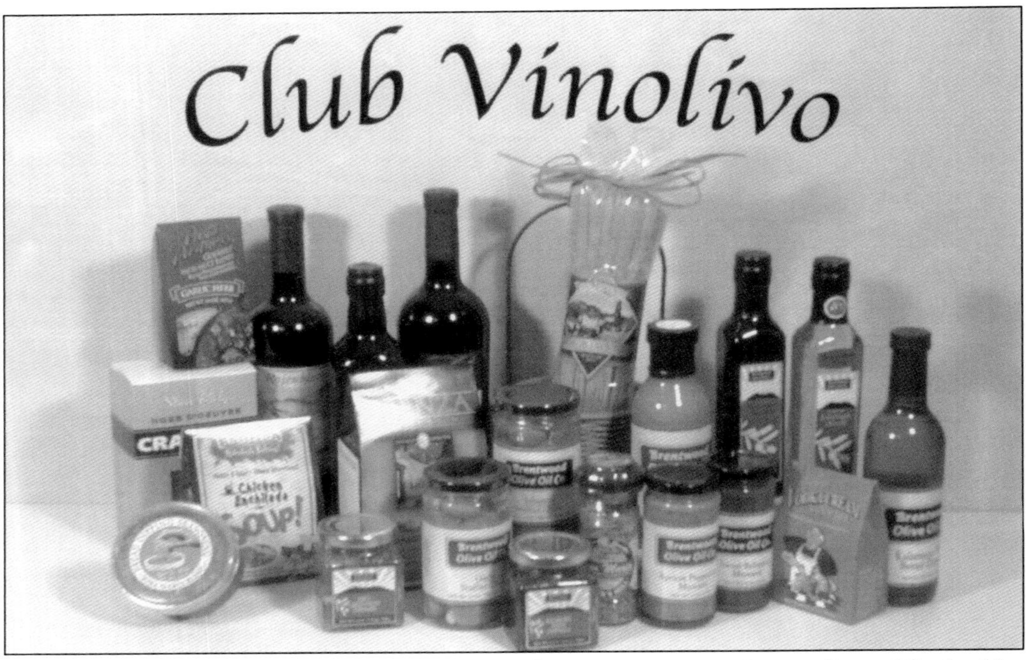

Olive production and products remain a thriving business in eastern Contra Costa. The healthy dietary value and gourmet interest in virgin olive oil helps drive the local olive oil industry. The Brentwood Olive Oil Company has created a new and exciting gourmet food club, "Vinolivo," that specializes in pasta, olive products, and regional food items.

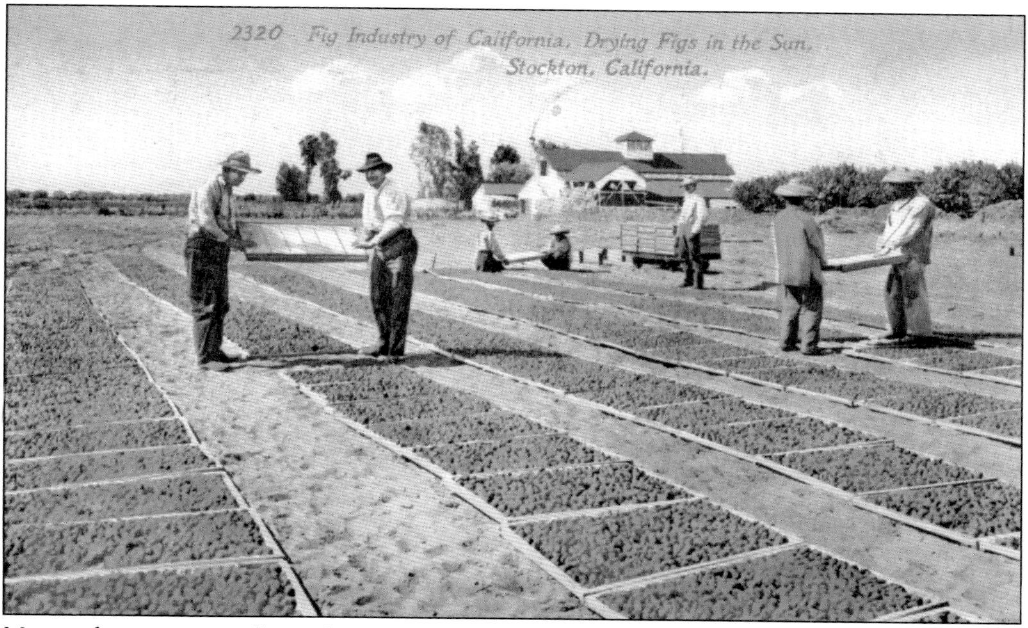

Men and women are all involved in drying figs in this promotional card. Note the Chinese and Caucasian laborers working side-by-side in this early image. Bloomfield farms, located in Brentwood, were known for their kadota (green) figs. In modern times, figs were crated in egg cartons and air-freighted to New York City. In earlier times, figs were dried much like peaches and apricots for preservation.

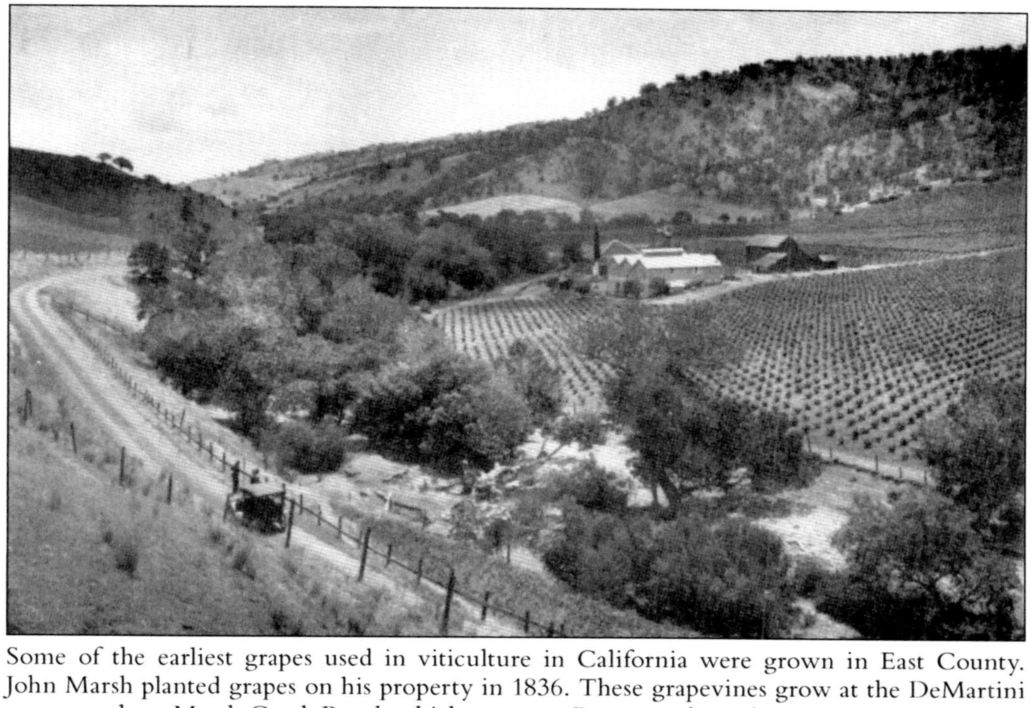

Some of the earliest grapes used in viticulture in California were grown in East County. John Marsh planted grapes on his property in 1836. These grapevines grow at the DeMartini property along Marsh Creek Road, which connects Brentwood to Clayton.

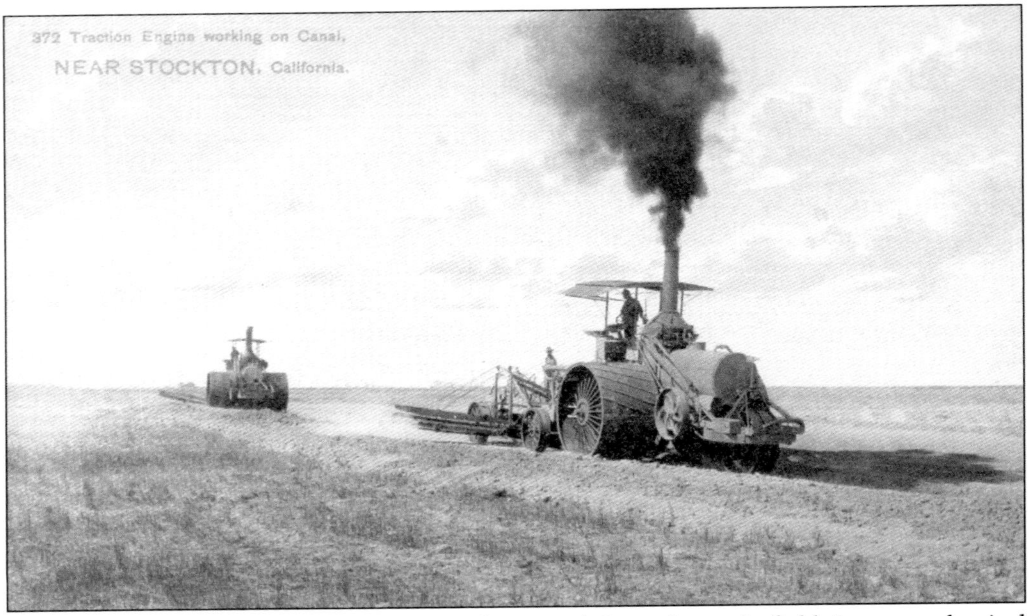

Smoke belches from early steam tractors as they travel through a grain field. It was mechanical innovations like the steam tractor that allowed large British agricultural concerns like the Balfour Guthrie Investment Company to turn 12,616 acres of the Los Medaños tract to greater productivity.

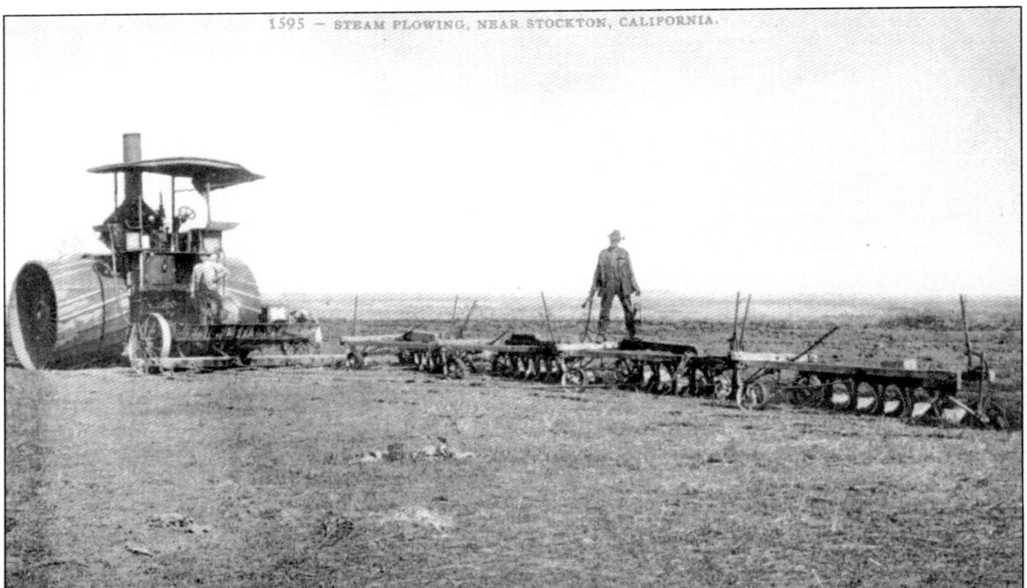

Every disc, plow, cultivator, and spring tooth implement can be harnessed to the steam tractor with ease. One man can do all this. Gone are the 24-horse teams. Note the wide, steel treads on the tractor, ensuring its grip over the long, flat plain.

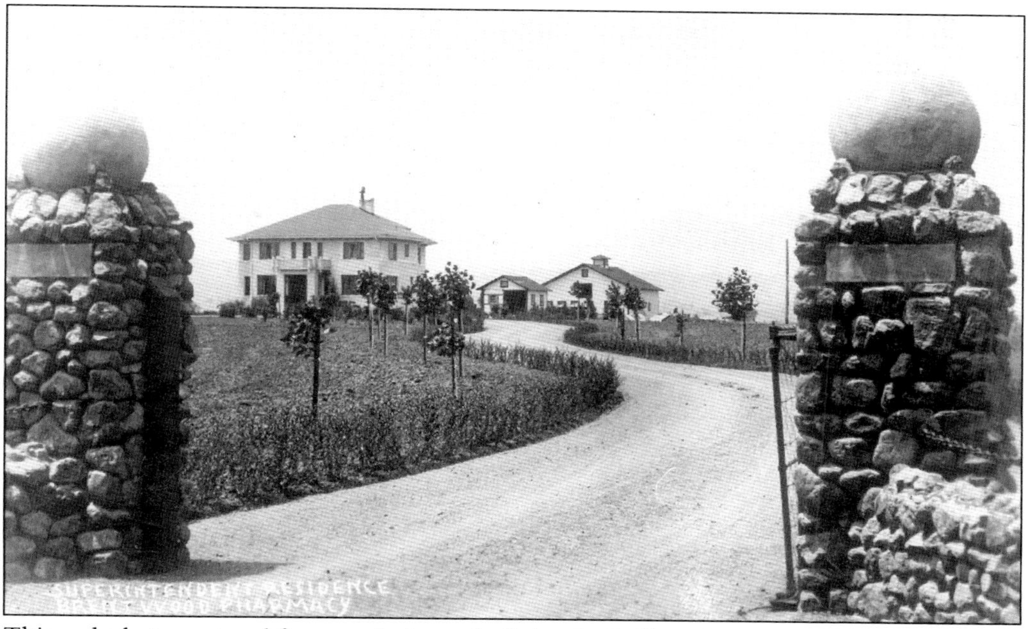

This real-photo postcard features the home built by the Balfour Guthrie Investment Company *c.* 1913 for its superintendent. It was located on the corner of Walnut Boulevard and Balfour Road. It served as the Brentwood Hospital from 1929 to 1931.

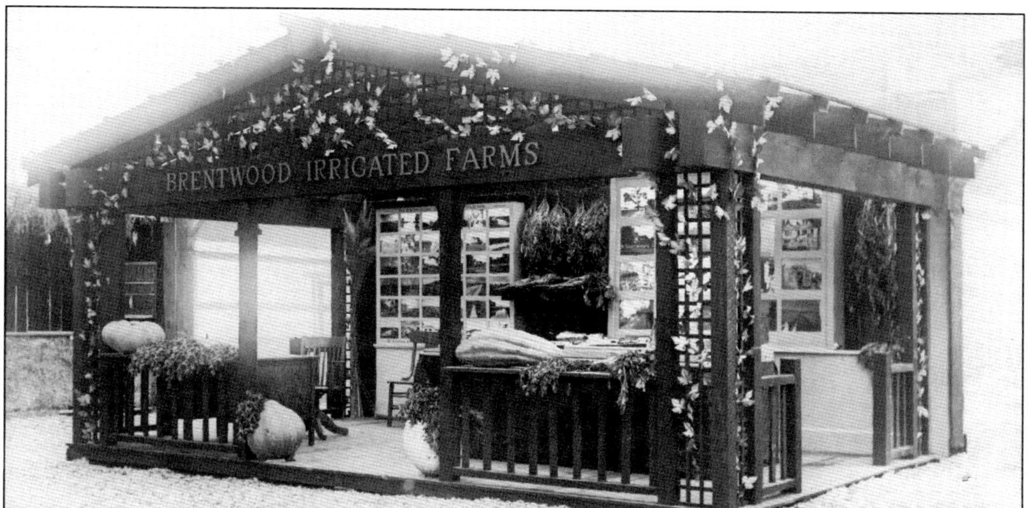

Brentwood Irrigated Farms created this fair display featuring the bounty of the region. An irrigation system was the key to the Balfour Guthrie Investment Company's success. Brentwood inherited the extensive water system and expanded water deliveries to properties throughout the region.

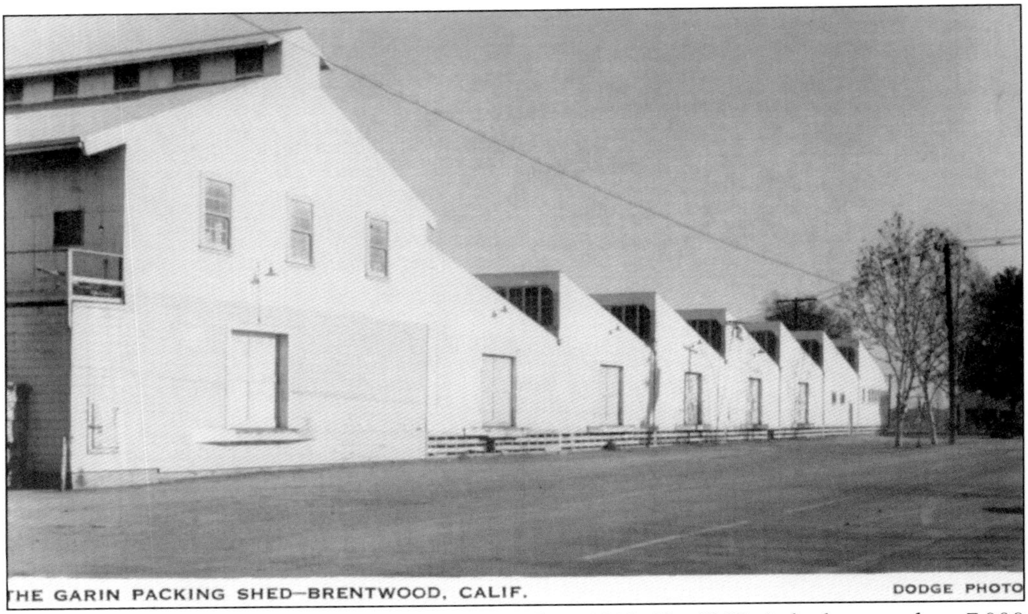

The H. P. Garin Company came to Brentwood in 1923. By 1935, it had more than 7,000 acres producing cauliflower, cabbage, lettuce, peppers, peas, tomatoes, and other vegetables. Its agribusiness operations experienced early farm labor strikes by the International Workers of the World during the Depression.

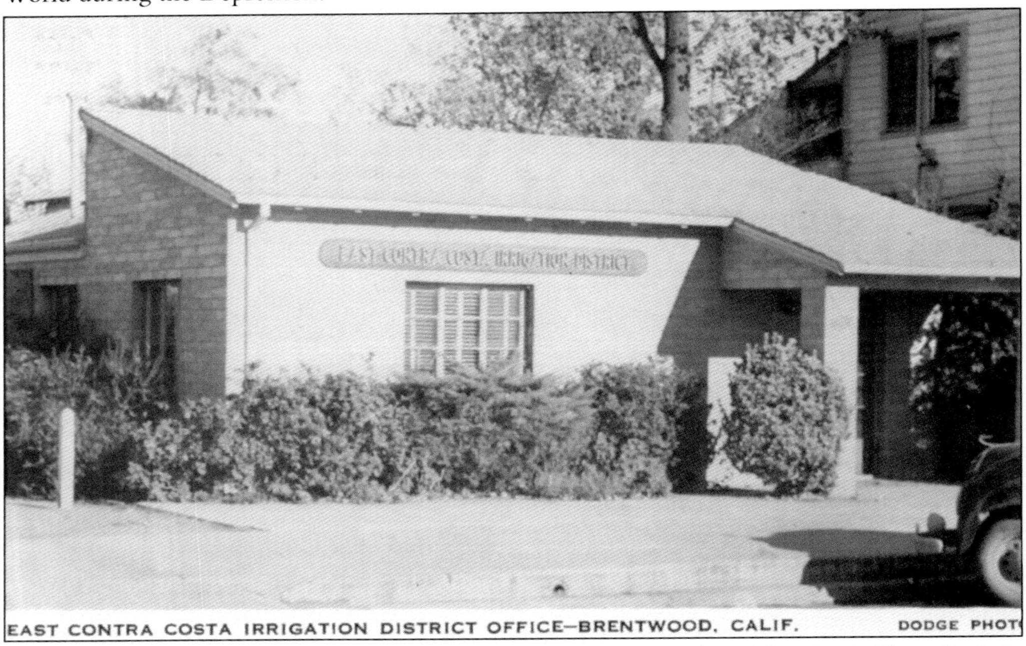

The irrigation network and private water delivery system developed by the Balfour Guthrie Investment Company in 1914 became the East Contra Costa Irrigation District in 1926. It consolidated Lone Tree, Knightsen, and Brentwood Irrigation Companies. The area continued its preeminence in quality produce through continued delivery of water from the San Joaquin Delta. Farmers paid for water measured in feet over time.

A postcard from Byron features the California state flower, the golden poppy. Generic postcards picturing wildflowers were a staple in the stationer's trade. This postcard was sent to friends in Brentwood urging a visit.

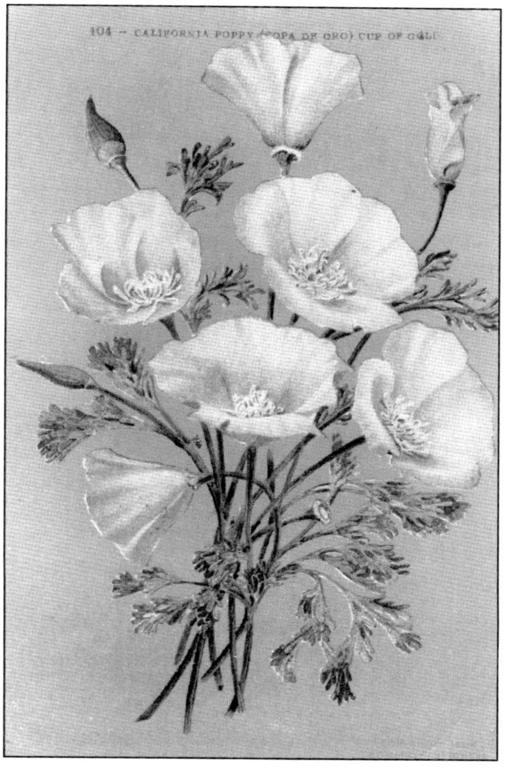

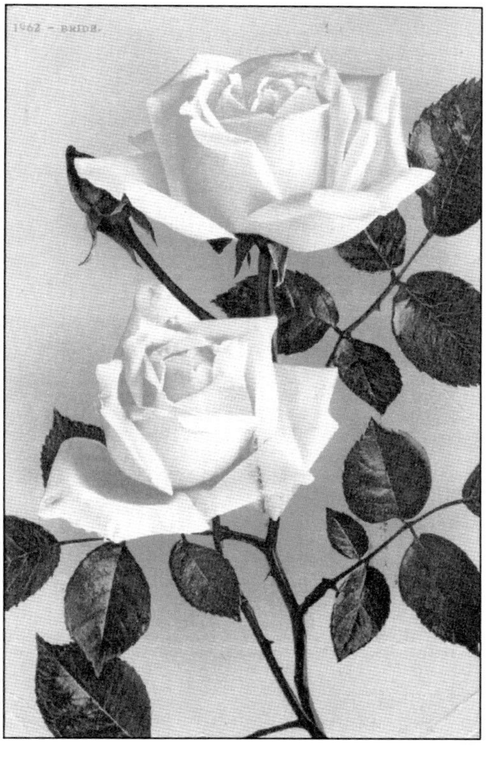

All farming is not agriculture and husbandry. Commercial cultivation of flowers for domestic enjoyment is conducted on a small scale. Herbs and flowers were grown and transported to San Francisco by train.

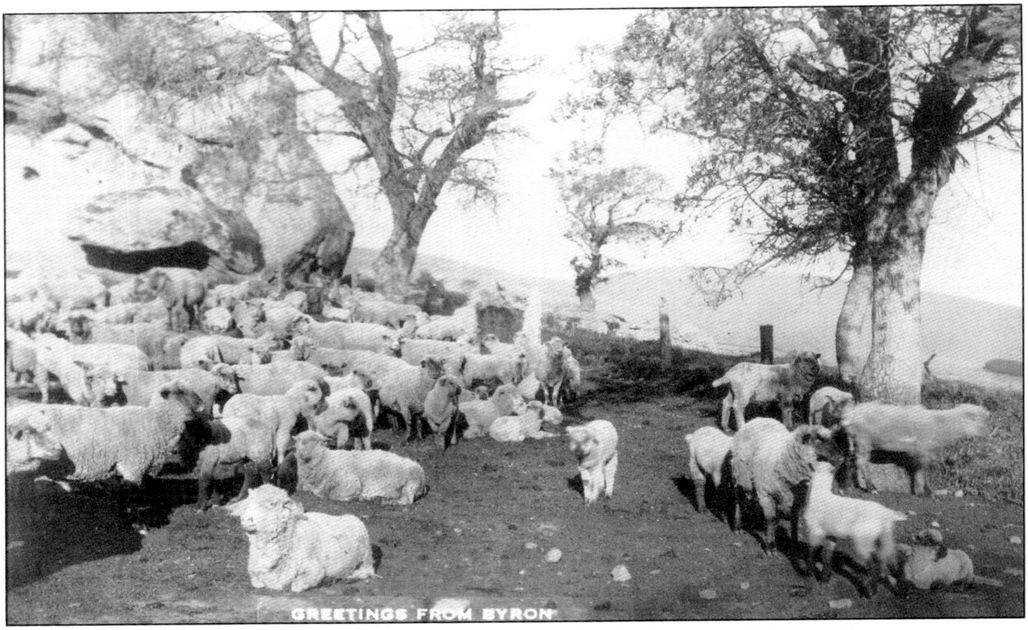

Natural grasses and volunteer wheat creates grazing land where combines and tractors cannot follow. Basque and Spanish families raised herds of sheep in the Vasco region. Sheep belonging to the Pimentel and Santana families graze near the Vasco caves.

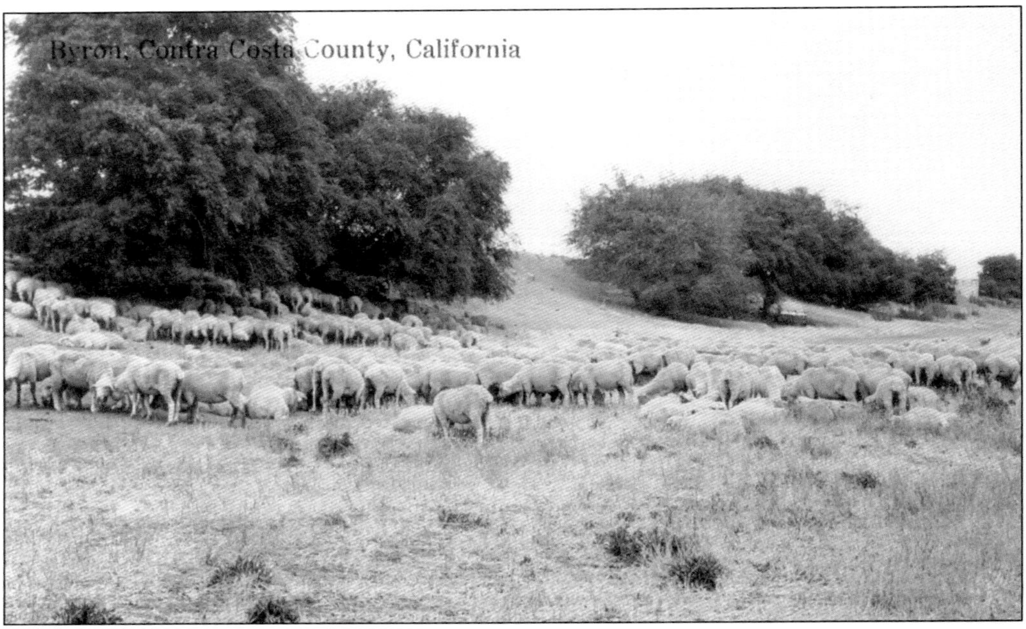

Sheep found their way onto fallow lands and late alfalfa fields to graze near Byron. This sheep herd, belonging to Oliver Armstrong, provided one of the few rural postcards featuring Byron.

Three

Civic Pride and Public Buildings

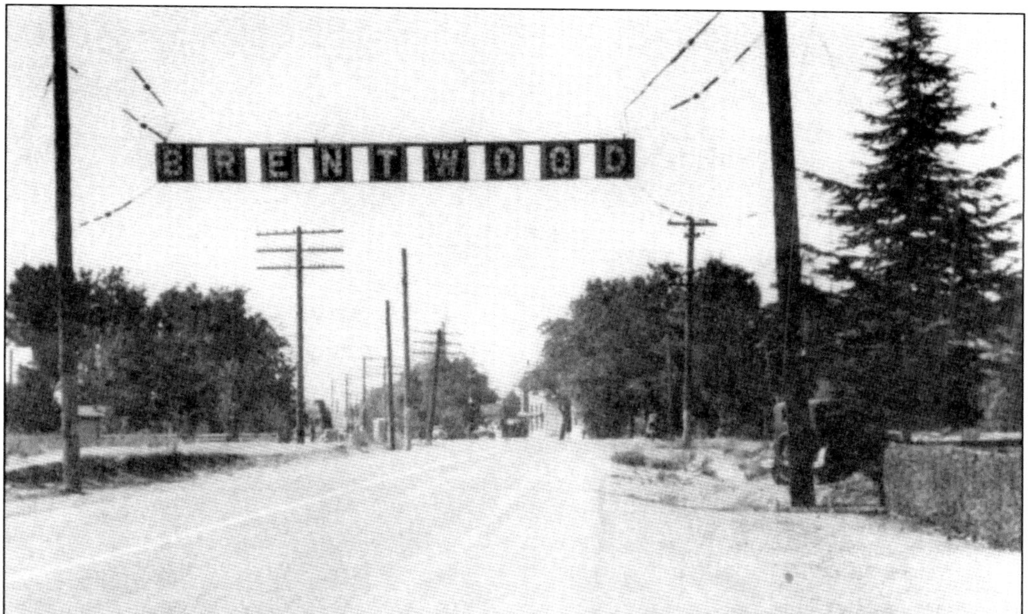

People arriving in Brentwood from the south side of town are greeted with a warm welcome. This illuminated sign spanned Railroad Avenue, today's Brentwood Boulevard, in the 1920s and 1930s. Note the individual light bulbs. The bright electric lights must have been visible from Eden Plain.

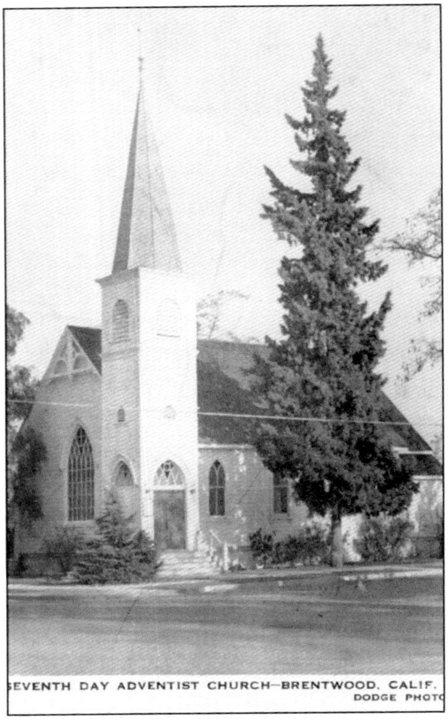

The Seventh Day Adventist Church was one of many houses of worship in the core area of Brentwood. Later it would serve as a First Baptist church and was located across the street, facing the Catholic church at the intersection of First Street and Maple Street.

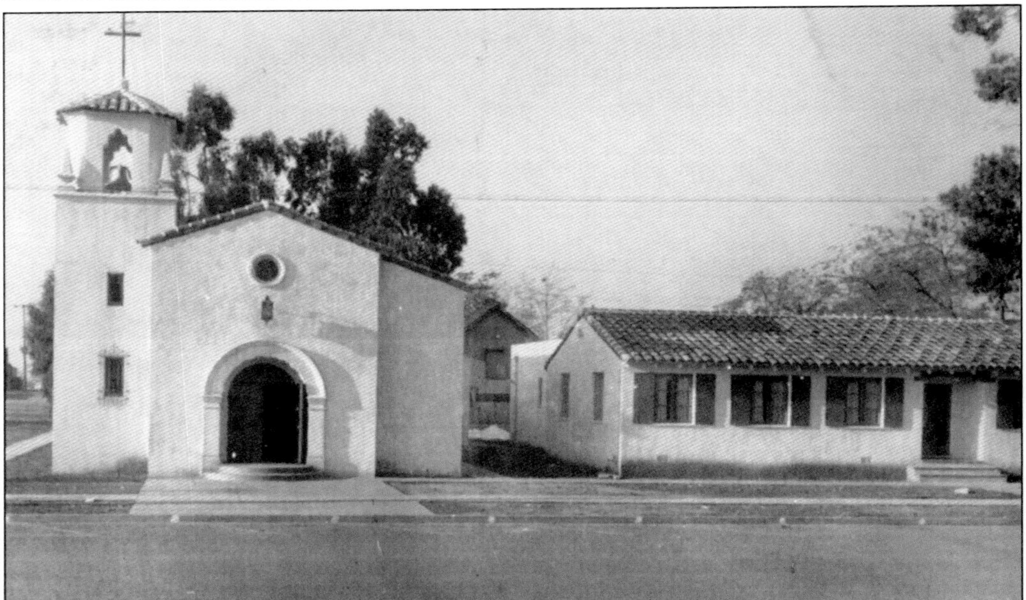

The Immaculate Heart of Mary Catholic Church and Pastorate Building and the First Adventist Church face each other on opposite corners. The Catholic church was dedicated in 1949 and served the community for over 50 years. The church moved to a new facility on the corner of Central Avenue and Fairview Avenue in 2005. The original building is a real estate office as of this writing.

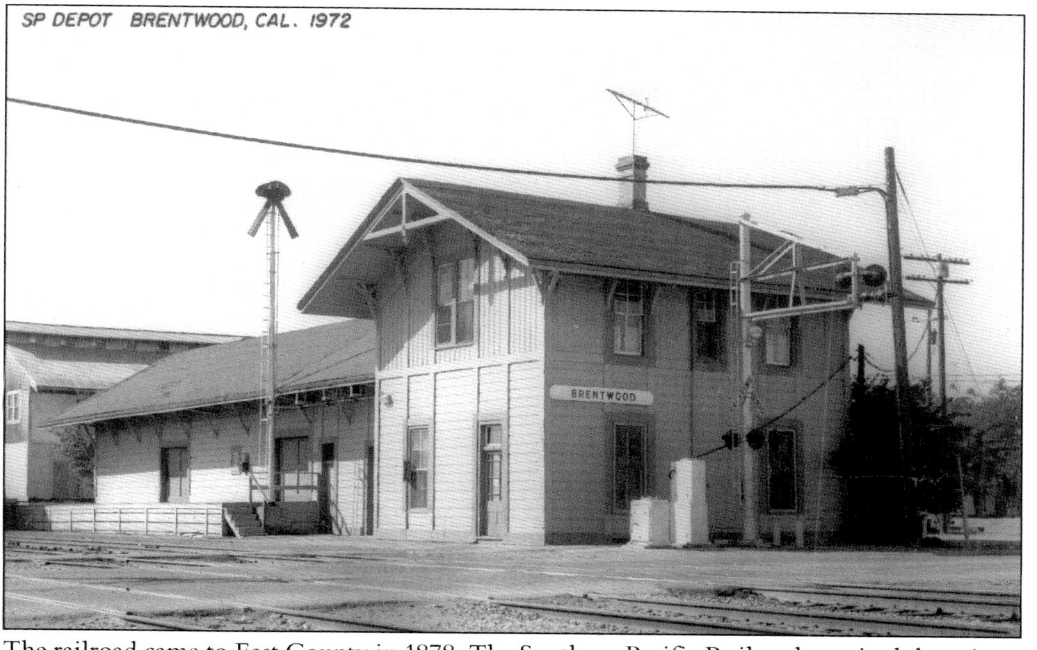

The railroad came to East County in 1878. The Southern Pacific Railroad acquired the private road and built the easily recognizable SP Yellow depot. Produce and passengers embarked on the train lauded as the "Road of a Thousand Wonders" by early promotional brochures.

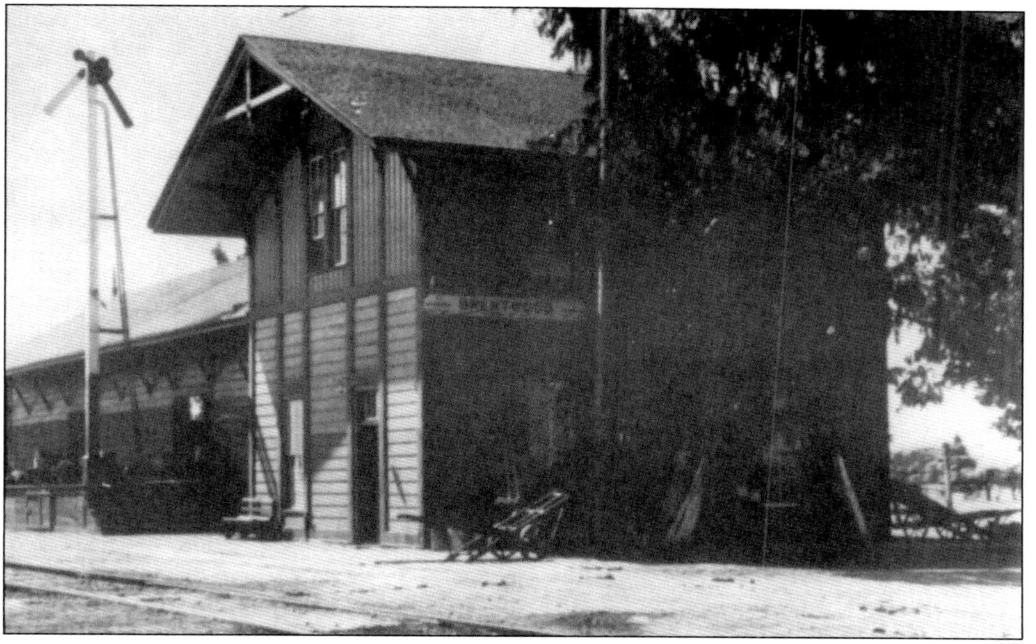

Over time, the original depot suffered from disuse and neglect. At one time, eight trains a day stopped at the depot. Today the Brentwood depot is gone, and it is no longer even a flag stop. Passengers must go to Antioch, Martinez, or Stockton to catch the Amtrack train.

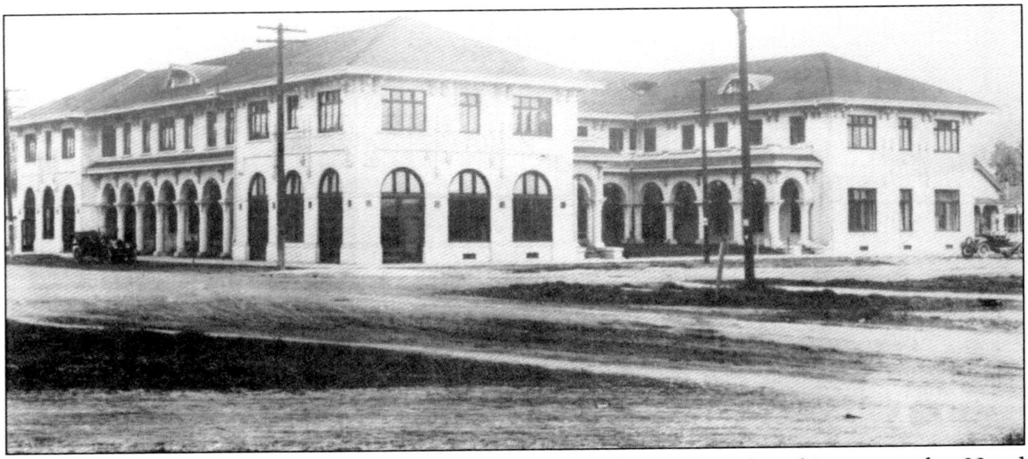

This real-photo postcard captures the crown jewel of Brentwood architecture, the Hotel Brentwood. The Balfour Guthrie Investment Company purchased 12,616 acres surrounding Brentwood in the first decade of the 20th century and immediately entered into a building campaign. The hotel had two separate restaurants, bars, and private room accommodations.

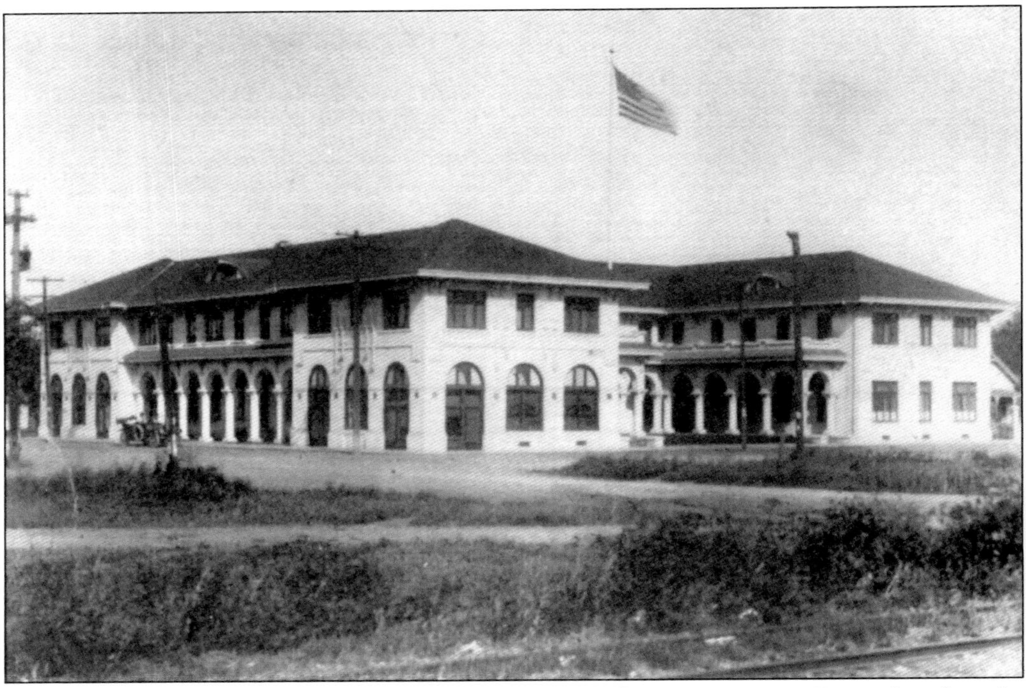

Hotel Brentwood dominated Oak Street in Brentwood for over 50 years. Empty lots face the hotel where restaurants and saloons will soon be built. The reputed cost of the building in 1913 was $50,000.

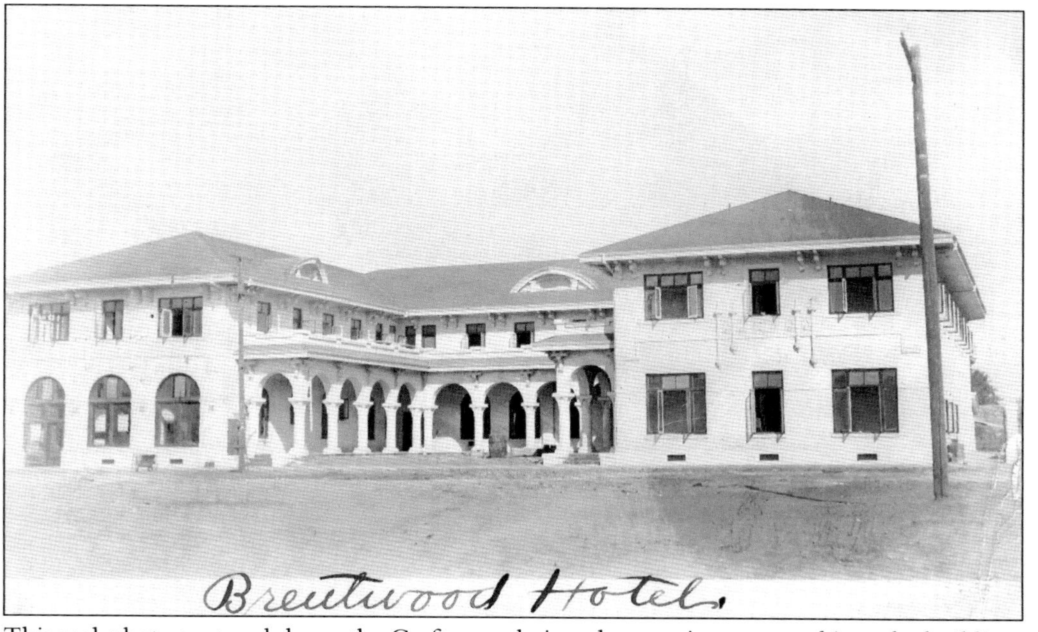

This real-photo postcard shows the Craftsman design elements incorporated into the building, including simplicity, openness, form following function, details, and clean lines. Also seen is the stylistic influence of art nouveau in the Hotel Brentwood.

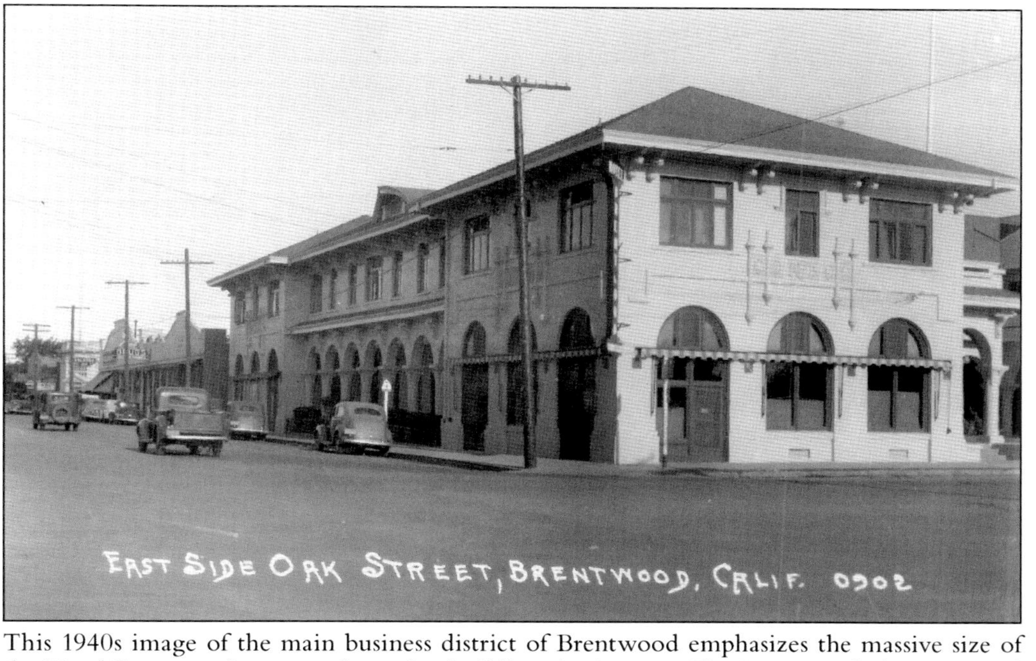

This 1940s image of the main business district of Brentwood emphasizes the massive size of the Hotel Brentwood compared to other buildings in the area. The Brentwood Pharmacy and Ken's "Bad Boy" Market are to the north. The Bank of America, now the Brentwood Press Building, is in the distance. The pharmacy and market buildings have artificial facades to enhance their image. The hotel needs no such artifice.

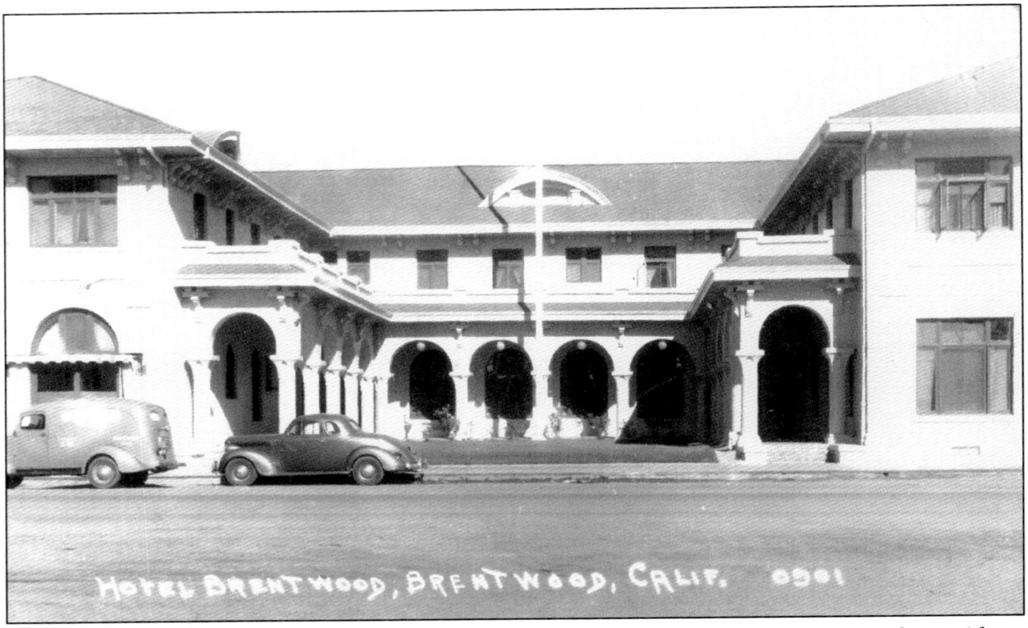

This interior courtyard image shows the Hotel Brentwood's archway-covered corridors. Corporate shareholders visiting from Great Britain, local shopkeepers, and field workers all drank, ate, and stayed at the hotel. The numbers of postcard images of the hotel are second only to the John Marsh house in popularity.

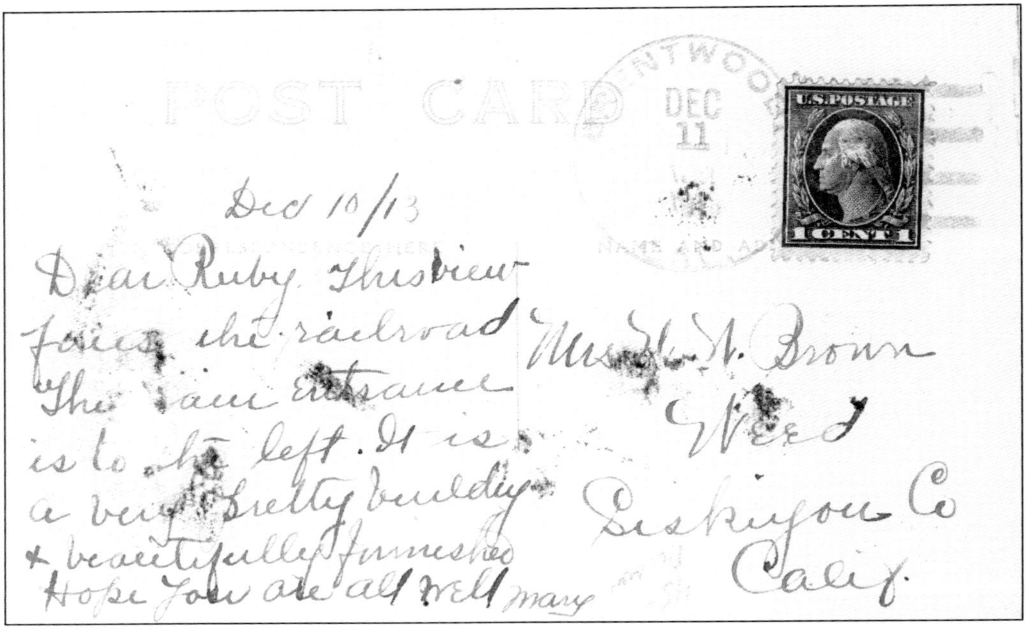

This postcard reads, "Dec 10/13 Dear Ruby. This view faces the railroad. The main entrance is to the left. It is a very pretty building and beautifully furnished. Hope you are all well. Mary."

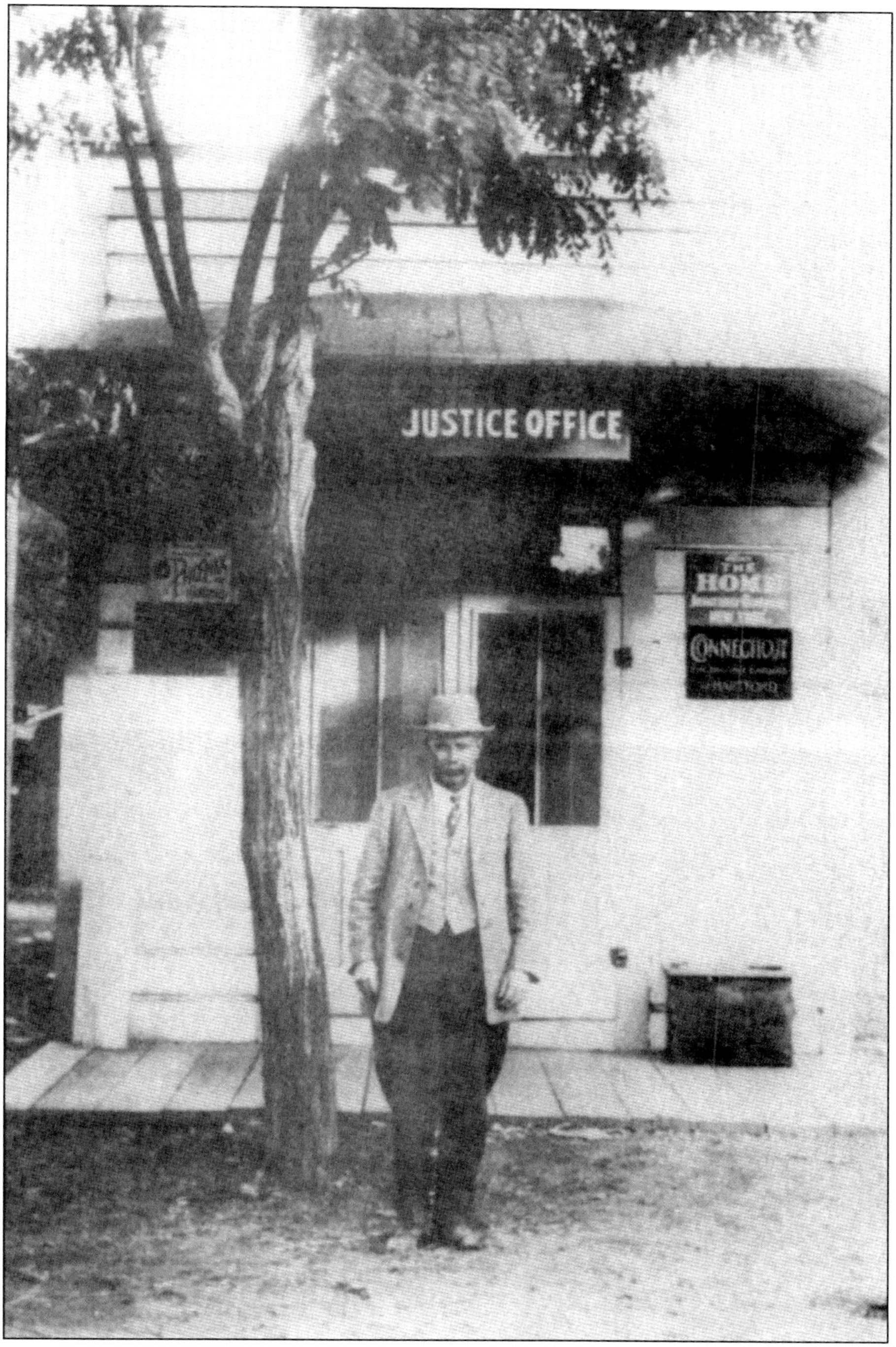

Justice and the rule of law came early to Brentwood. A small town of 200 voting citizens did not lack in civic pride. Judge Robert Wallace stands in front of his office at the corner of Railroad Avenue, now Brentwood Boulevard, and Oak Street. Judge Wallace was elected justice of the peace in 1900. He served over 30 years in that position and 32 years as Liberty Union High School trustee.

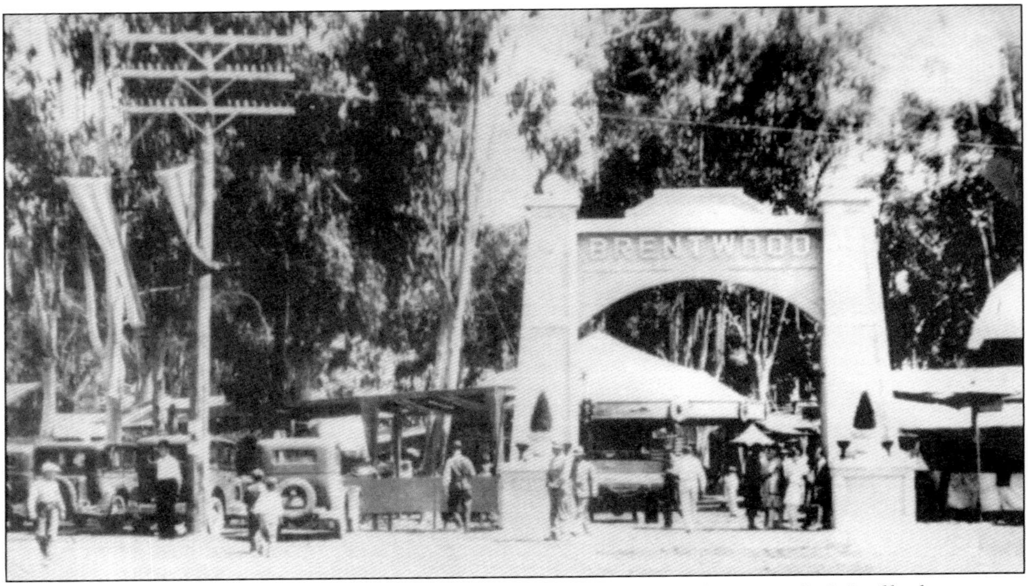

Brentwood had the first public park in eastern Contra Costa County. Originally known as Brentwood Grove, the park, called Brentwood Park today, is still the center of civic events for the community. This image was taken during the three-day Apricot Festival sponsored by the chamber of commerce during late June from 1928 to 1937.

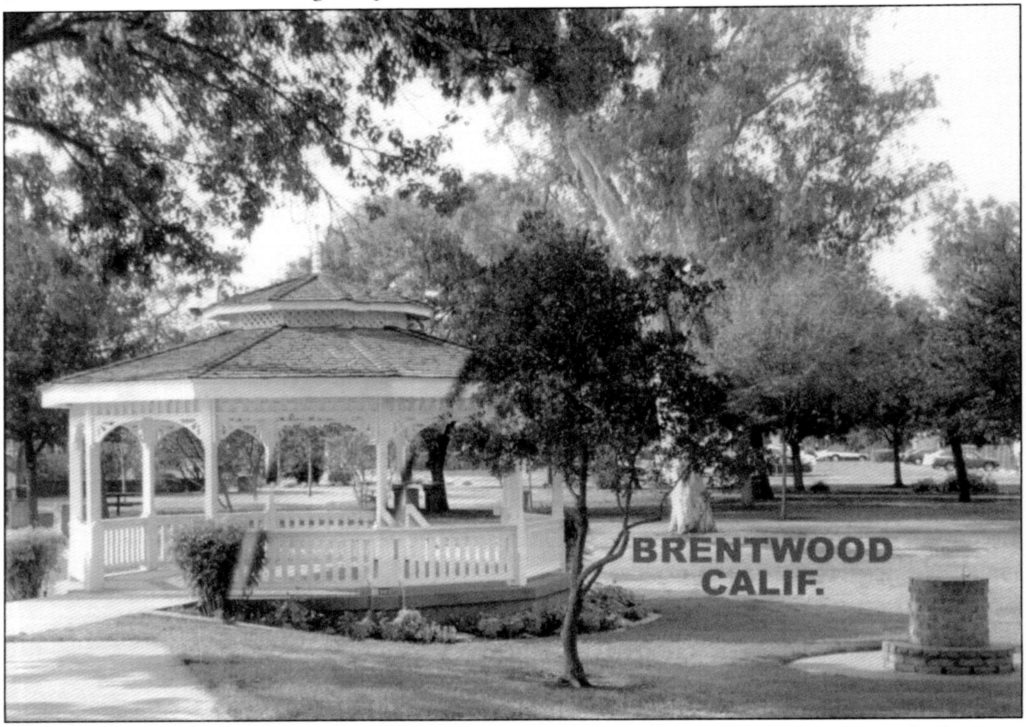

This image shows Brentwood Park as seen today. The gazebo, although rebuilt, hails from the original Brentwood Grove days when municipal bands were in fashion. The chamber of commerce still sponsors a summertime event, the Cornfest, each July.

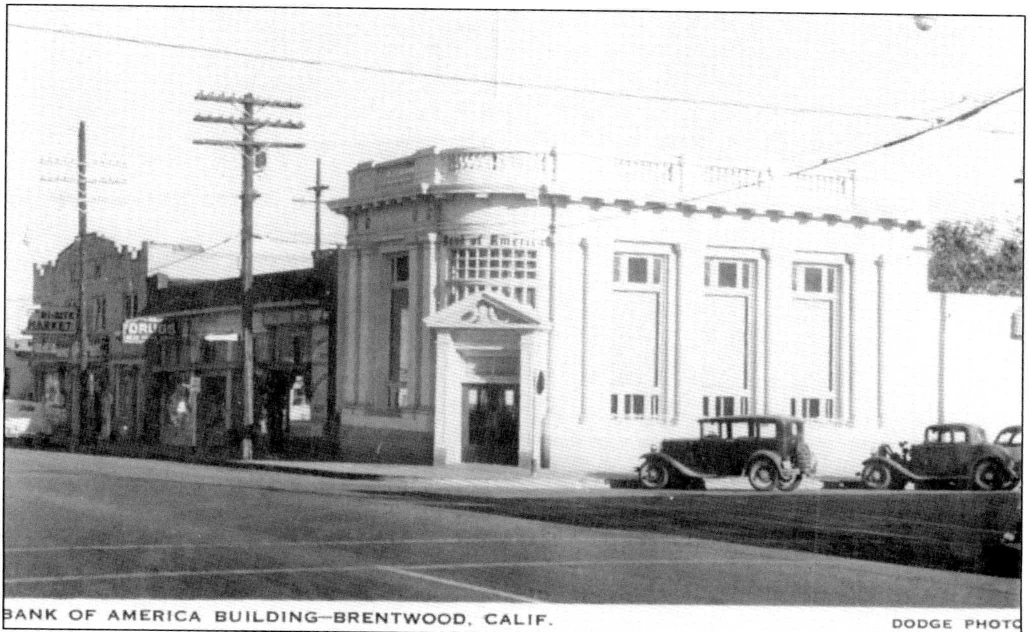

This imposing edifice was originally the Bank of Italy building. The Bank of Italy and its successor, the Bank of America, were instrumental in financing agriculture in California. Known initially as the "Bank of the Little Guy," the bank grew to be a giant that fueled the California economy.

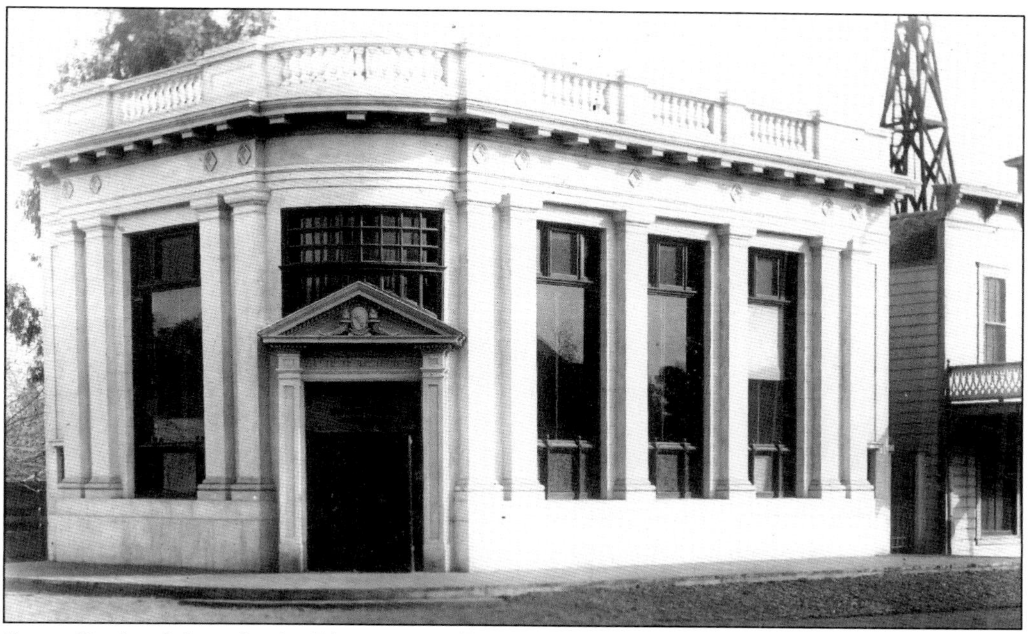

Every Bank of America building in small-town California must resemble this structure in Brentwood. It and the Hotel Brentwood were the two anchors of the business district. It seemed impossible that the bank would outgrow these quarters, but the bank moved across the street to a new, modern building in the 1960s.

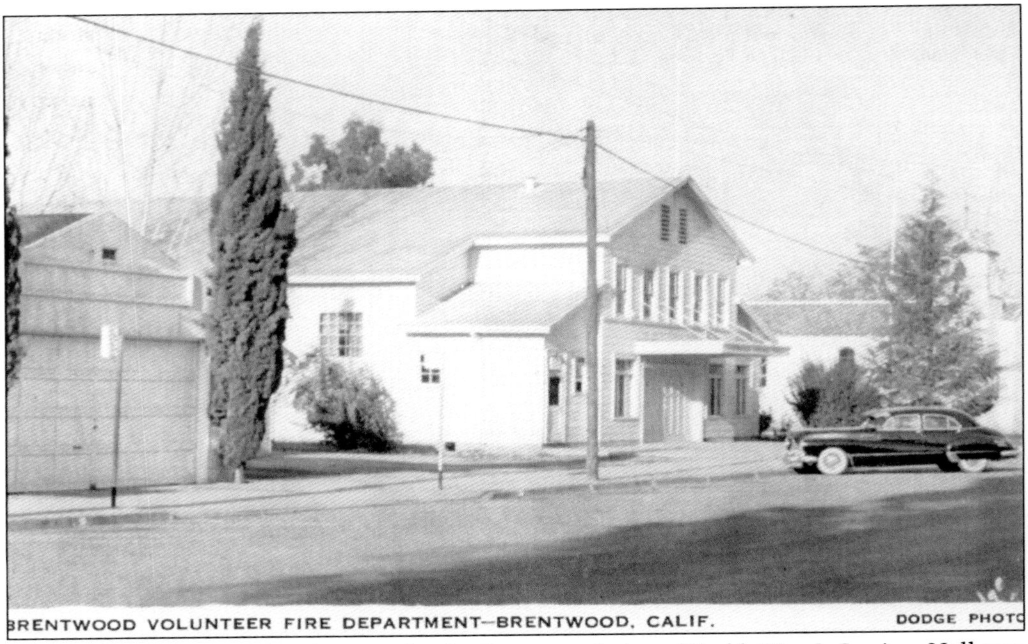

The American Legion has been active in Brentwood since World War I. Legion Hall was constructed in 1924 at a cost of $16,860 with state bond funds. Next door is the original volunteer fire department building. Together these buildings have hosted many volunteer firefighters' balls, high school reunions, and high school classrooms in times of need.

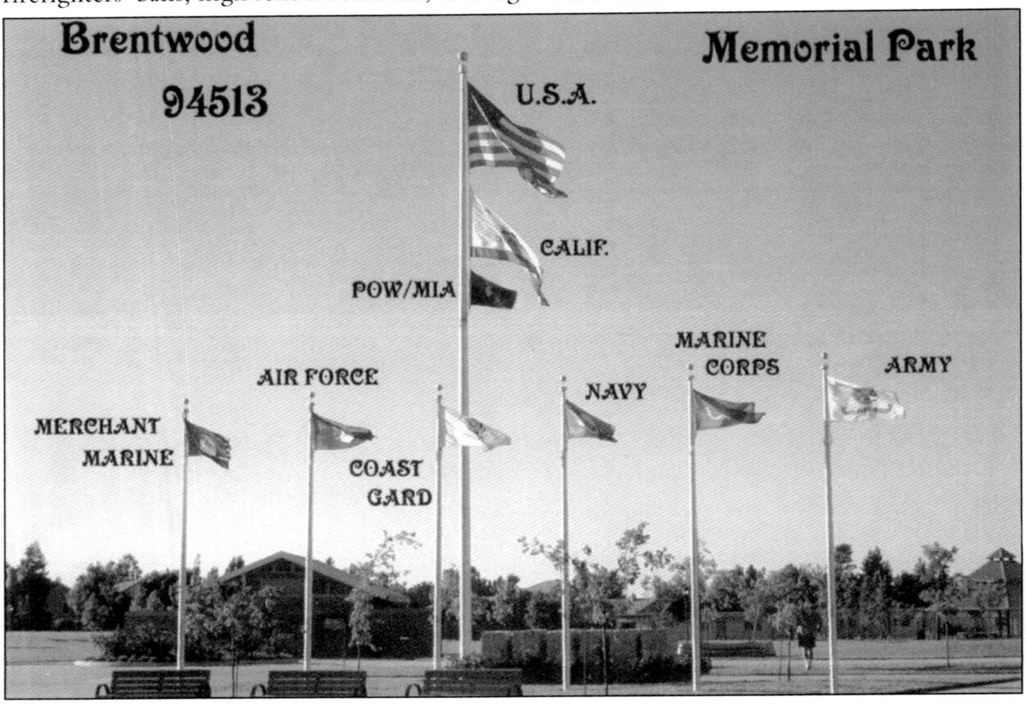

Brentwood's citizens and veterans remember members of the armed forces. Memorial Park honors those who have lost their lives in times of war or in the service of their country.

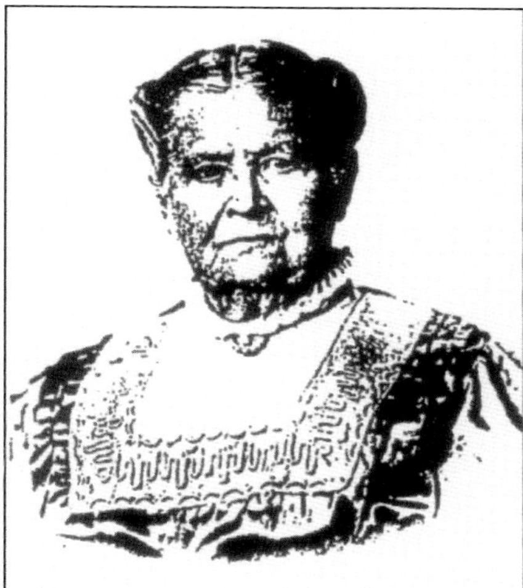

Mrs. Frances E. Donner Wilder
July 8, 1840 - November 21, 1921

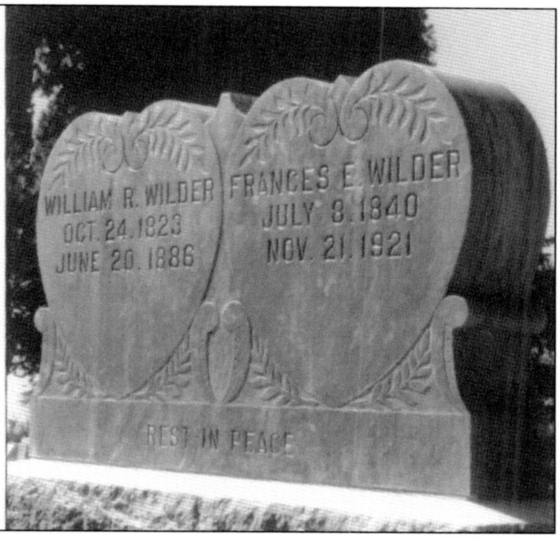

One of the most famous pioneer immigrant parties arriving in California is the ill-fated Donner Party. One of the two daughters of Tamsen and George Donner married and settled in Byron. Frances Donner Wilder, the elder of the two surviving Donner children, married a few years after her rescue. She and her husband, William Wilder, farmed and raised their children here. They are both buried at Union Cemetery.

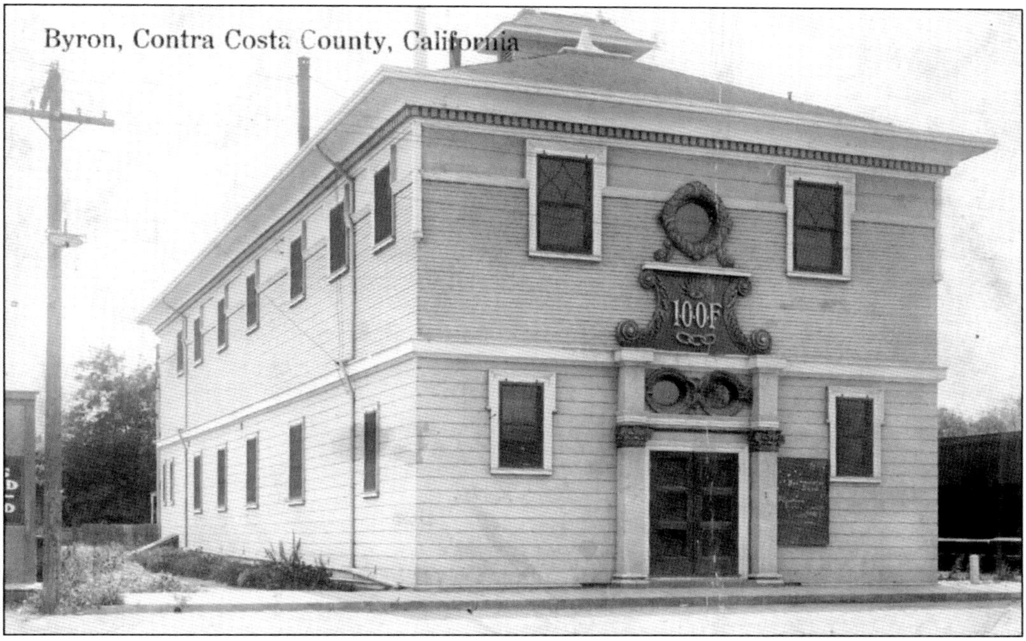

Fraternal organizations are a large part of rural life. The International Order of Odd Fellows building in Byron served the lodge and community for many years. It was here that survivors of the great Byron train wreck were treated. It was also from here that Japanese Americans from the area were collected during World War II prior to their transportation to internment camps.

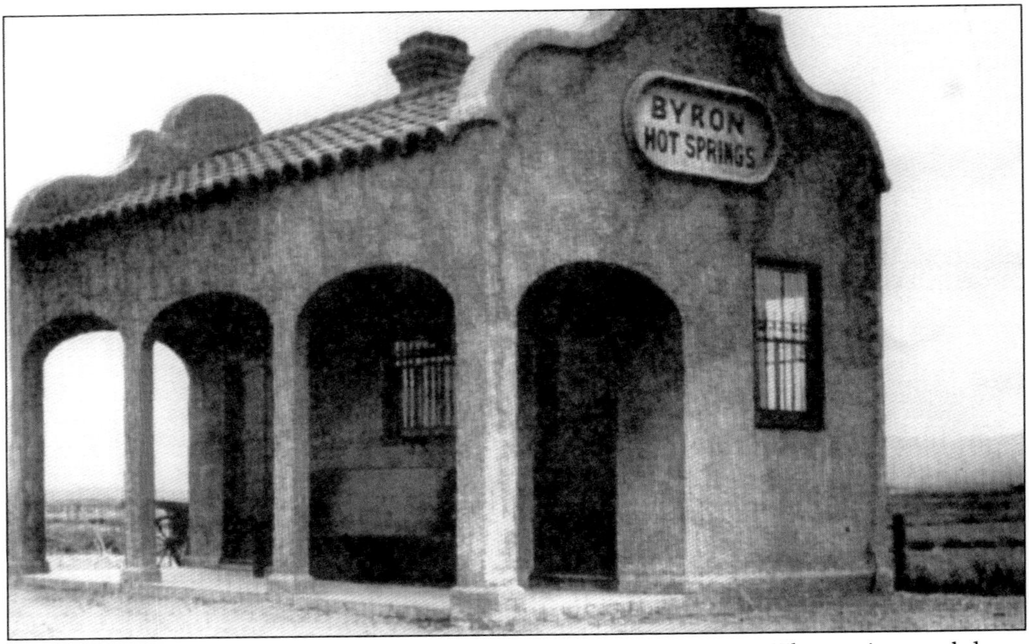

For those disembarking for the Byron Hot Springs, this is the station. The carriage and, later, the estate wagon would meet eight trains a day as passengers came to the "home of health." Many invalids were carried from the train on a stretcher and loaded onto a Byron Hot Springs's transport. A week later, the recovered patient would walk to the train station, cured of what had ailed him.

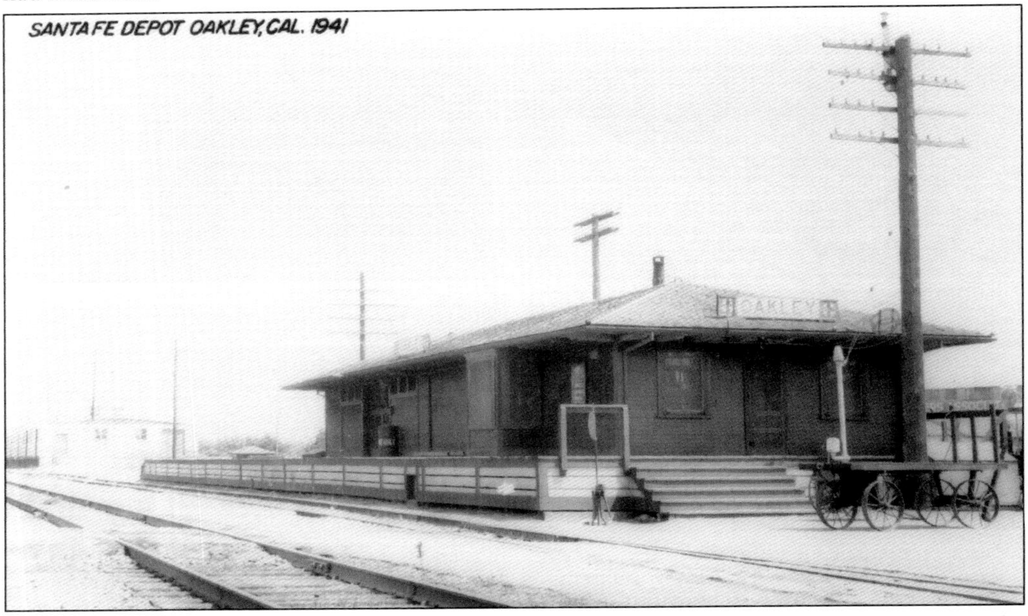

Oakley had a train station serviced by the competing Santa Fe Railway. Santa Fe depots had a distinctive style not unlike the Southern Pacific railroad stations. Here passengers and freight boarded for the route that followed the San Joaquin and Sacramento Delta and San Pablo Bay, terminating in Oakland.

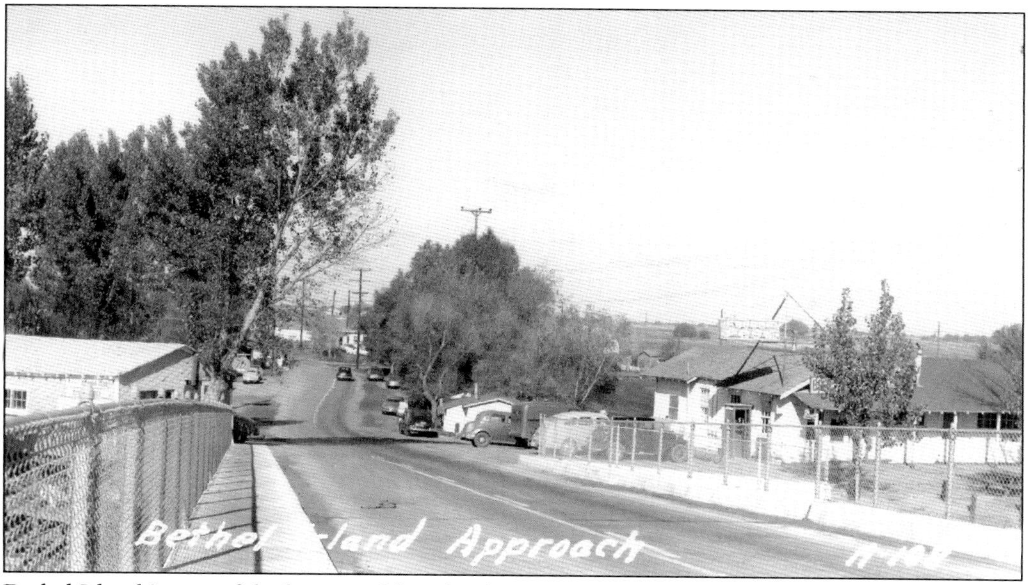

Bethel Island is one of the largest of the islands recovered from the San Joaquin and Sacramento Delta. The levees, built primarily by Chinese labor, were constructed after the completion of the Transcontinental Railway. The acres behind the levees have continued to sink, placing property and homes well below the existing river level.

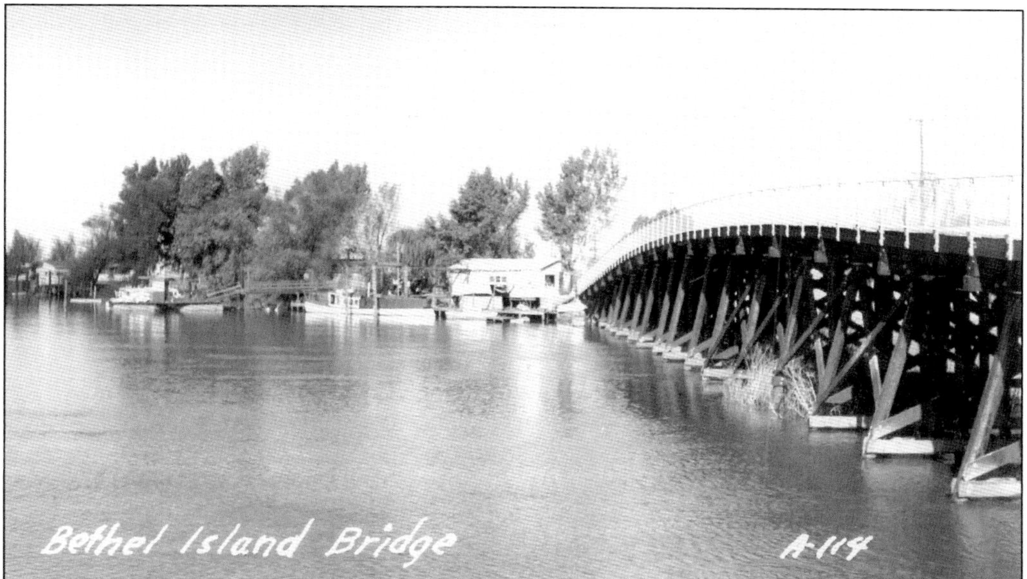

Bethel Islanders are justly proud of the approach bridge to their island. Unlike most small islands in the delta, their island home is accessible without a ferry ride. No tall ships arrive at Bethel Island, and it is outside of the main shipping channel. It is the perfect leisure delta community.

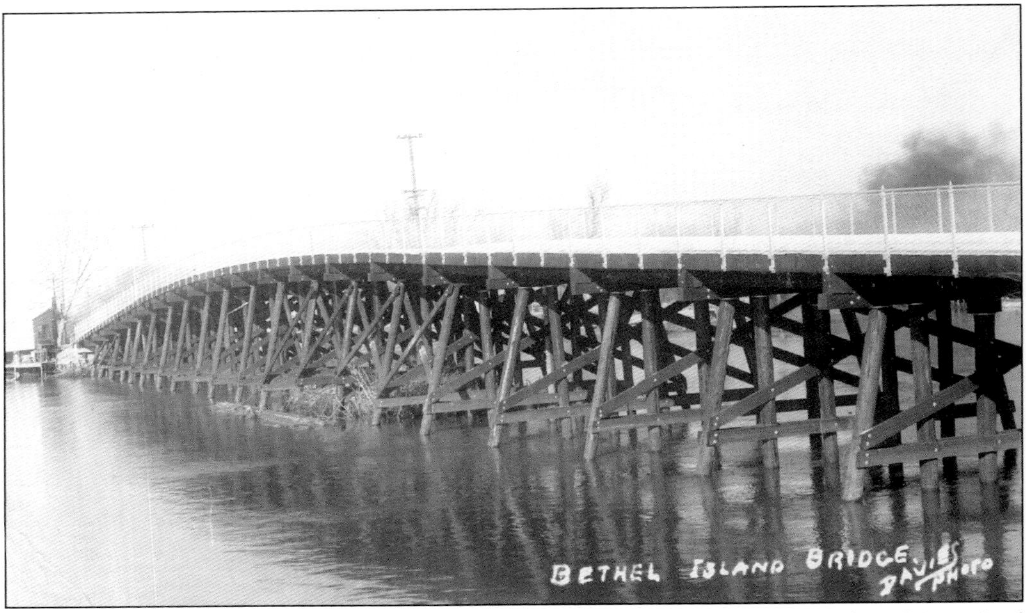

Just beyond the Bethel Island Bridge, one can see the San Joaquin Yacht Club and its retired ferry clubhouse. Also hidden away are clamshell dredges that first dredged for gold in the Mokulemne River. They are now pressed into levee reclamation service. Here, too, are muskrats, beavers, river otters, and other wildlife left unmolested in river byways and habitats.

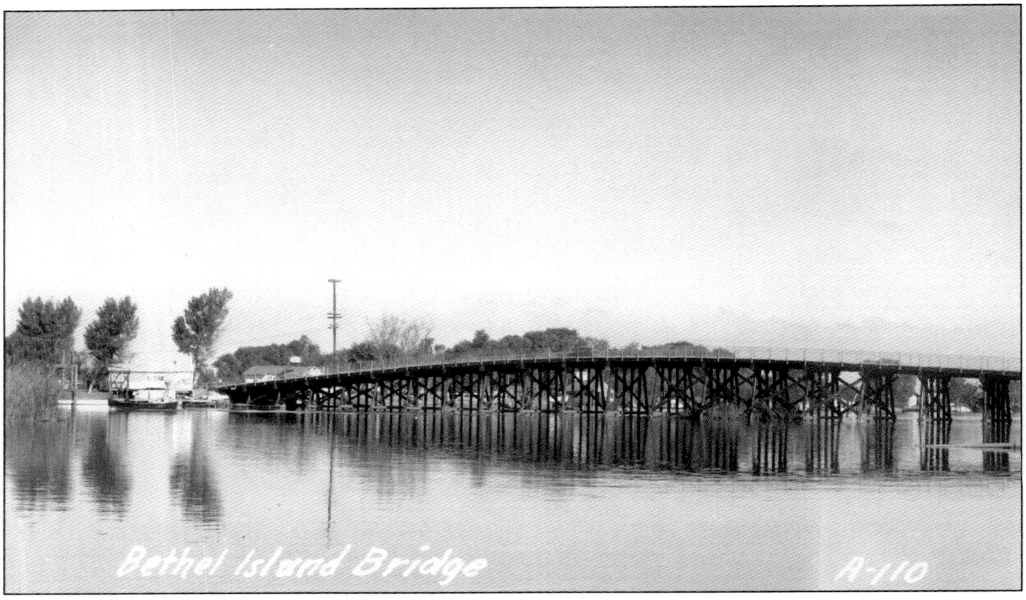

The "gateway to the delta" and its 1,000 miles of waterways has long been the recreational booster motto of Bethel Island. In its time, the island has been home to small farms and dairies. Its soft peat land has even been used as a horse farm for retired San Francisco streetcar horses and police mounts.

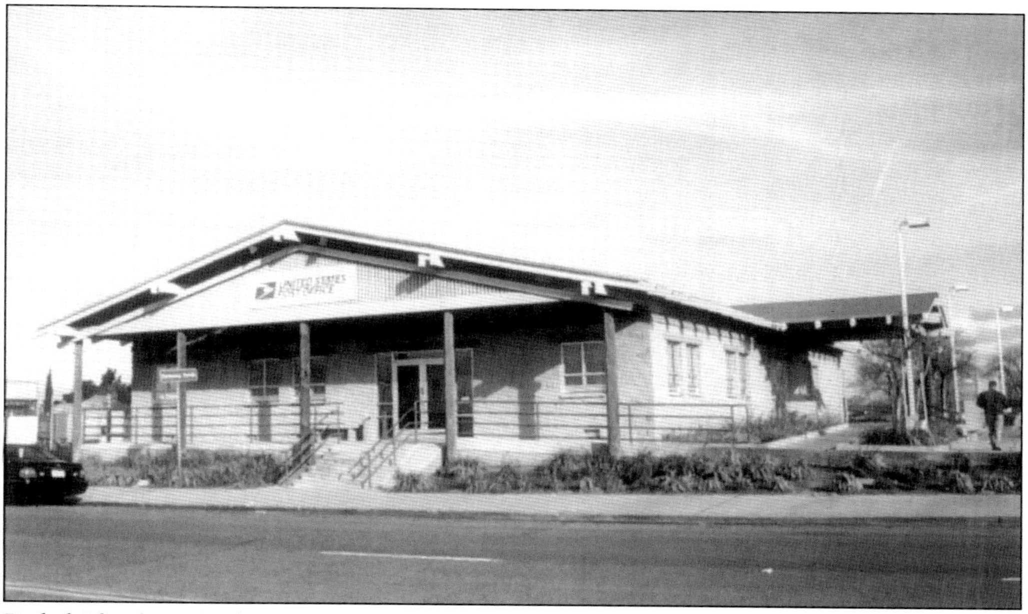

Bethel Island received a new U.S. post office building in the 1944 to replace the small office that was previously occupied. Both home, rural route, and post office mail delivery is available. The postman even delivers the mail to remote California Delta island dwellers by boat.

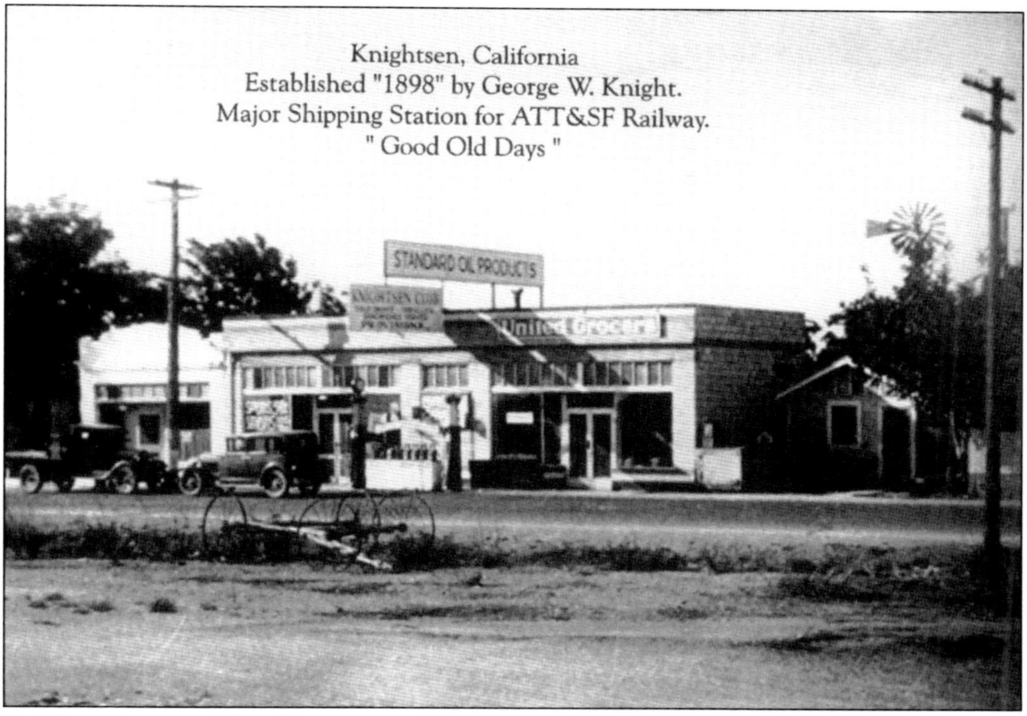

Knightsen is one of the oldest communities in eastern Contra Costa County. It was originally established as a shipping point for the Santa Fe Railway. The railroad depot is still active at harvest with a cooling station and facilities to ship car after car of sweet yellow and white corn.

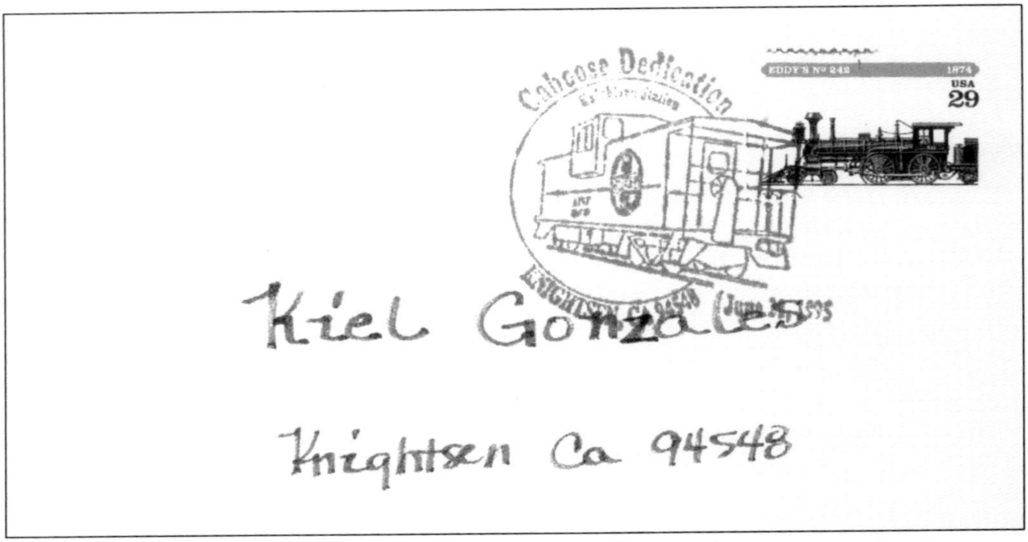

Philatelists (stamp collectors) love small-town post offices, and commemorative issues are heavily collected. Dedication of a railroad caboose in June 1995 was an occasion for a special commemorative issue in Knightsen.

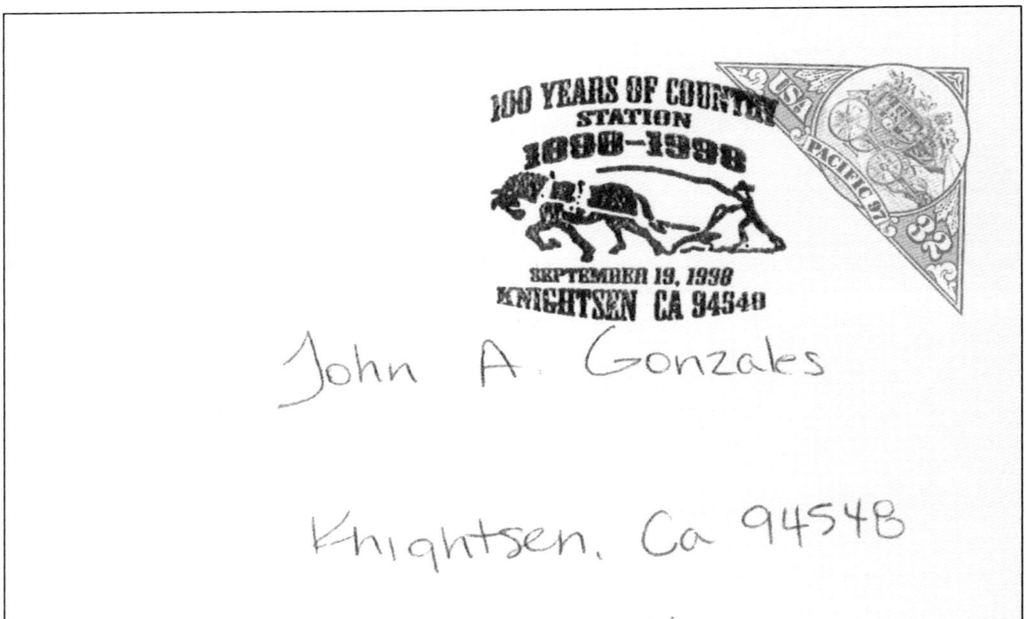

Commemoration of a country post office located in Knightsen for 100 years provides another excuse for civic pride and celebration. Many original buildings in Knightsen are still standing, suggesting that the community may avoid suburbanization and become a historic district.

Four

Commercial Districts

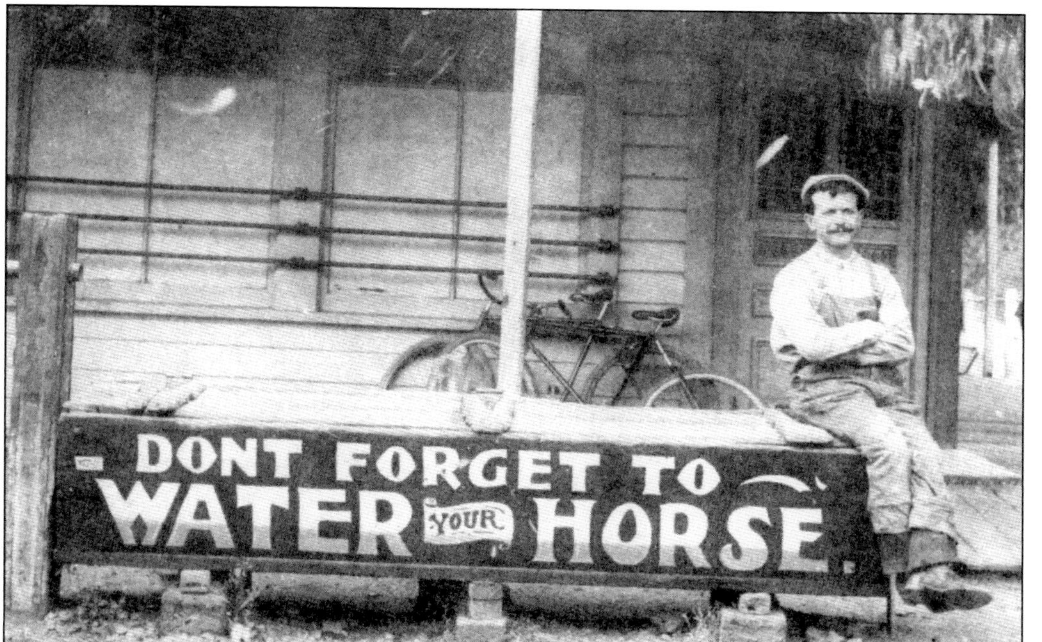

Don't forget to water the horse, but note the bicycle behind the water trough. The proud proprietor of Torre's Saloon, Jimmie Torre, poses in front of his establishment. This photograph was taken *c.* 1910.

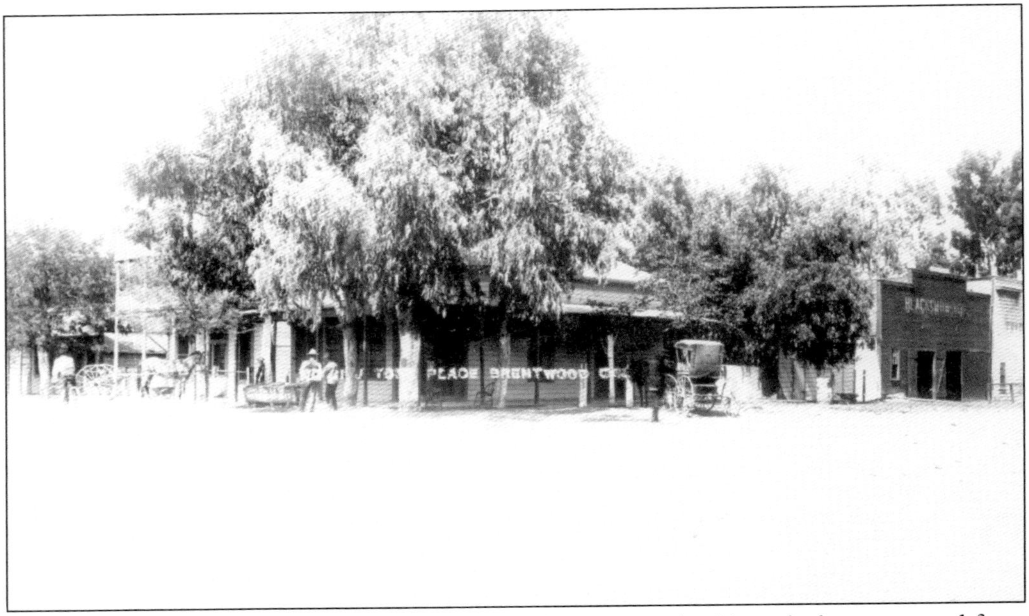

Jimmie Torre poses outside his Torre's Saloon and Ice House in this real-photo postcard from 1910. This establishment was Brentwood's first saloon as built and owned by Louis Bacagallupi in 1881. Bacagallupi sold the bar to Torre in 1888. Today Torre's Saloon, now called Sweeney's, continues to extend hospitality at the corner of Oak Street and First Street.

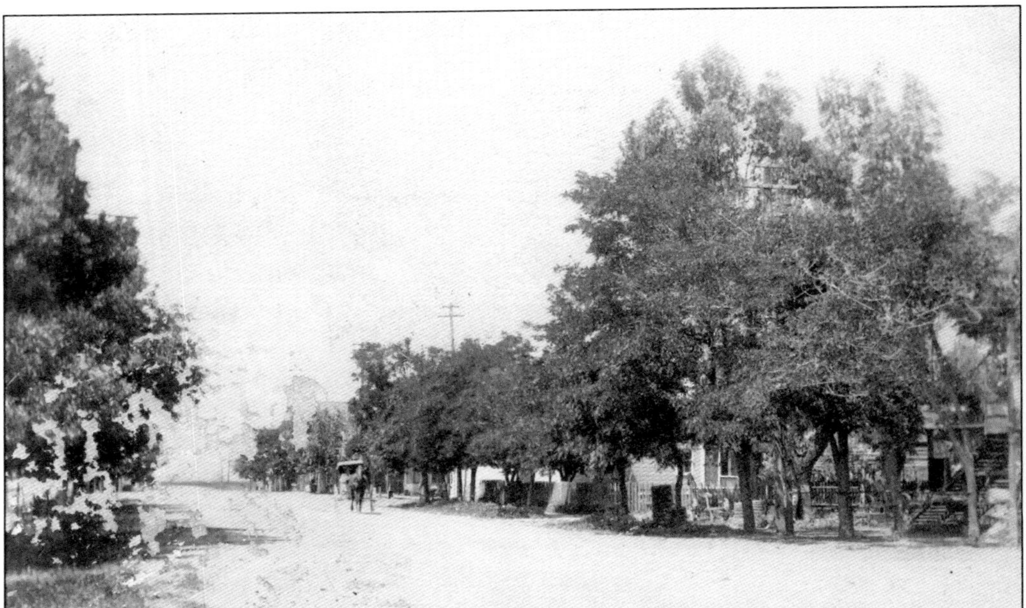

Looking north along Oak Street from Torre's Saloon, a tree-lined Brentwood is depicted before the arrival of the Balfour Guthrie Investment Company. A sole horse-and-buggy travel down the street. It is paved with hard gravel, not asphalt, and has no stop signs, curbs, or sidewalks.

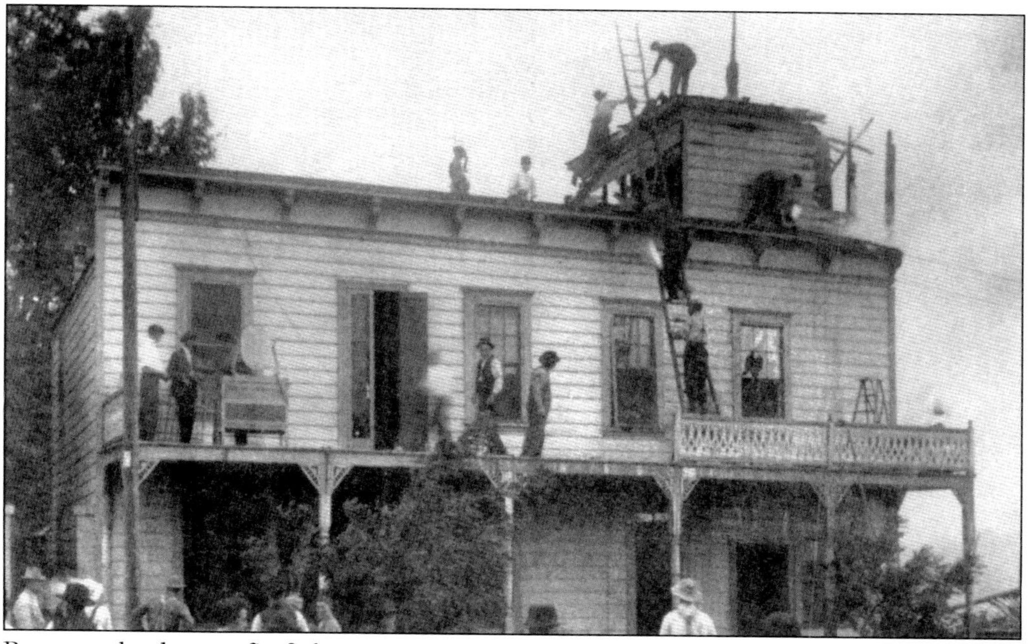

Brentwood volunteer firefighters attempt to save Diffin's Boarding House in 1915. Note the bucket brigade of water passes from hand to hand and pours water on the flames. No fire trucks, water pumps, or hoses are in sight. Diffin's was on First Street next to the Bank of Italy building.

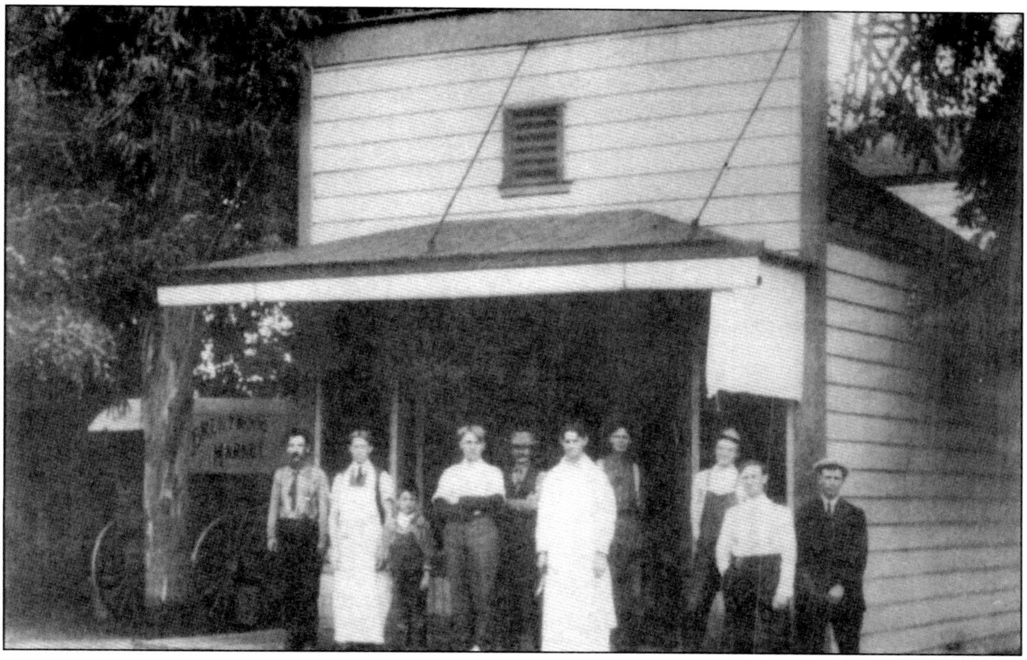

The grocers, butchers, and staff of the Brentwood Market proudly wait to offer their services in front of their establishment in downtown Brentwood. They only do take-out orders. Note the wagon to the left of the building for home deliveries.

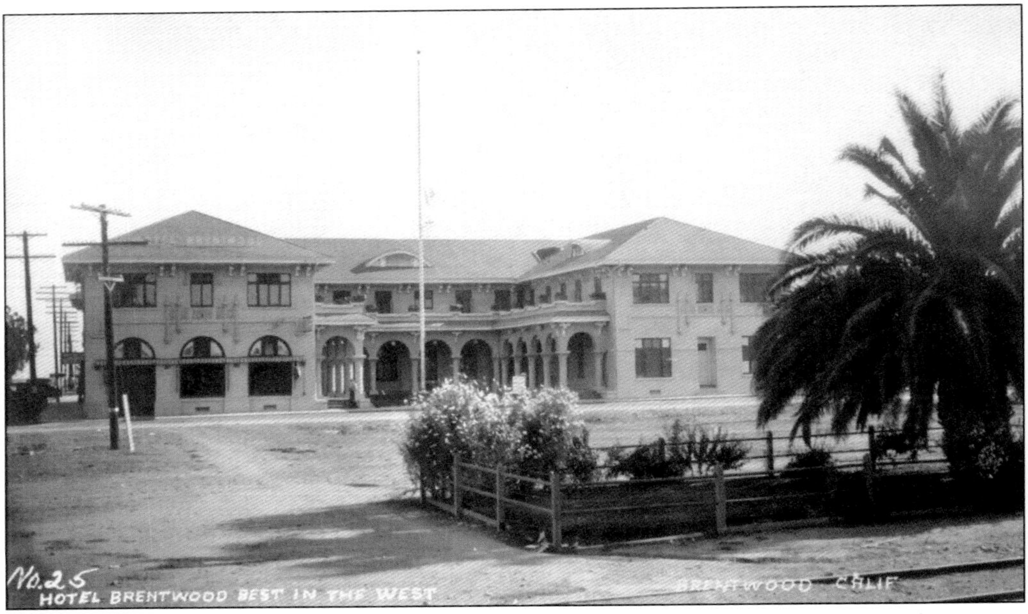

Real-photo postcards were popular from the 1890s through the third decade of the 20th century. As camera equipment became lighter and more easily transportable, photographers left their studios and controlled environments for the open air. Photographs were taken and developed in wagon darkrooms. Townspeople clamored for images showing civic improvements.

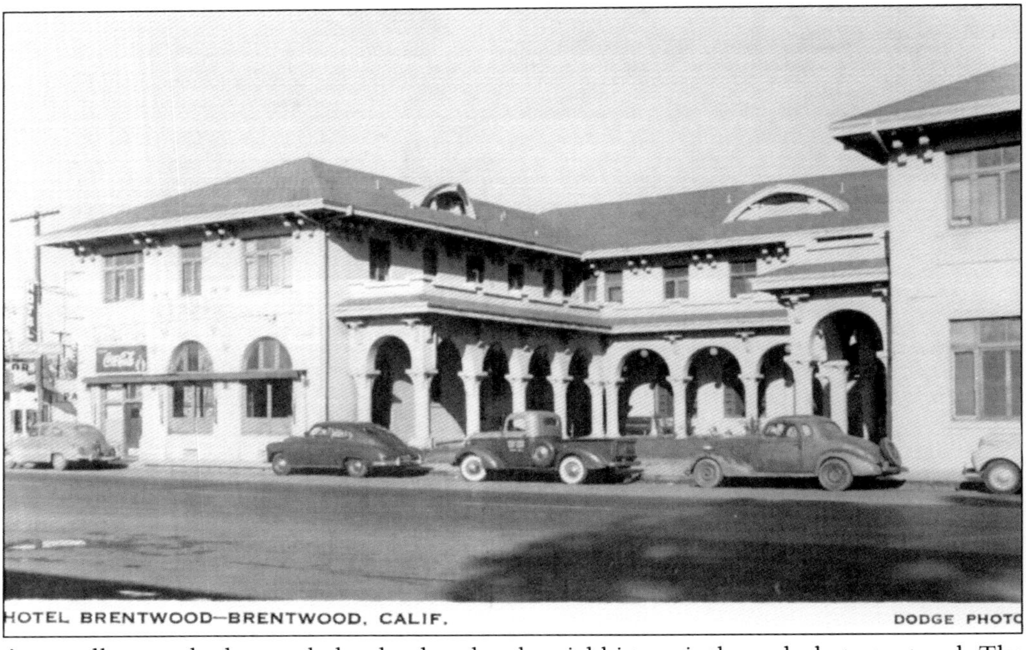

An excellent method to study local cultural and social history is the real-photo postcard. The economic improvements or social transition of a community can be captured in popular images of the time.

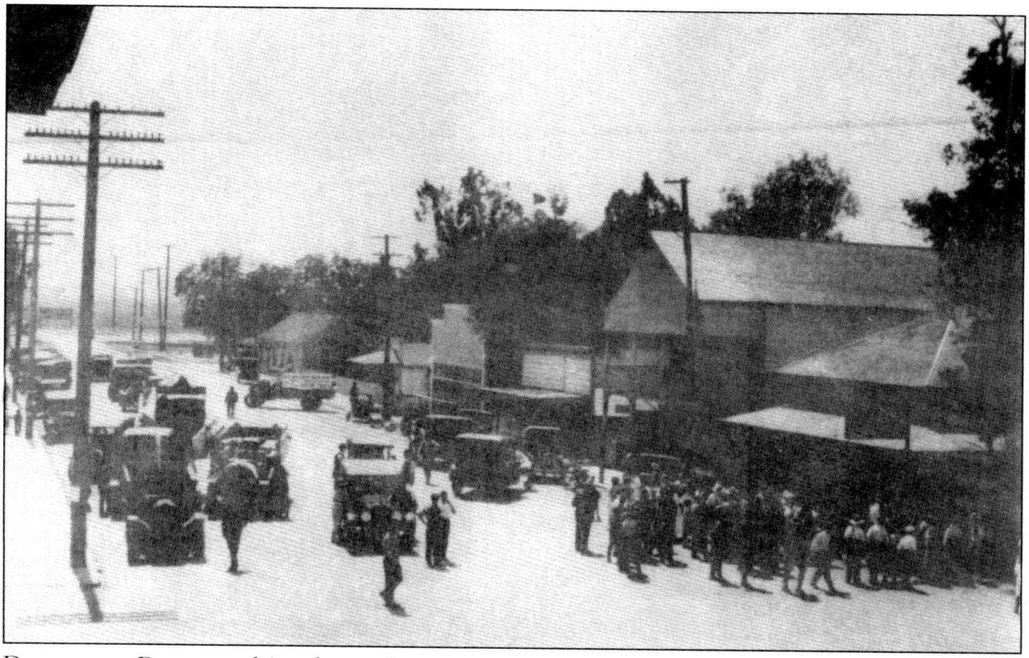

Downtown Brentwood is a busy place, and there is not a horse-and-buggy to be seen. The main commercial street, Oak Street, is still unpaved and sports wooden sidewalks in this real-photo postcard. Oak Street was paved in 1915.

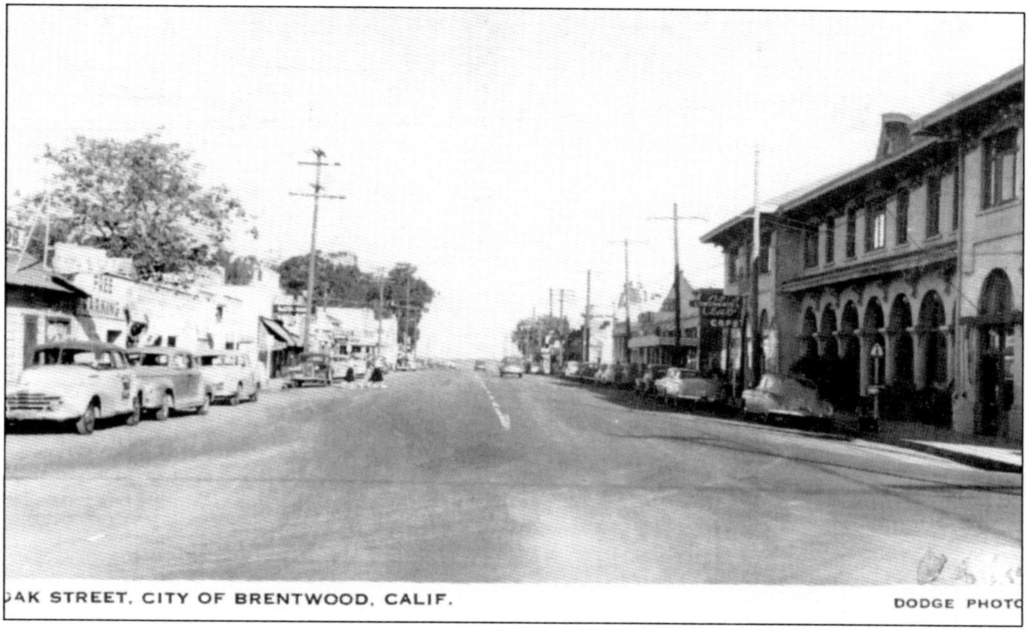

Oak Street in Brentwood in the 1940s has changed a great deal since the 1920s. The streets are paved, the sidewalks are cement, and parking is at a premium. Note the sign on the left advertising free parking, as this is still the case on all Brentwood streets as of 2007.

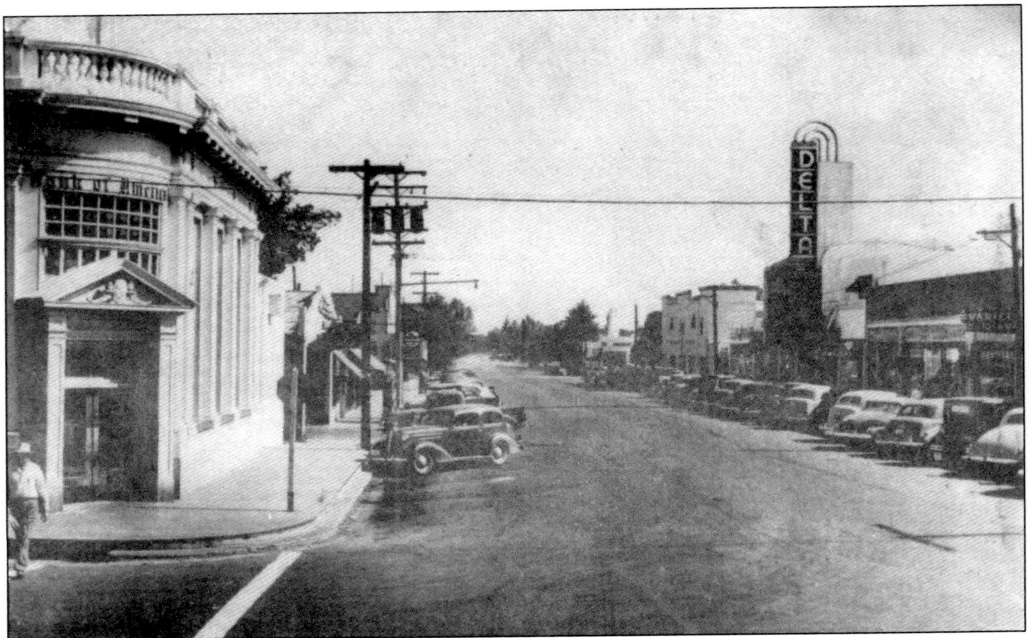

First Street in Brentwood features the keystone building housing the Bank of Italy (later Bank of America), built in 1913, and the Delta movie theater, built in 1938. Next to the Delta theater was an ice cream fountain and a dry goods store. A dime store completed the block.

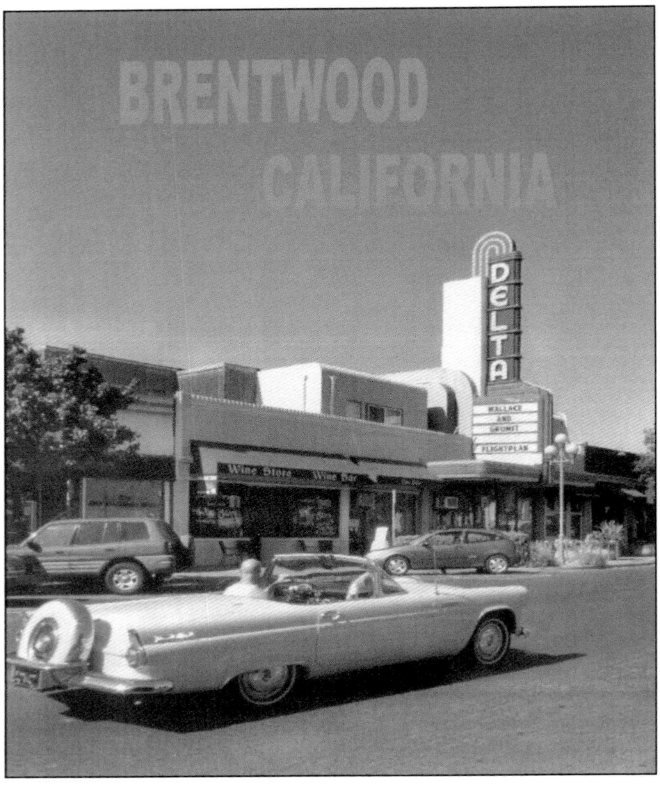

A person can still cruise First Street in Brentwood in a classic car. Gone are the Spanish-language pictures shown only on Tuesdays and Wednesdays, and English-language films on Fridays, Saturdays, and Sundays. Today first-run movies with matinees are shown daily.

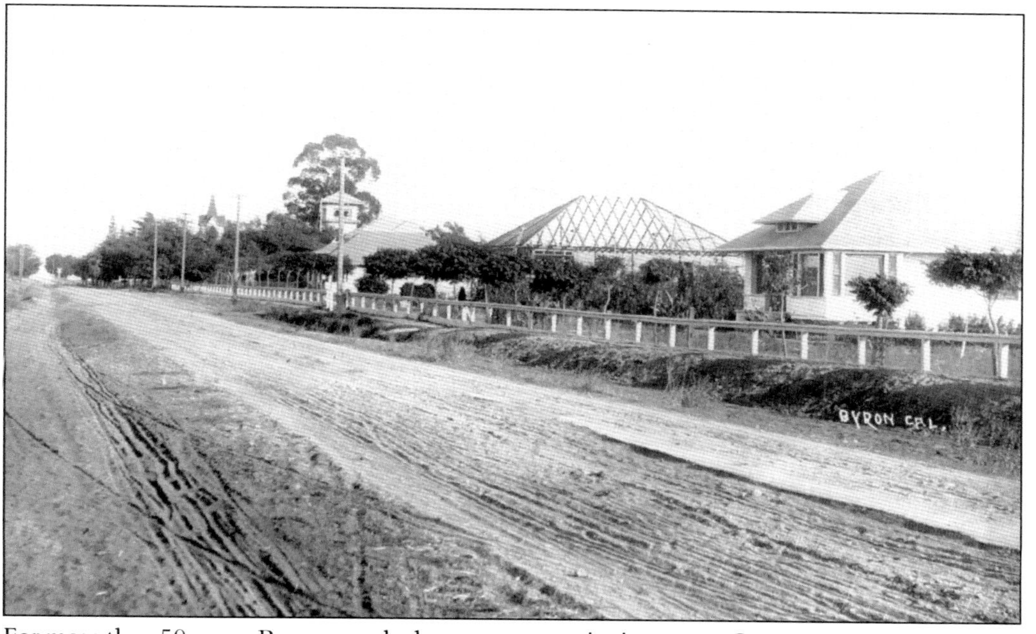

For more than 50 years, Byron was the largest community in eastern Contra Costa County. This image captures what is now Camino Diablo Road. The second-story bell tower of the Byron school is the tallest building on the street. The Pimentel home is shown under construction. The bare roof joists have yet to be papered and shingled.

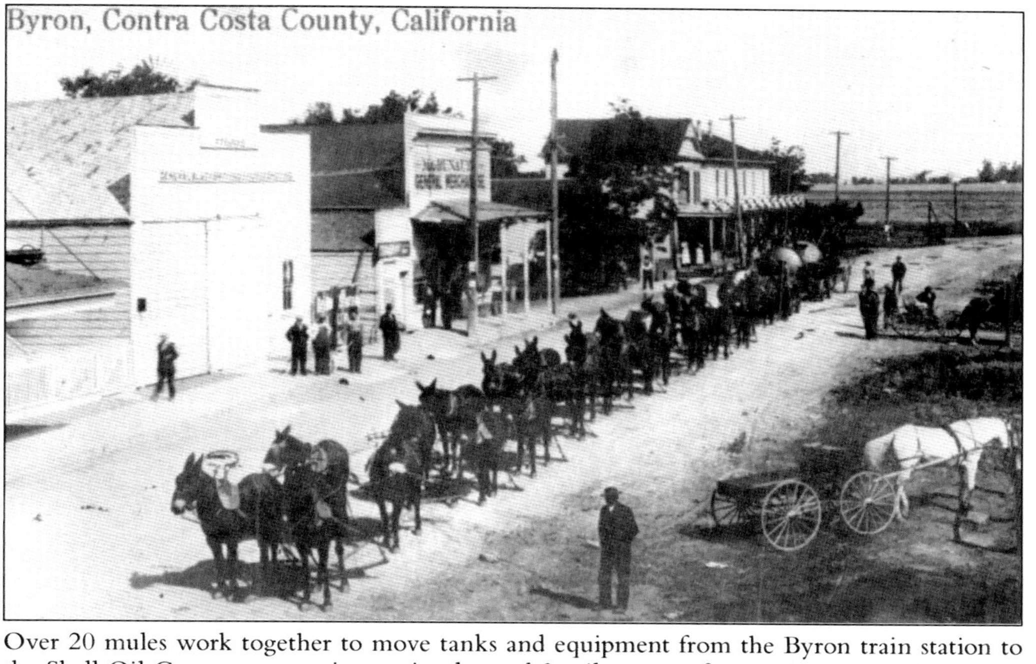

Over 20 mules work together to move tanks and equipment from the Byron train station to the Shell Oil Company pumping station located 3 miles west of town. Townspeople stepped in line behind the mule train and walked in procession to the oil station in celebration of the equipment arrival.

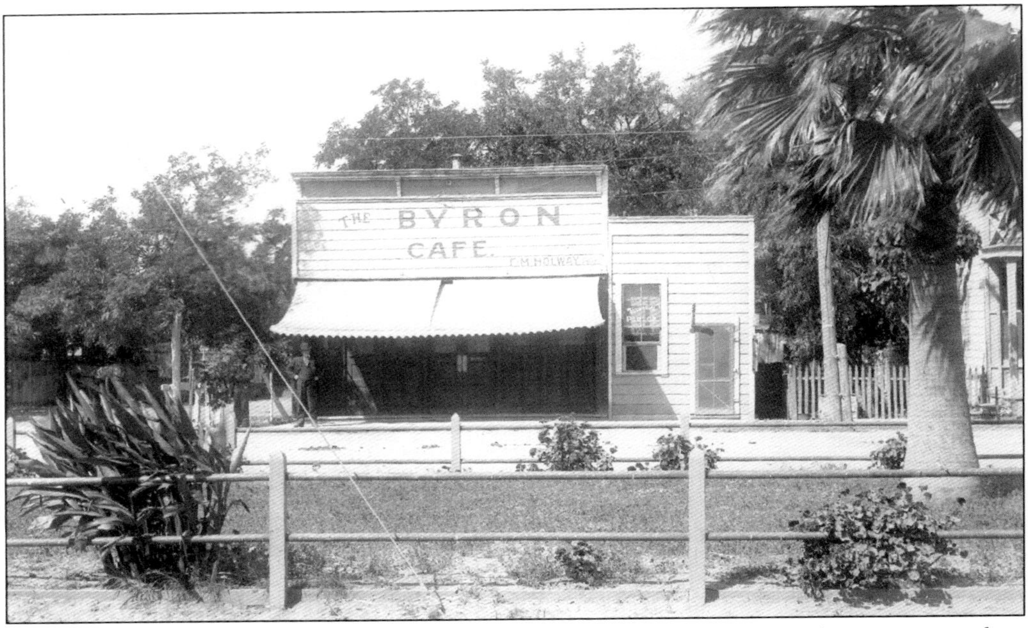

There has always been a Byron Café for local farmers, businesspeople, and visitors to gather. Fred Holway's café was located on Main Street in Byron across from the community park. Note the palm trees, pepper trees, and grass. This is Fatty Arbuckle's preferred restaurant for dessert when visiting the Byron Hot Springs.

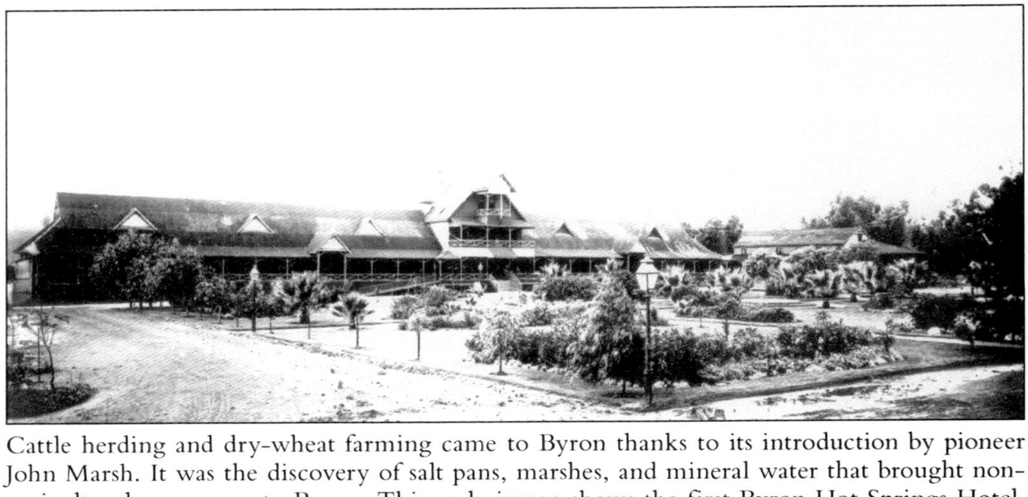

Cattle herding and dry-wheat farming came to Byron thanks to its introduction by pioneer John Marsh. It was the discovery of salt pans, marshes, and mineral water that brought non-agricultural commerce to Byron. This early image shows the first Byron Hot Springs Hotel. Fire destroyed the building in the late 1890s.

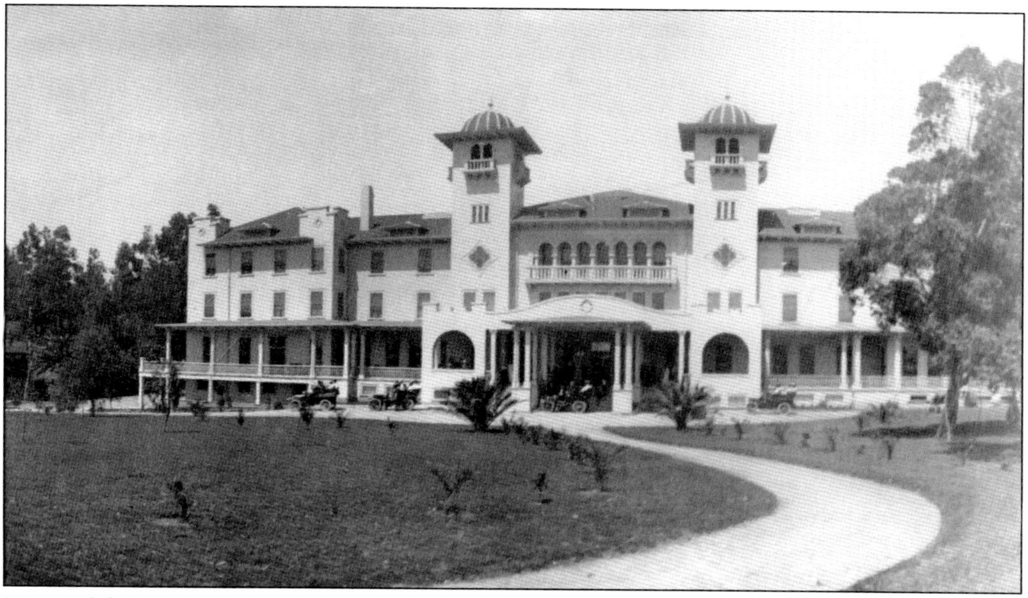

Demand for mineral water cures, accommodations, rest and relaxation, and retreats for visitors from all over California requires a new, larger facility at the hot springs. This beautiful Moorish-style building (constructed in 1902 and burned in 1912) is both a private sanitarium and a hospital that catered to guests requiring licensed medical treatment and hydropathy cures.

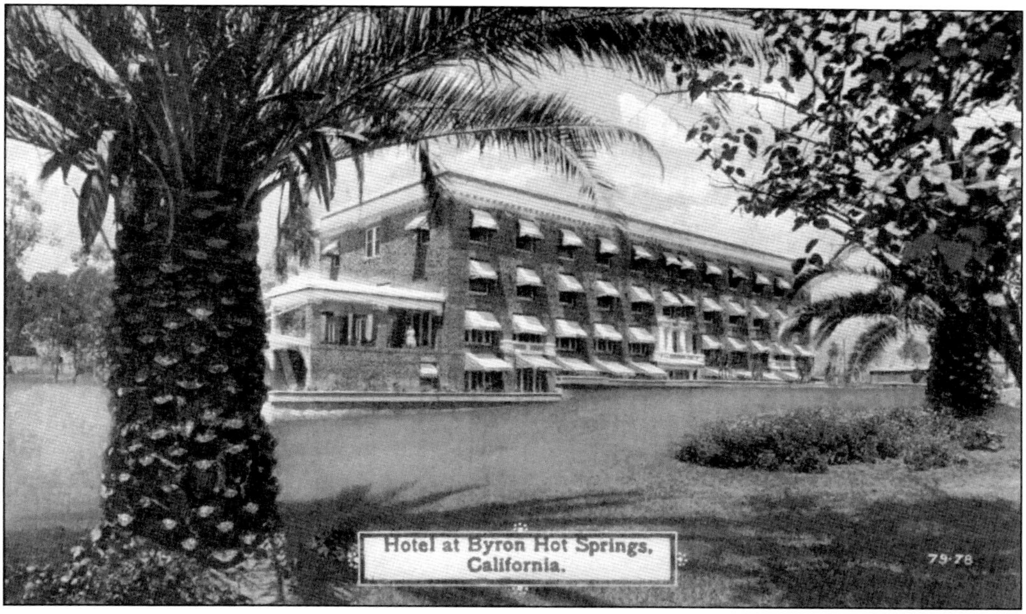

The reputation of the Byron Hot Springs as a destination resort expanded beyond the West as California welcomed the world to the Panama-Pacific International Exhibition in 1915. This multistory hotel opened in time to accommodate exhibition guests seeking a health and recreational spa for weekend and weeklong vacations.

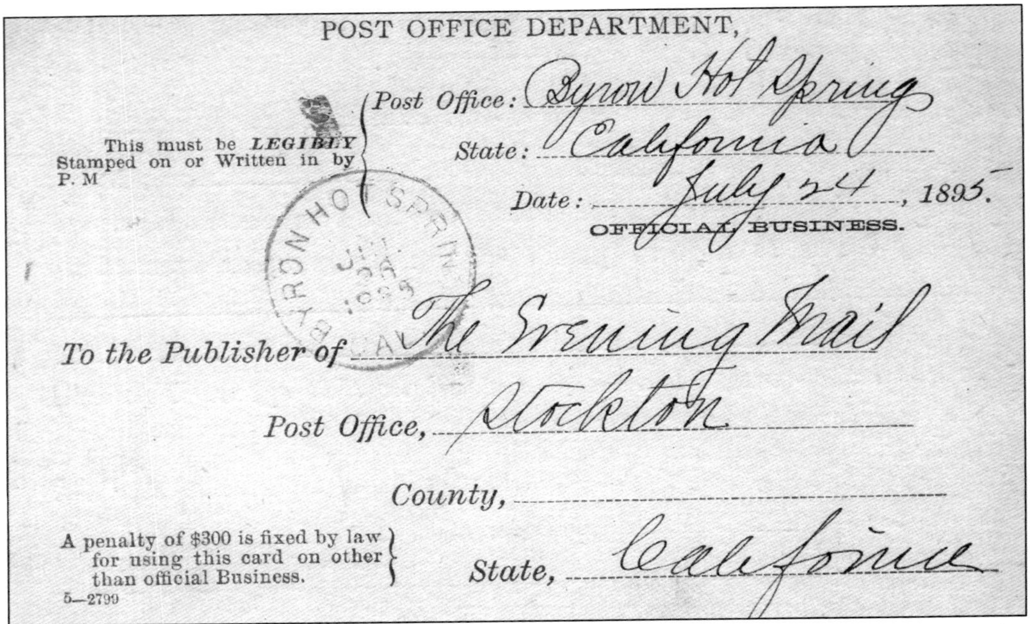
POST OFFICE DEPARTMENT,

This must be LEGIBLY Stamped on or Written in by P. M

Post Office: Byron Hot Springs

State: California

Date: July 24, 1895.

OFFICIAL BUSINESS.

BYRON HOT SPRINGS JUL 26 1895 CAL

To the Publisher of The Evening Mail

Post Office, Stockton

County,

A penalty of $300 is fixed by law for using this card on other than official Business.

State, California

5—2799

The Byron Hot Springs had its own post office and postmaster separate from the community of Byron's U.S. post office. Its official identification as a U.S. rural post office was granted in 1889.

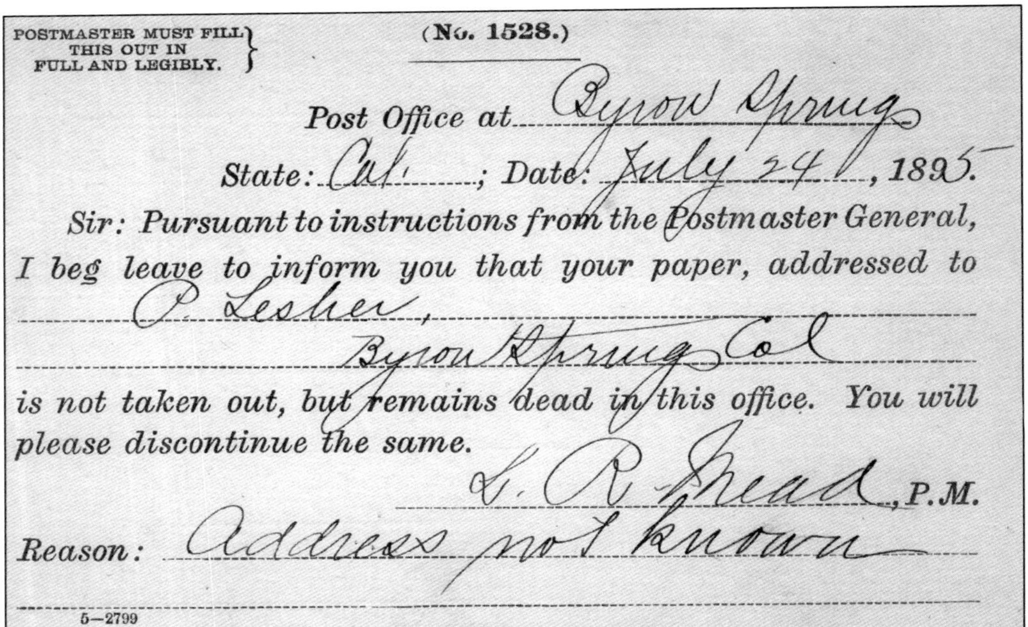
POSTMASTER MUST FILL THIS OUT IN FULL AND LEGIBLY.

(No. 1528.)

Post Office at Byron Springs

State: Cal. ; Date: July 24, 1895.

Sir: Pursuant to instructions from the Postmaster General, I beg leave to inform you that your paper, addressed to

P. Lesher,

Byron Springs Cal

is not taken out, but remains dead in this office. You will please discontinue the same.

L. R. Mead, P.M.

Reason: Address not known

5—2799

Decommissioned U.S. post office documents and postage franks are highly collected by philologists. The postmaster, Lewis Risdon Mead, who signed this dead letter notification, founded the Byron Hot Springs resort in 1868. The post office closed December 31, 1930.

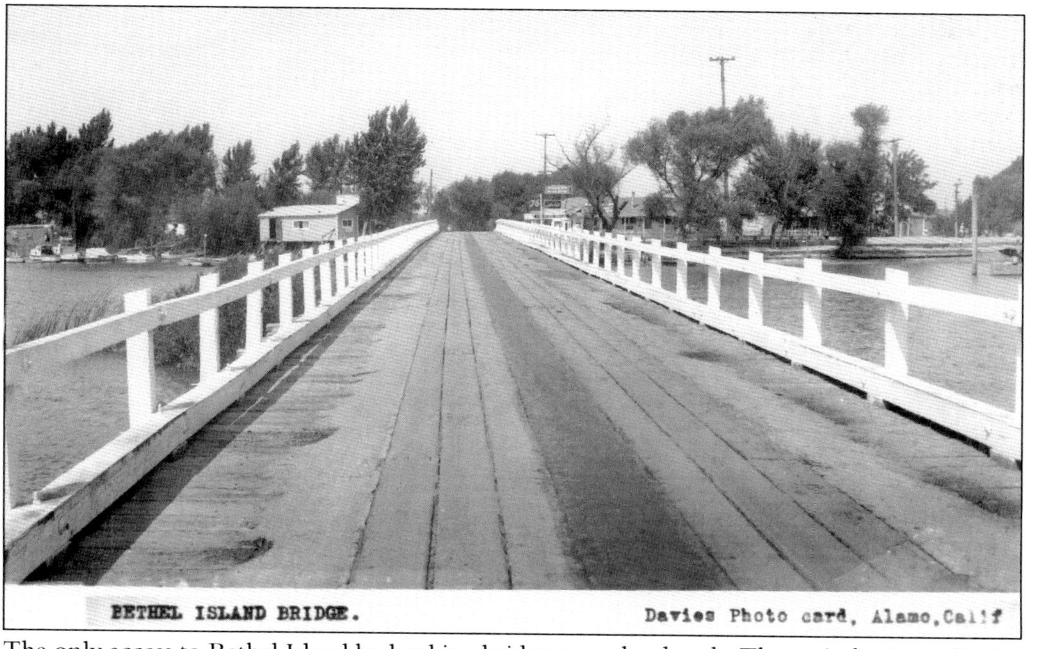

The only access to Bethel Island by land is a bridge over the slough. The main business district of the community can be seen at the end of the bridge. Most of the island's commerce is water, marina, and recreation related.

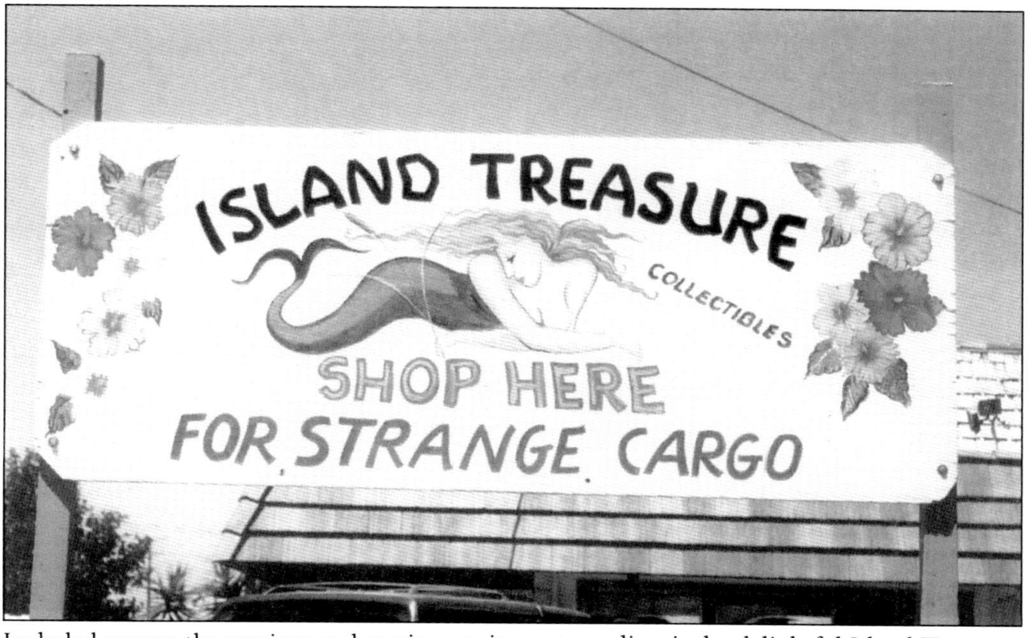

Included among the marinas and marine equipment suppliers is the delightful Island Treasures shop. Here a person can find yesterday's castaway transformed into today's antique. Mind the resident mouse chaser at the door.

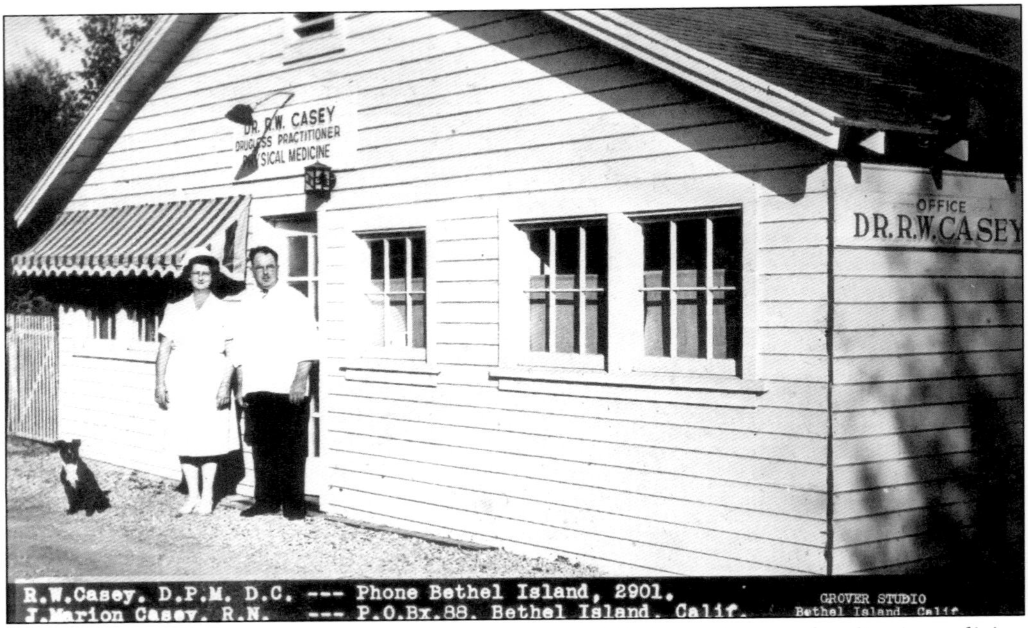

One of the few non-marine businesses in town was R. W. Casey, doctor of podiatric medicine and chiropractic. His wife, J. Marion Casey, aided him professionally as a registered nurse. There is no indication of the pooch's name or pedigree.

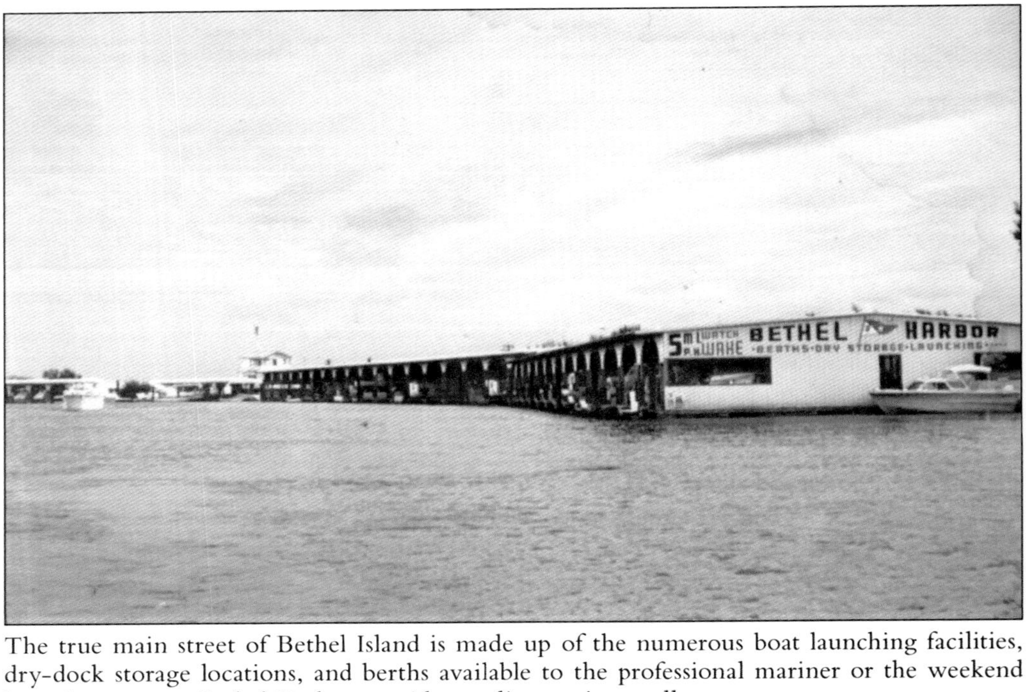

The true main street of Bethel Island is made up of the numerous boat launching facilities, dry-dock storage locations, and berths available to the professional mariner or the weekend houseboat renter. Bethel Harbor provides quality service to all.

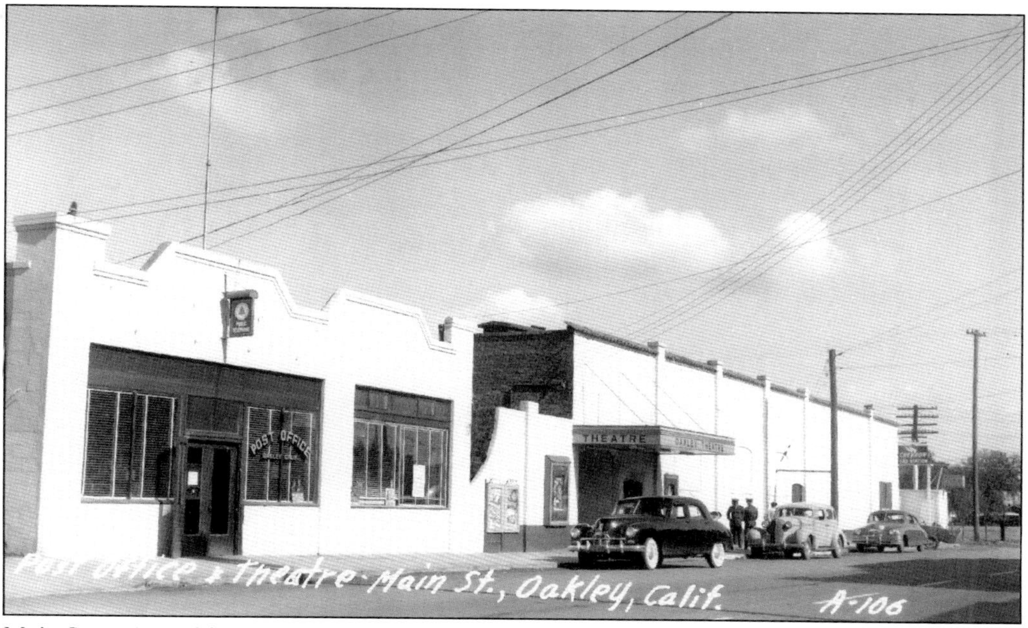

Main Street in Oakley is a thriving community as this 1940s image of the business district shows. Uniformed service men wait outside the Oakley movie theater for the film *Outpost in Morocco* (1949), starring George Raft, to begin. Across the street is the Santa Fe railroad depot.

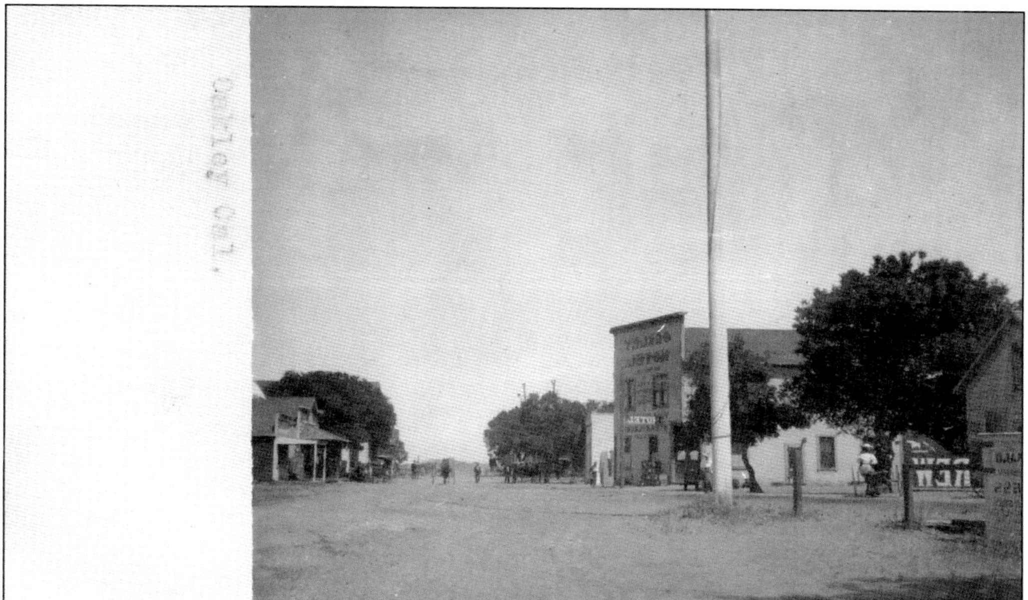

Downtown Oakley has grown along California State Route 4 over the years. This early real-photo postcard is an anomaly. It is not an actual photographic print but a contact print and probably the original glass photo–plate size. Note all the words and images are reversed.

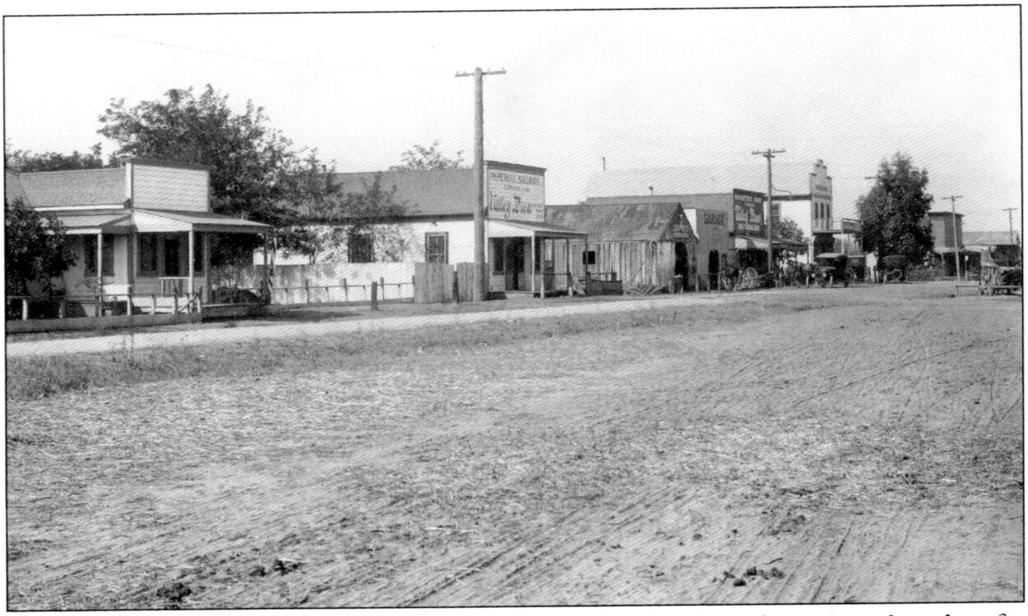

The town of Knightsen was established originally as a shipping depot for grain and produce for the Santa Fe railroad. Many of the buildings seen in this image are still standing, some in a sad state of repair. The entire community is a historic-district-in-waiting, including the home of its founder, George W. Knight. This is the earliest known image of Knightsen Avenue, taken around 1913.

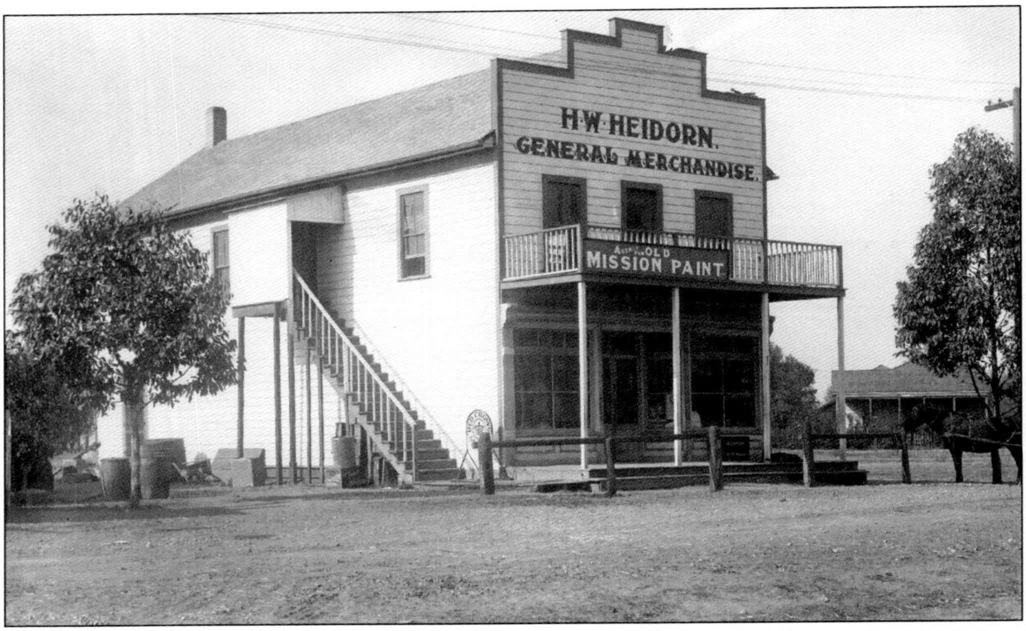

At the heart of the Knightsen commercial district stands the H. W. Heidorn building, established in 1904. General merchandise was sold downstairs, and the proprietor and his wife lived upstairs. Over 2,500 gallons of raw milk was shipped daily on the Santa Fe Railroad to San Francisco creameries from this busy dairy center.

Five

Domestic Life and Tranquility

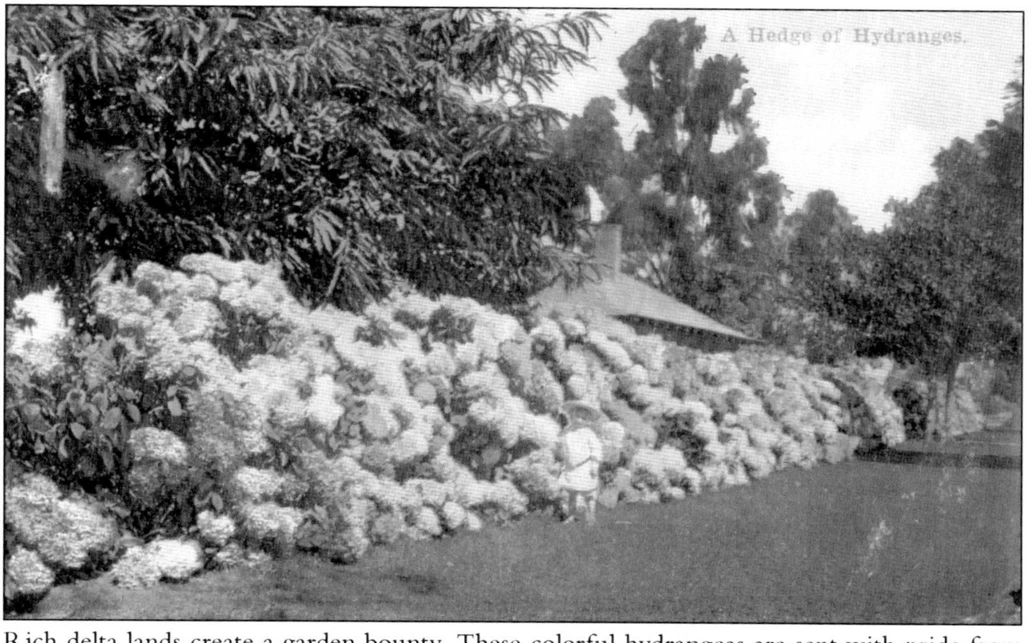

Rich delta lands create a garden bounty. These colorful hydrangeas are sent with pride from Oakley, which was founded in 1898. A child stands in front of the floral display, another sign of domestic happiness.

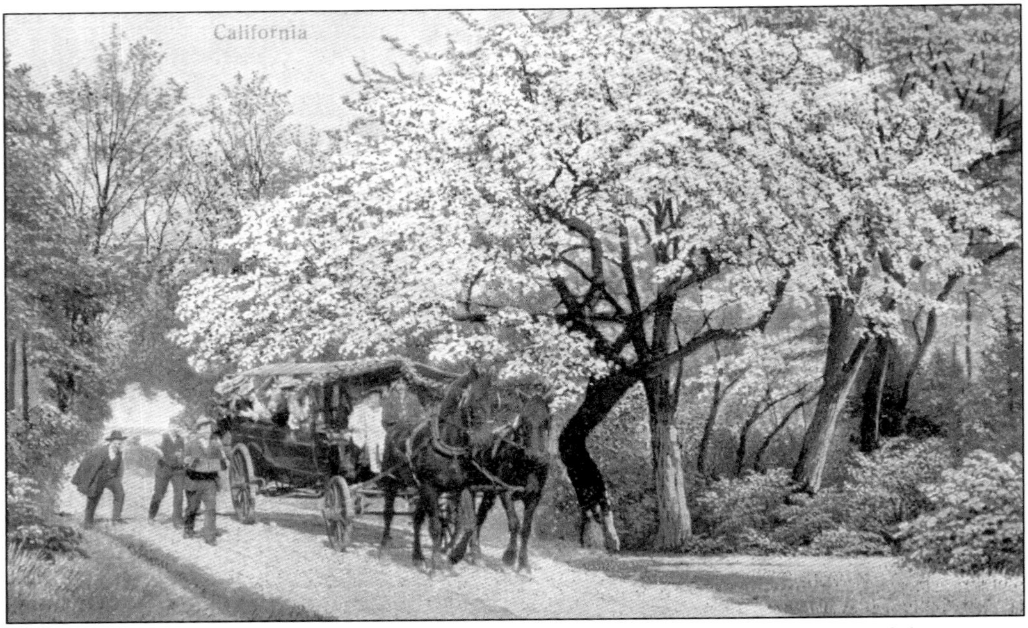

Dramatic arbor displays and trees bursting with color in early spring are some of the greatest joys in eastern Contra Costa County. A buggy ride and later an automobile ride east from Clayton along Marsh Creek Road to Borden Junction would look much like this in February.

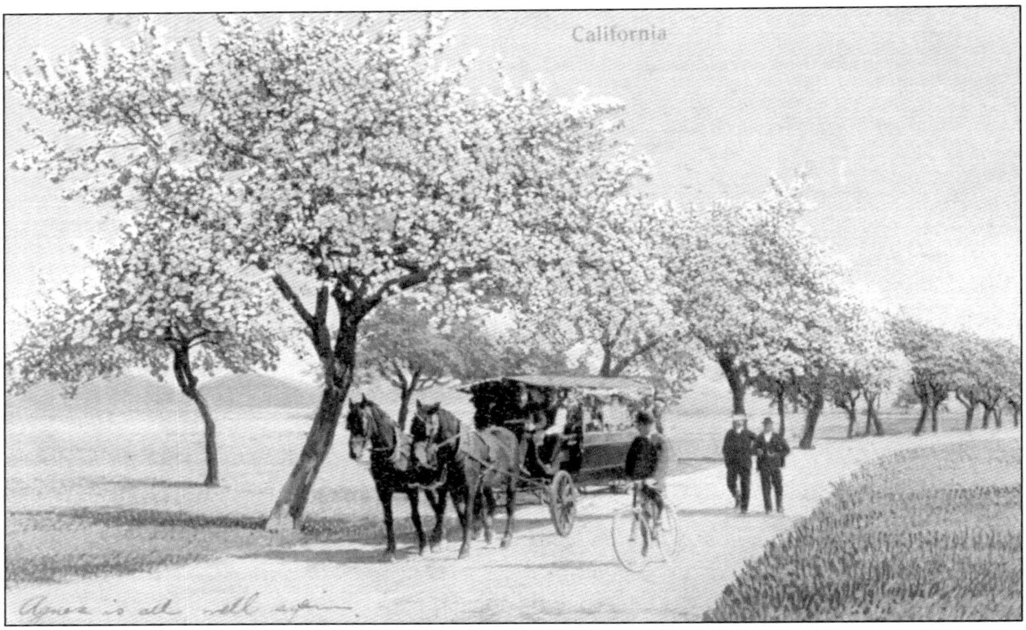

Driving horse-drawn wagons along tree-lined country roads has its pleasures. It is the popularity and number of bicycles that causes the dirt and gravel roads to be paved. This one-lane byway will soon see multiple asphalt lanes as more people take to their two- and later four-wheel vehicles for Sunday drives to the country.

Contra Costa Hills

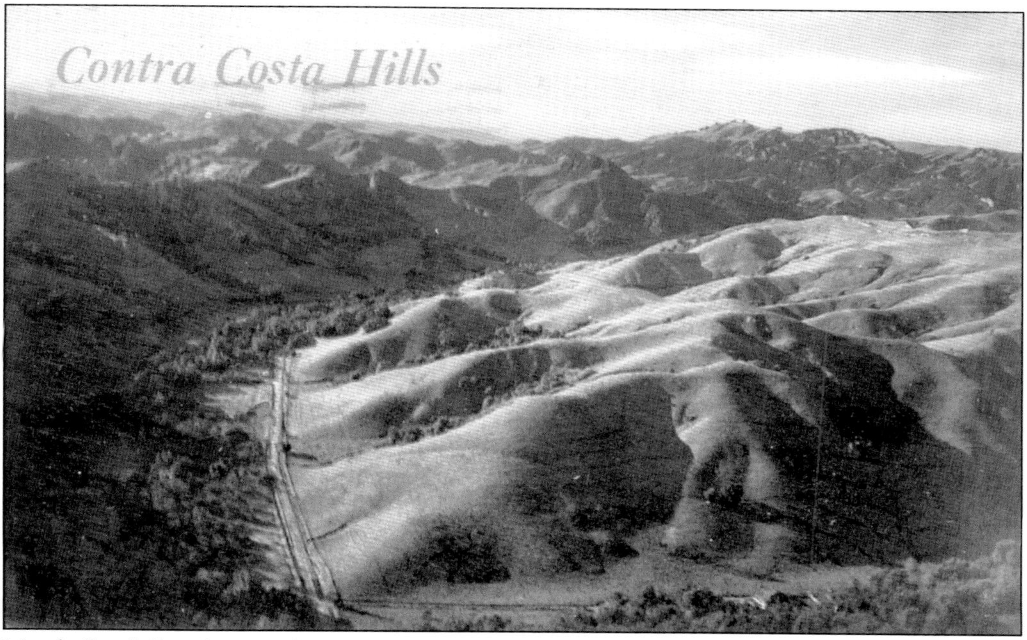

Marsh Creek Road, once the main connecting artery between East County and the Bay Area, winds its way through the coastal ranges and foothills. The view from the top of Mount Diablo reveals many hidden valleys, canyons, dry washes, and divides. It is the home of kit fox, red-legged frog, burrowing owl, and other species threatened or endangered.

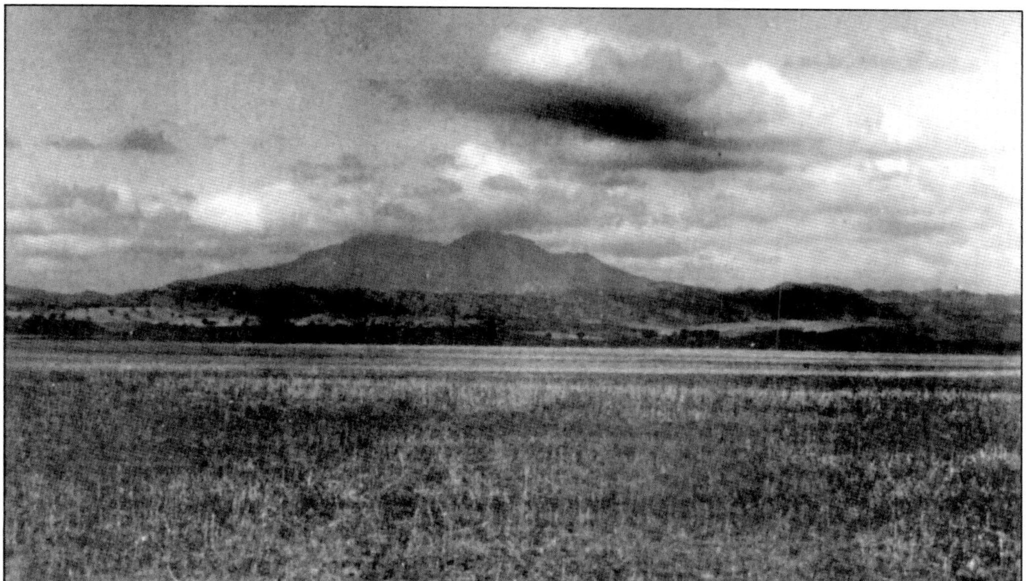

The eastern view of Mount Diablo (elevation 3,869 feet) dominates the Sacramento and San Joaquin River Delta and the Central Valley. Only from the east can one appreciate its imposing presence over man's efforts in the vast breadbasket. On a clear day, a person can see Mount Shasta, Mount Lassen, Yosemite's Half Dome, 35 of California's 58 counties, and 600 miles of the Sierra Nevada.

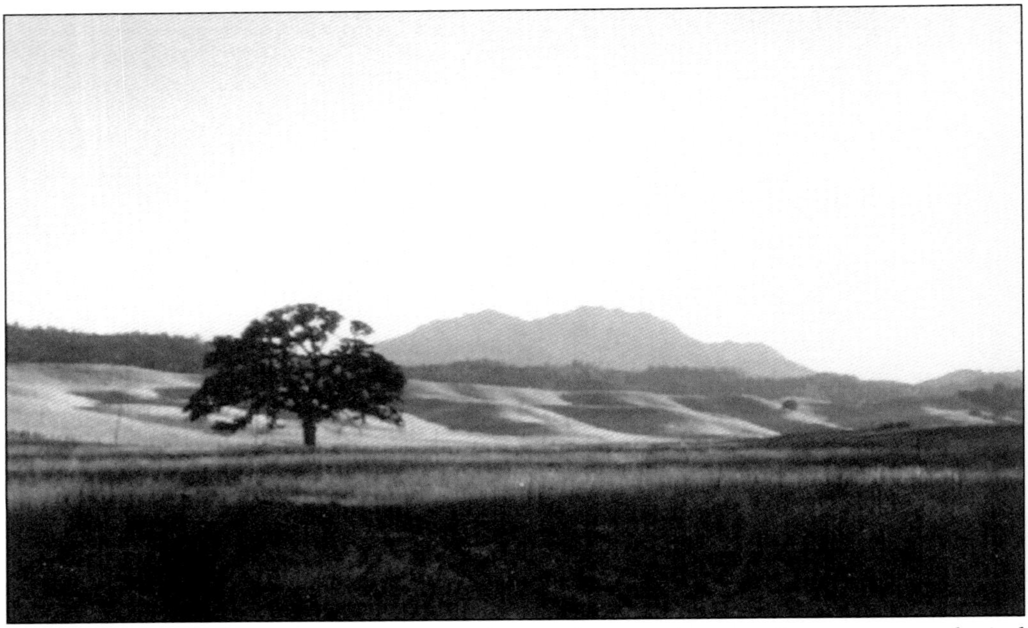

The "Devil Mountain" draws Brentwood close to the coastal range. The western geological edge of the Central Valley is Fairview Avenue on the western edge of the city limits. The city is on the cusp; part San Francisco Bay Area city, part Sacramento and San Joaquin Central Valley town.

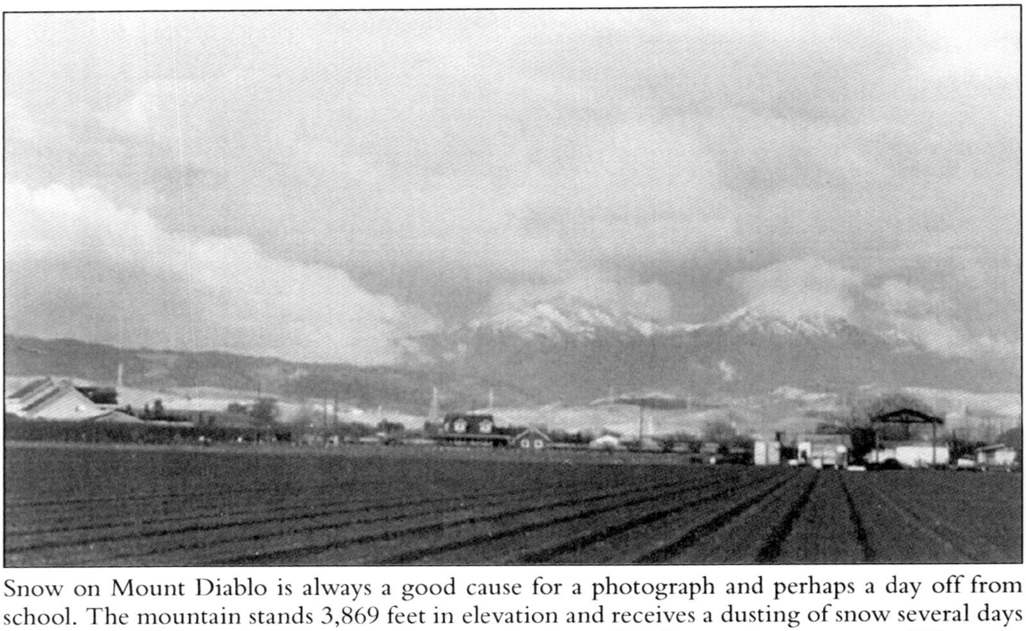

Snow on Mount Diablo is always a good cause for a photograph and perhaps a day off from school. The mountain stands 3,869 feet in elevation and receives a dusting of snow several days a year. From its summit, one can see across the Central Valley to the entrance of Yosemite Valley, a reflection of Mount Lassen to the north, and the Farlone Islands to the west.

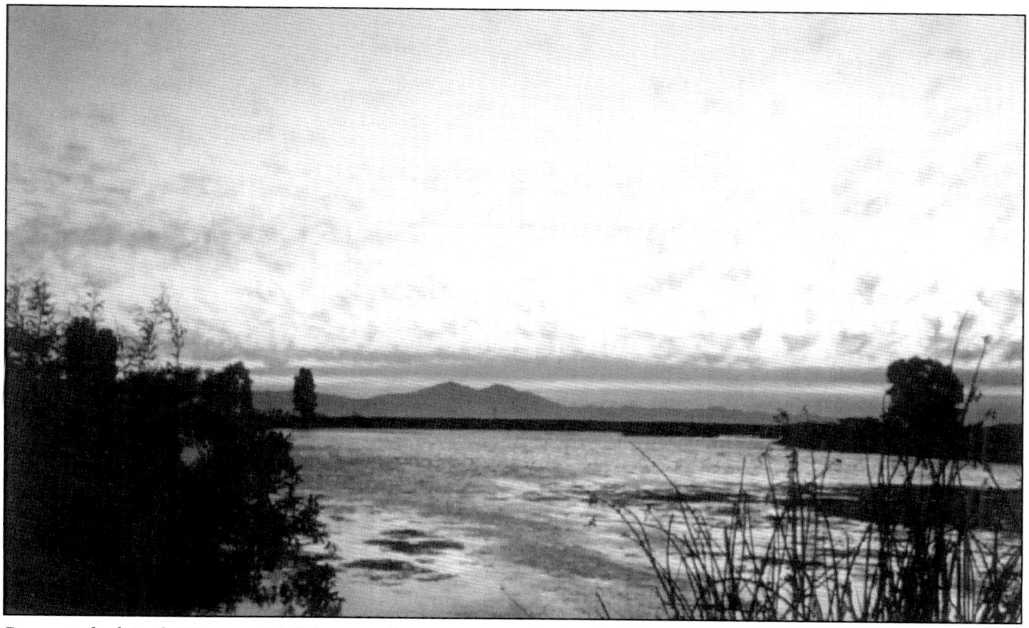

Sunsets behind Mount Diablo are the most scenic in California. Nothing compares with the apricot, red, and purple sunsets at the end of a hard day of wakeboarding. See the tule, hear the mocking birds, and watch the fish jump. The 10 million candlepower aerial navigation beacon at its top is visible for 100 miles.

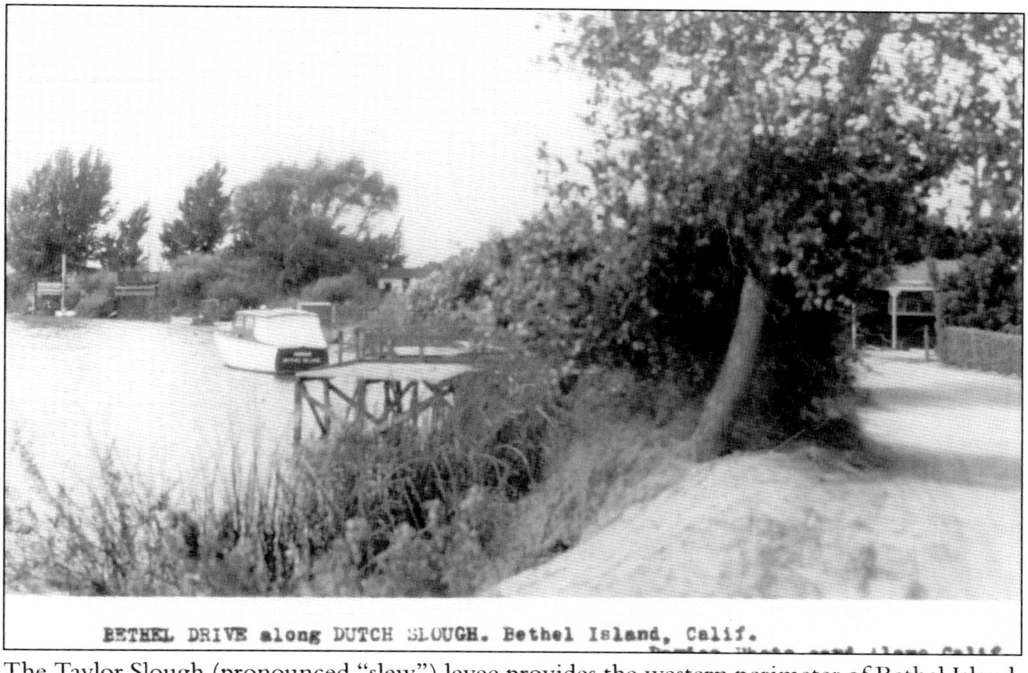

The Taylor Slough (pronounced "slew") levee provides the western perimeter of Bethel Island. This postcard shows the levee road, a dock, a cabin cruiser, and a home along the levee road. All delta tracts have roads along the levees, and the real estate is attractive for recreational, commercial, and residential development.

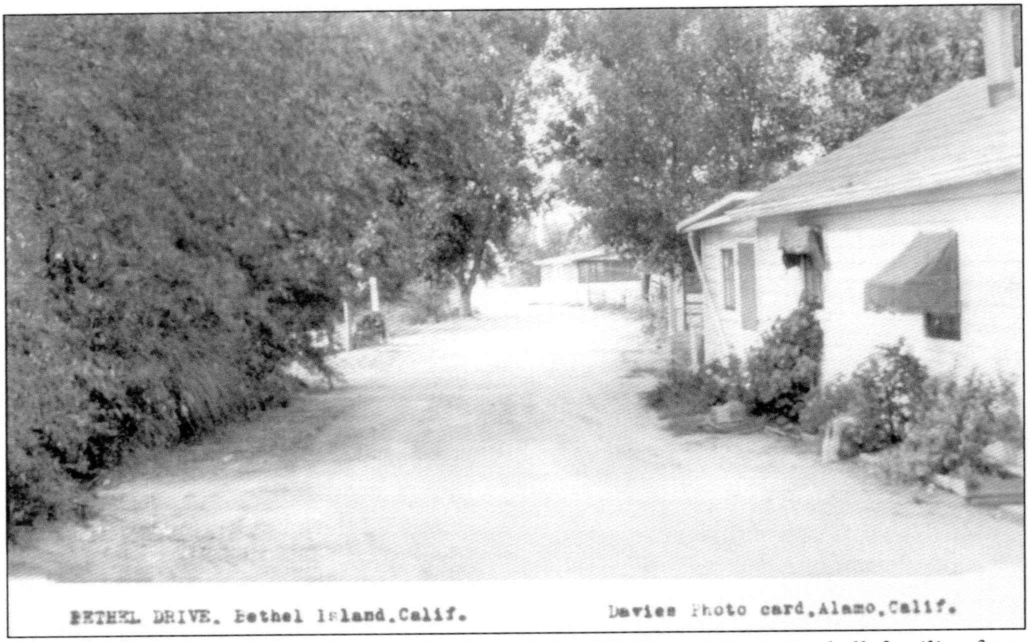

Bethel Drive acknowledges the contribution of the W. K. and F. C. Bethell families from whom the island takes it name. Chinese labor reclaimed 4,000 acres in 1872 at a labor cost of 12.5¢ per cubic yard. W. K. Bethell, J. C. Smith, and N. R. Harris increased the levee to 12 feet at its base, 4 feet high and 6 feet at the crown at a cost of $600 per mile.

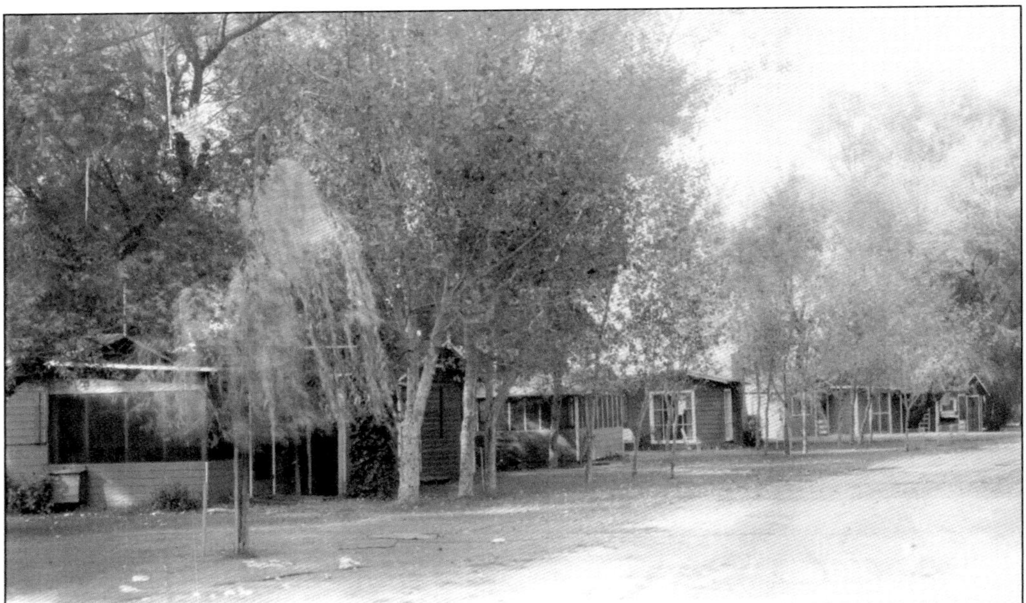

The cottages seen here may have begun as tent cabins and changing rooms. Jack and Blanche Farrar began leasing lots to permanent campers for $1 a year in 1940. Every day spent in the cabin was an additional 50¢. Many of these tents became substantial cabins over the years.

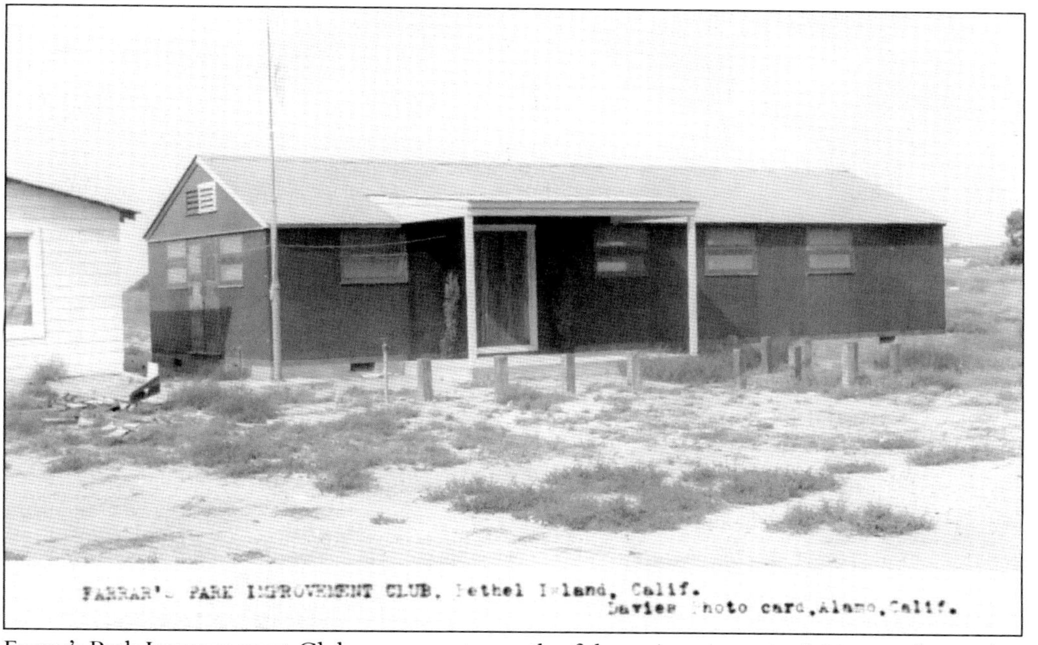

Farrar's Park Improvement Club was an outgrowth of the swimming, picnicking, and camping concessions. Farrar moved to Bethel Island to farm in 1930 and was the primary recreations developer of Bethel Island. He subdivided his property and sold small lots for as little as $50. The property was located between Bethel Island Bridge and Stone Road.

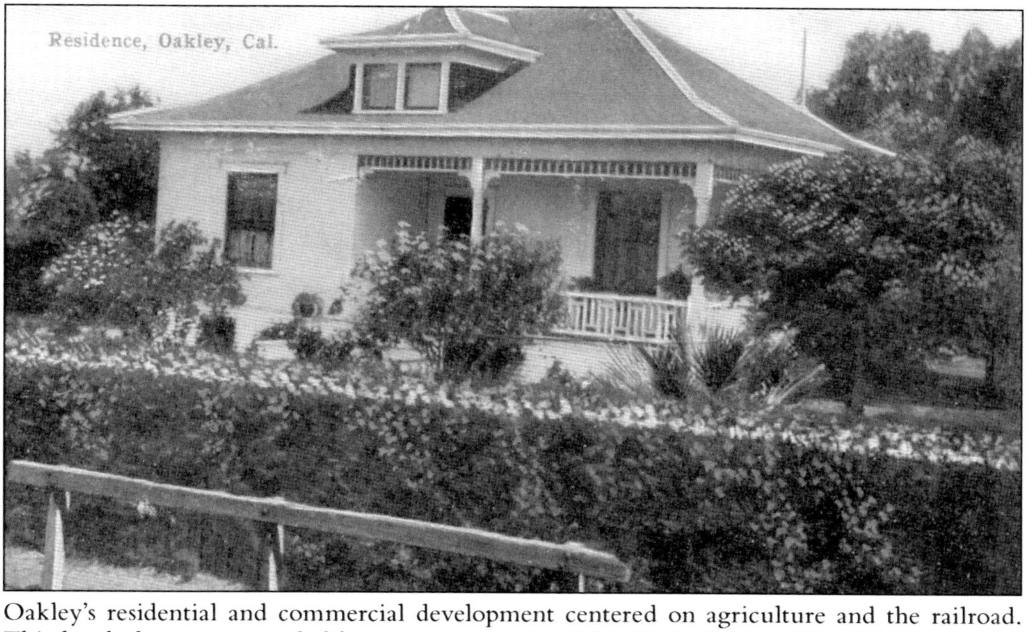

Oakley's residential and commercial development centered on agriculture and the railroad. This lovely home surrounded by oranges, roses, and border hedges typifies the best type of town house of the time. Note the rail hitching post for the horse in front. There would have been a stable in back for family transportation and perhaps a chicken coop.

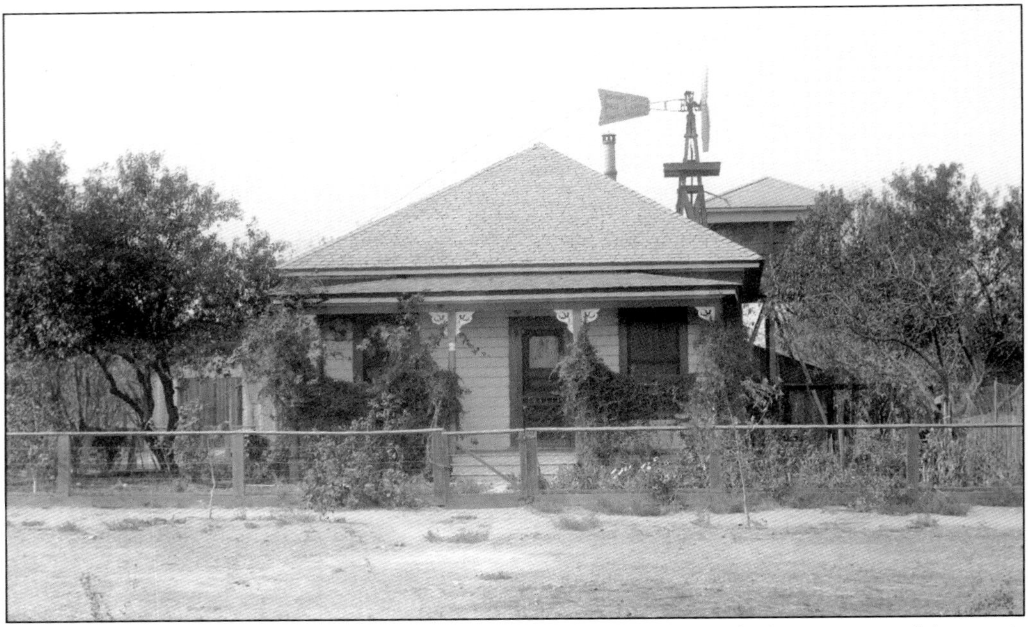

The Heidorn family kept two residences in Knightsen. This real-photo postcard image is of the country house on Delta Road where the family had a farm and spent the summer months. Cousins Margaret and Edna kept in touch by sending postcards by mail from Knightsen to Oakley.

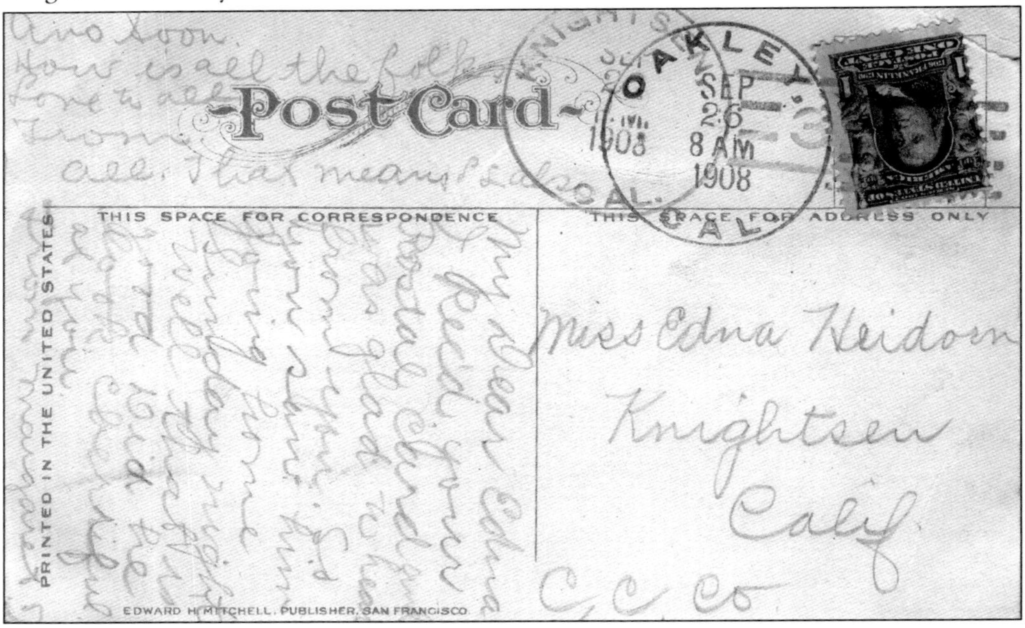

The postcard reads, "My Dear Edna. I rec'd your postal card and was glad to hear from you. So you saw him going home Sunday night. Well that is good. Did he look cheerful at you. Ano[other card] Soon. How is all the folks. Love to all. From all, that means and also from Margaret." Edna Hill (née Heidorn), 1892–1975, is remembered fondly as a local teacher of 54 years.

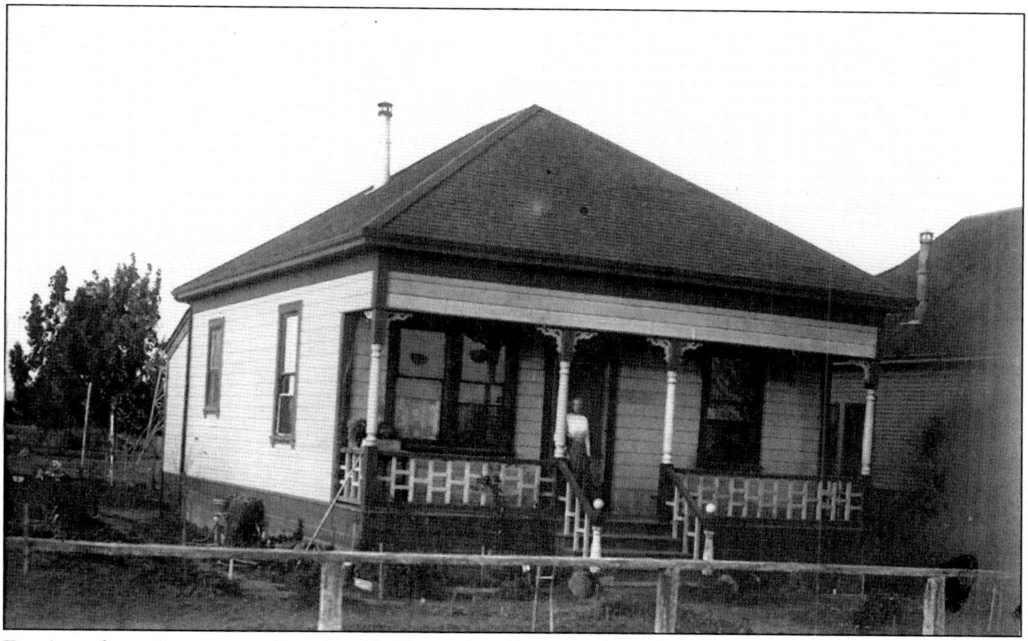

During the winter months, the Heidorn family moved back to Knightsen. Seen here is the correspondent on the porch in this real-photo postcard. Note the rail fence in front. The roads were paved with gravel in town, while roads around the farm were dirt and mud.

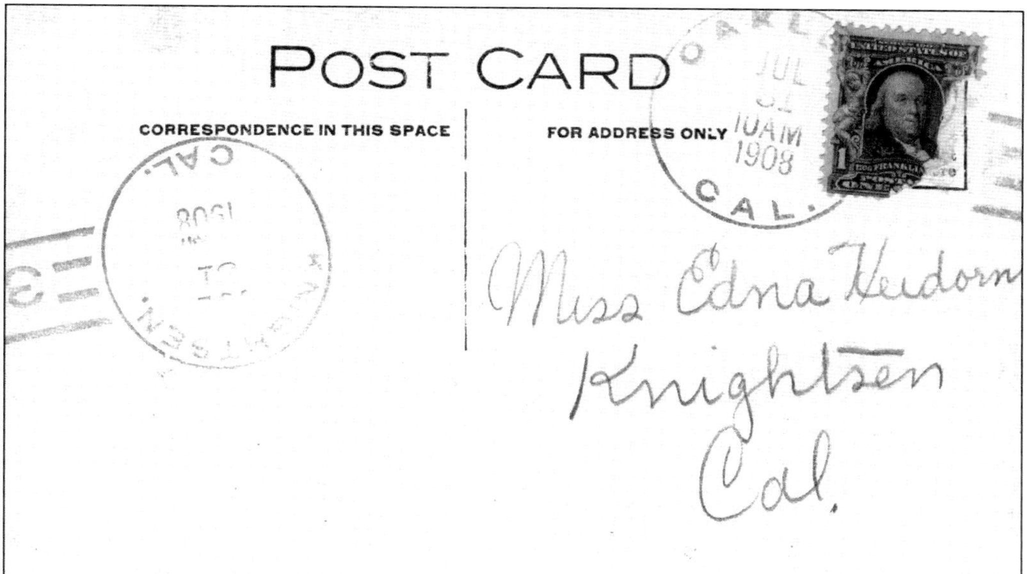

Margaret Heidorn does not provide a message this time to her cousin Edna. The postcard is dated July 1908 from both the Knightsen and Oakley post offices. The image on the cover must have been sufficient to convey the message, "We are in town, now." Edna Hill (née Heidorn) taught elementary school in Brentwood for many decades. The Edna Hill School is named in her honor.

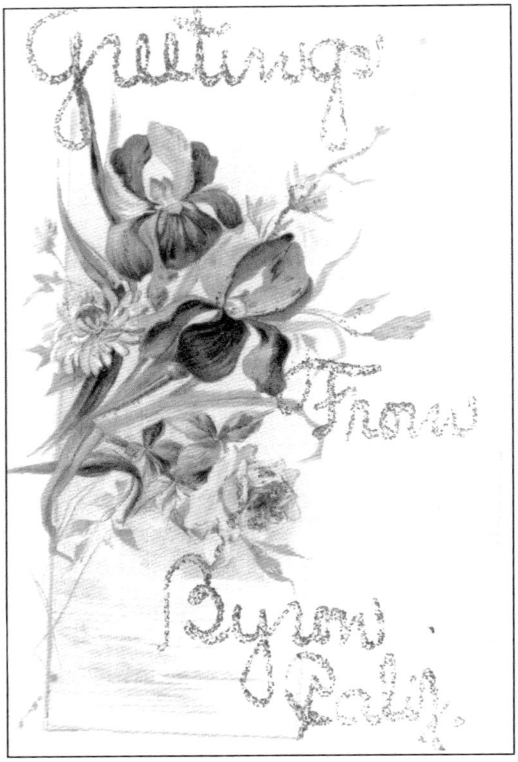

Embossed floral postcard stock from Europe was a favorite and carried by local stationers. Each stationer would customize the card stock to the local area. This iris flower image, made and sold in Byron, uses paste and glitter to extend "Greetings from Byron Calif." It is sent from Byron to Brentwood urging friends to visit.

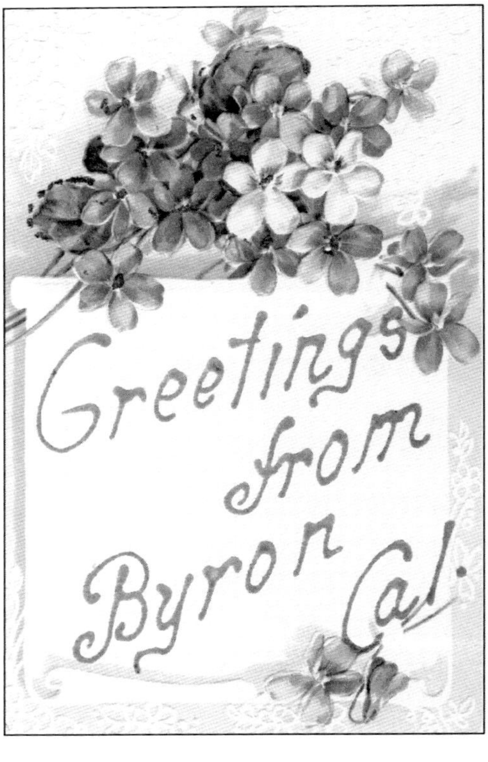

One card was not enough. A second card extends "Greetings from Byron Cal." The printed message on the back describes the embossed purple, blue, and white violets in three languages: Spanish, Russian, and German. The sender adds her own note in English encouraging her friend to write if she cannot visit soon.

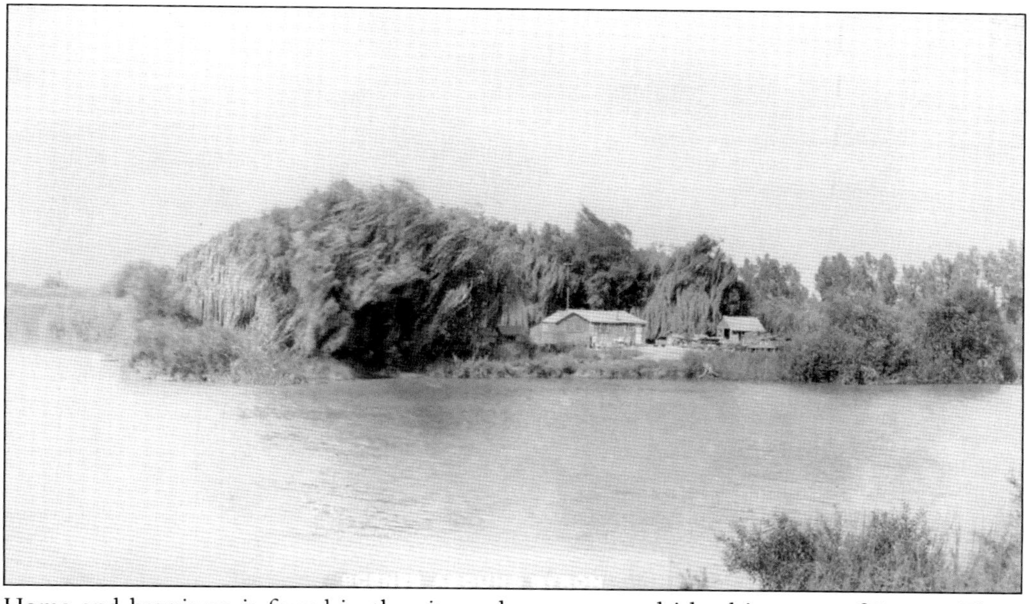

Home and happiness is found in the city and on a personal island just east of Byron. There are 55 man-made islands in the San Joaquin and Sacramento Delta, some unnamed and most devoted to agriculture. Many have a family or two living on them. This postcard shows a home and outbuildings on Middleton Island.

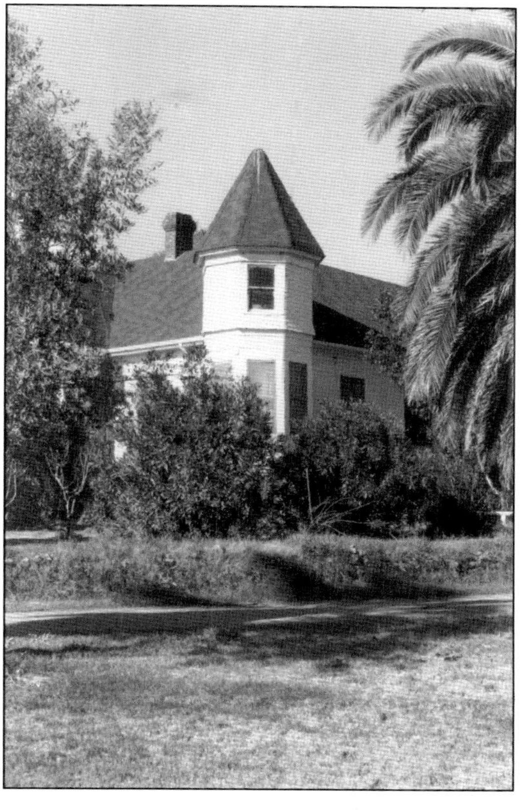

In contrast to a modest house on a reclaimed island in the slough, described above, is this beautiful Queen Anne–style home at the Byron Hot Springs. Lewis R. Mead built the Mead Mansion for his first wife, Blanche Durant Mead. She kept it as her sole and separate property until her death the day after Christmas in 1905. It had no kitchen. All meals were taken at the hotel.

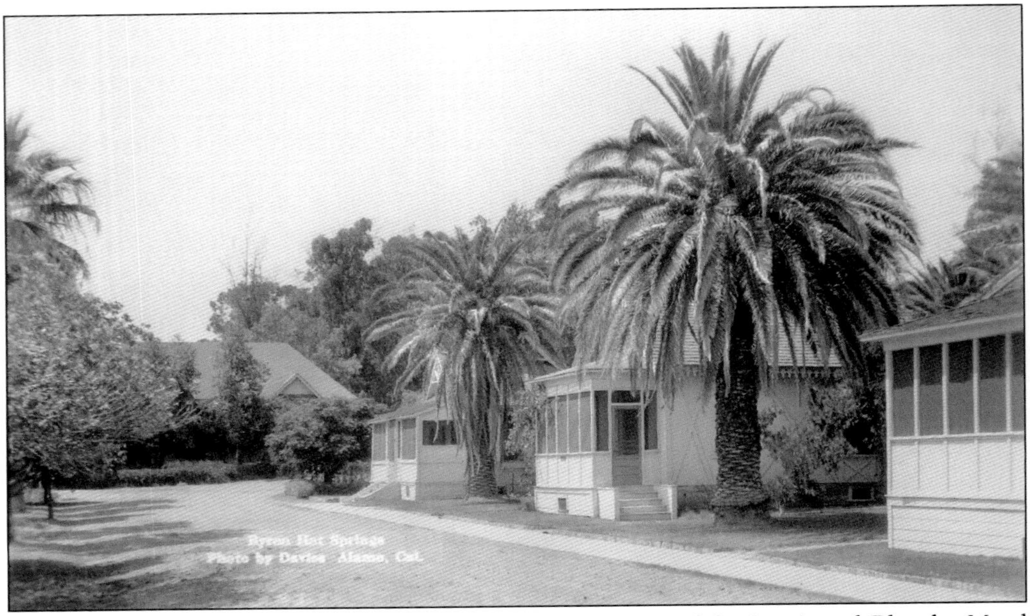

Several cottages lined the perimeter of the Palm Court east of the Lewis and Blanche Mead residence. These cottages were rented while the resort was in operation. Later, Byron families lived in the houses on yearly leases. Each had a name and was remodeled many times over the years. The last cottages were torn down in the 1980s.

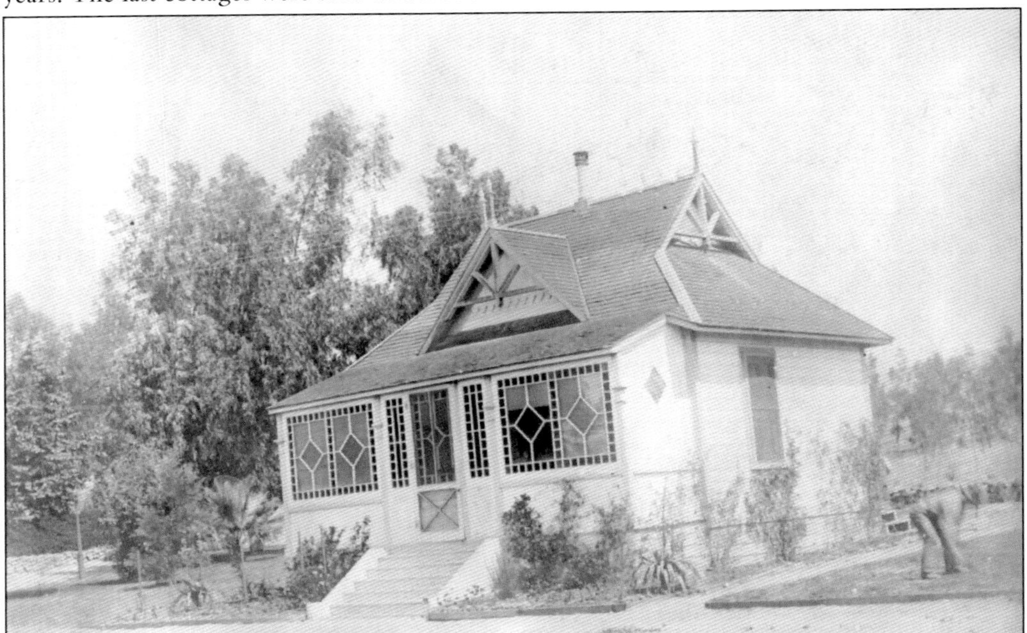

The cottages at the Byron Hot Springs were as cute and desirable as they could be. Most originally had stained-glass windows similar in design to the more elaborate windows in the Mead Mansion. Later the glass was removed and replaced with screens for better ventilation.

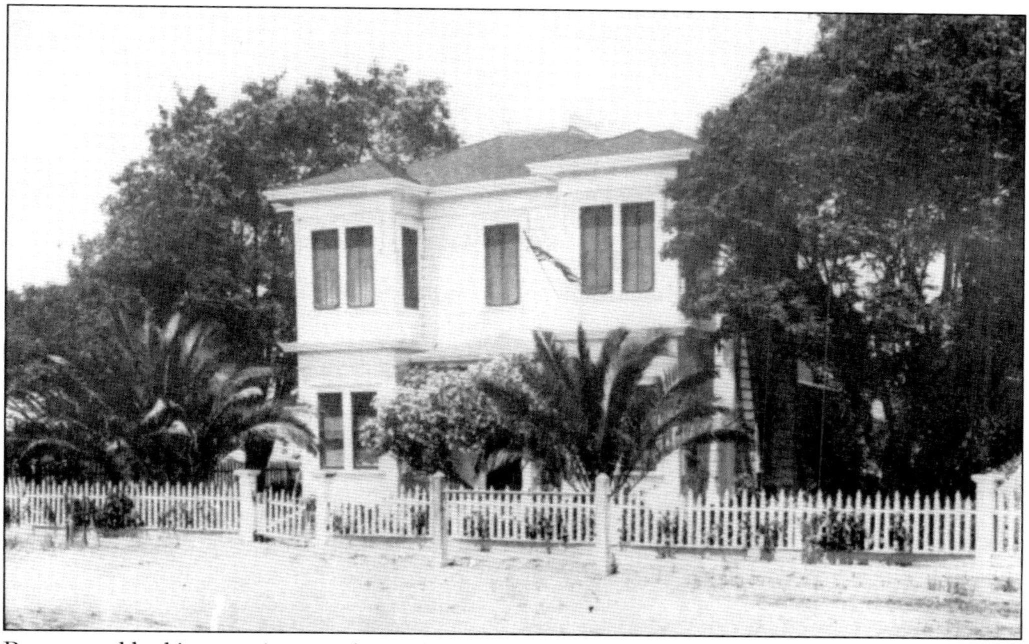

Brentwood had its mansion row located on Railroad Avenue, now Brentwood Boulevard. This two-story "stick" Victorian was built in 1886 on a quarter-acre lot by Judge Robert Wallace. It was within walking distance to the justice office and the Hotel Brentwood. It is now a real estate office.

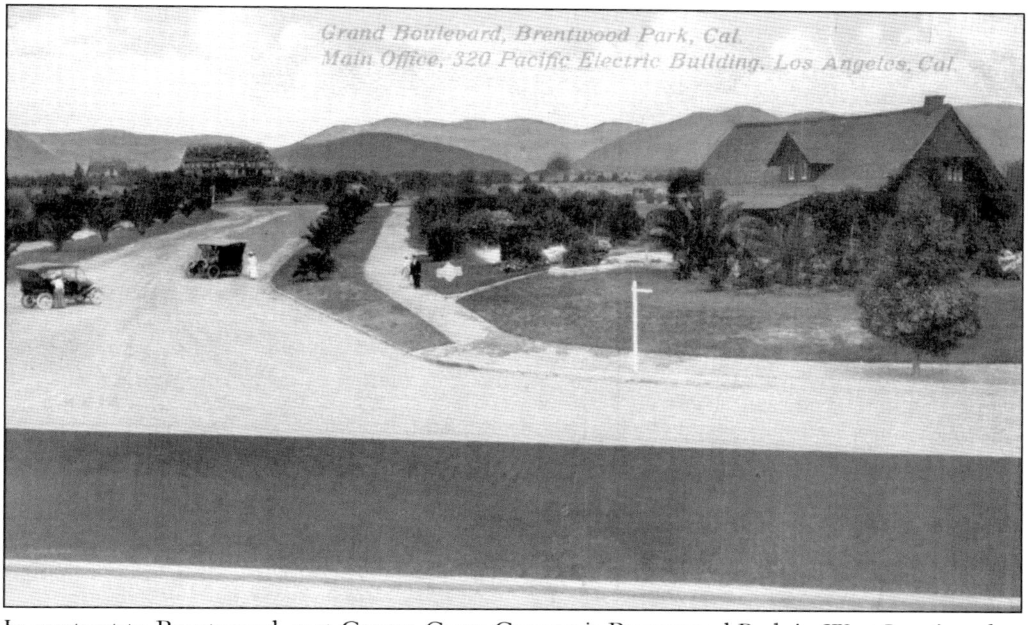

In contrast to Brentwood, east Contra Costa County is Brentwood Park in West Los Angeles. This postcard from *c.* 1917 shows Brentwood Park in development. Wilshire Boulevard on the south and Sunset Boulevard on the north border the present-day Brentwood District in Los Angeles. It extends from the San Diego Freeway (Interstate 405) on the east to Pacific Palisades city limits on the west.

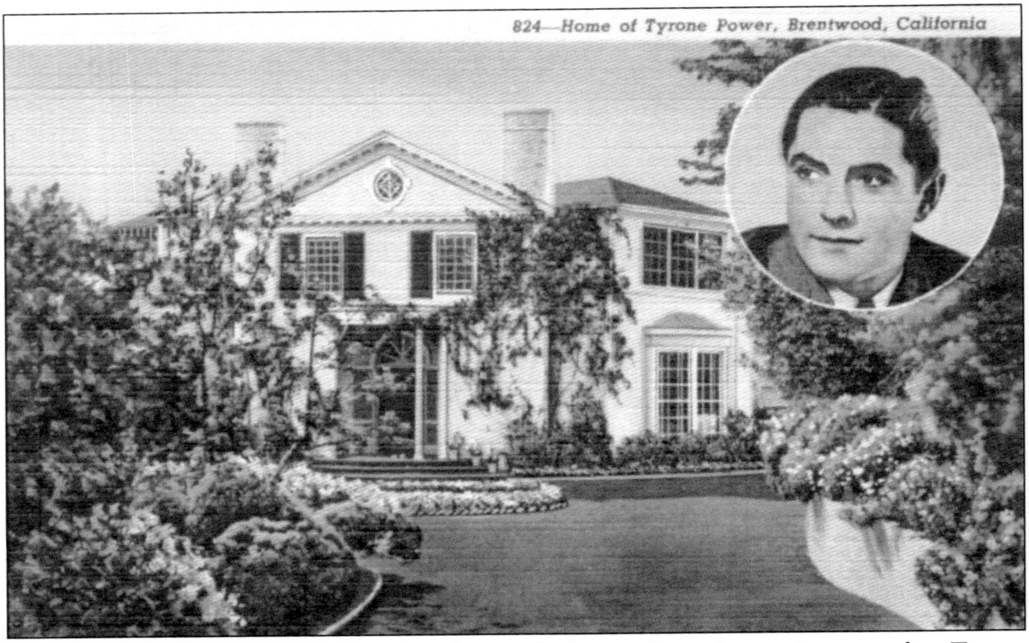

The Brentwood District of West Los Angeles was the home of popular movie stars such as Tyrone Power (shown here), Shirley Temple, Clark Gable, and Joan Crawford. Homes were all custom-built in various styles, including Colonial, California ranch, Scandinavian, Tudor, and bungalow.

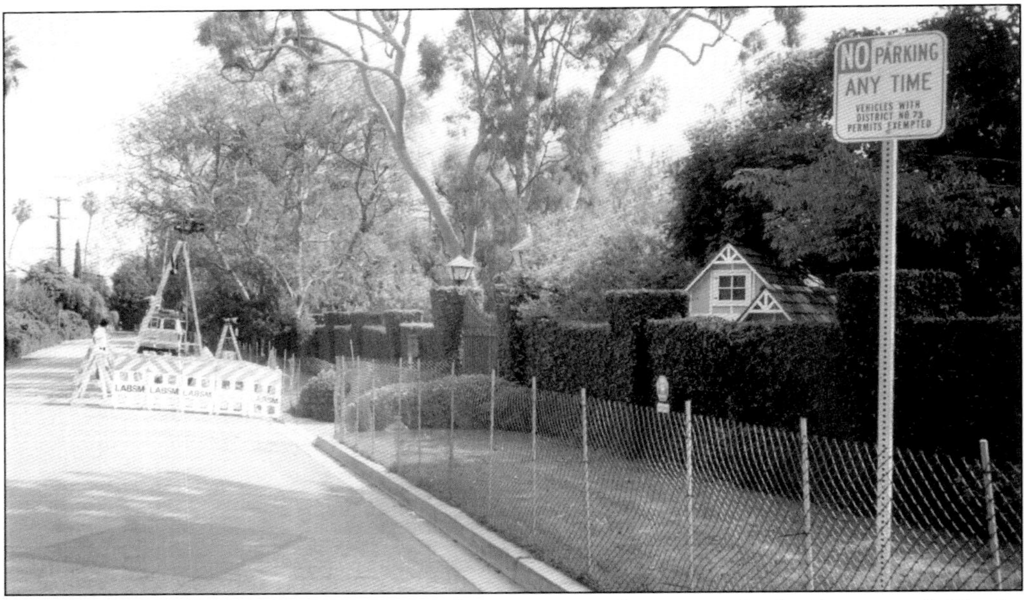

This contemporary real-photo postcard of O. J. Simpson's property in the Brentwood District of West Los Angeles shows the cyclone fence, no parking signs, and crime-scene tape used to discourage onlookers during the famous 1990s murder trial. O. J. has since sold the property. The new owners tore it down and replaced it with a new, larger, multistory home.

Six

Country Schools and Education

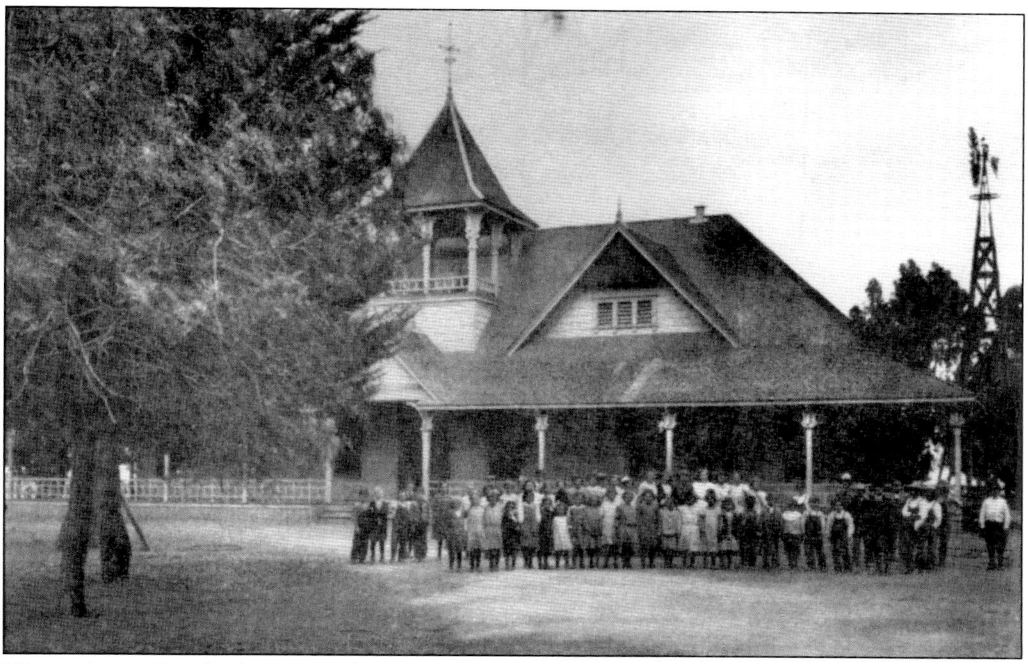

The entire student body and teachers appear proudly in front of the first Brentwood Elementary School, established in 1879. This is a real-photo postcard of the photographer taking the school picture. Note the camera tripod leg and lens bellows almost hidden in the trees to the left.

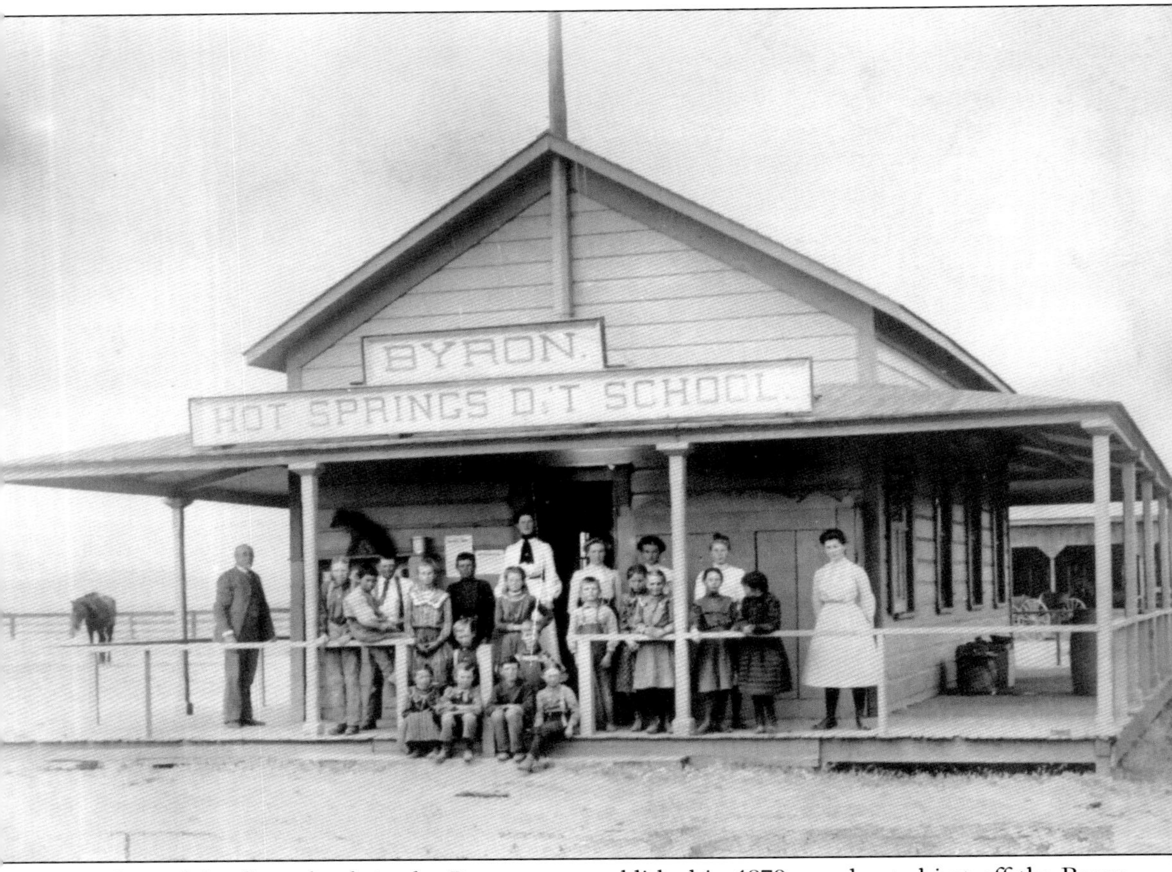

One of the first schools in the Byron area, established in 1879, was located just off the Byron Hot Springs property where the Byron Airport stands today. The land on which the school was located was originally part of the 160-acre John Samuel Armstrong homestead. Armstrong, who allowed the school to be built on his land, stands on the porch just to the left of the building.

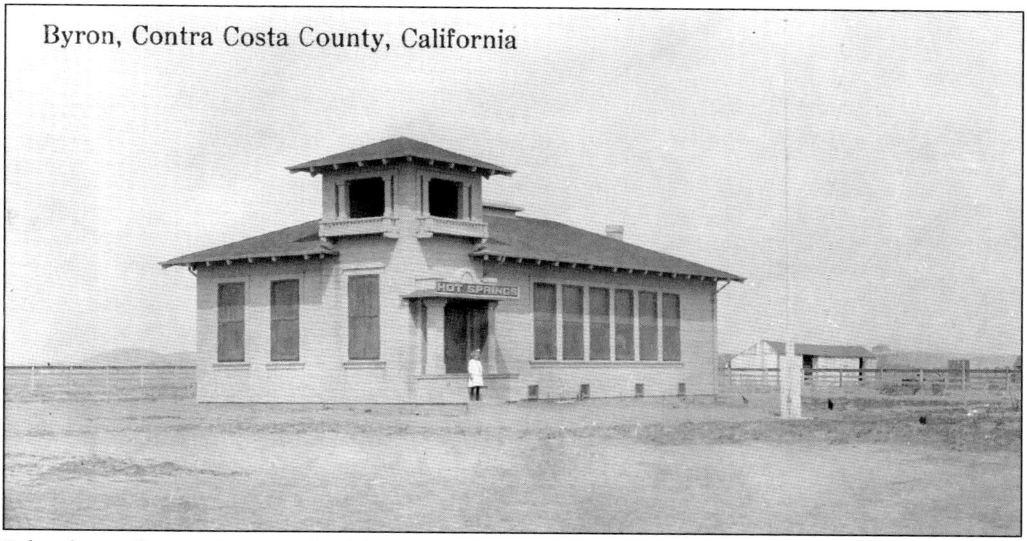

School enrollment increased with sanitarium and resort growth at the Byron Hot Springs. More than 50 people lived on the hot springs' property to support the domestic needs of business. A second school was to be built to accommodate the increasing enrollment of the original school on Byron Hot Springs Road in the 1920s. The school building still exists and is a private residence.

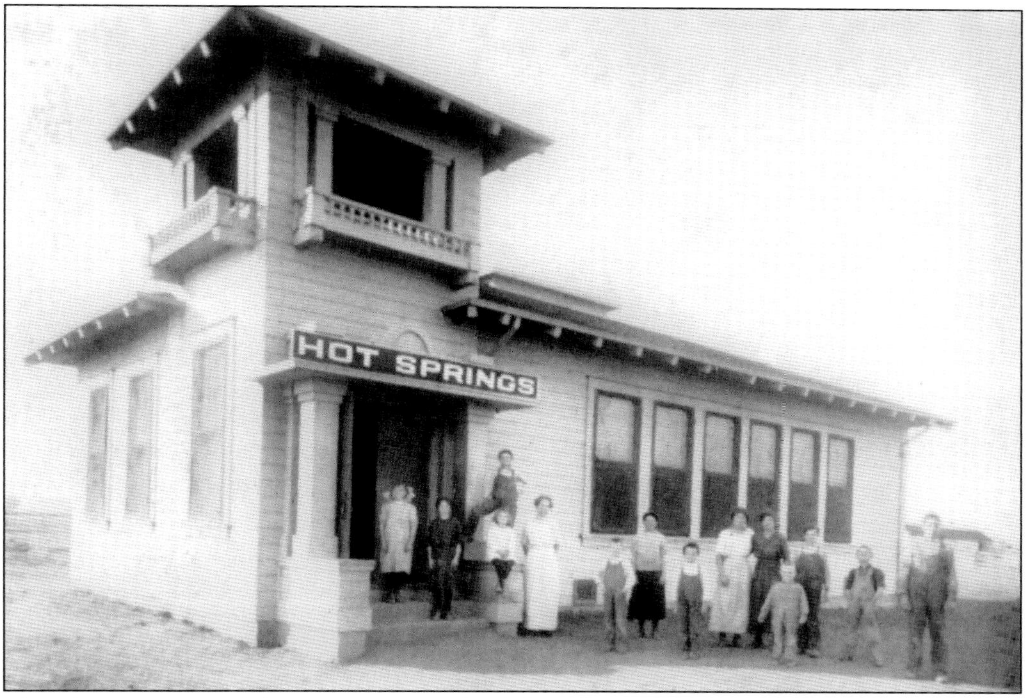

This close-up view of the Hot Springs School shows teachers and students posing in front of their one-room schoolhouse. Note the small shed and paddock for horses to the right rear of the schoolhouse. Students either walked or rode their horse-drawn cart to class. The school closed in 1943 and the student body was absorbed into the Byron Union School District

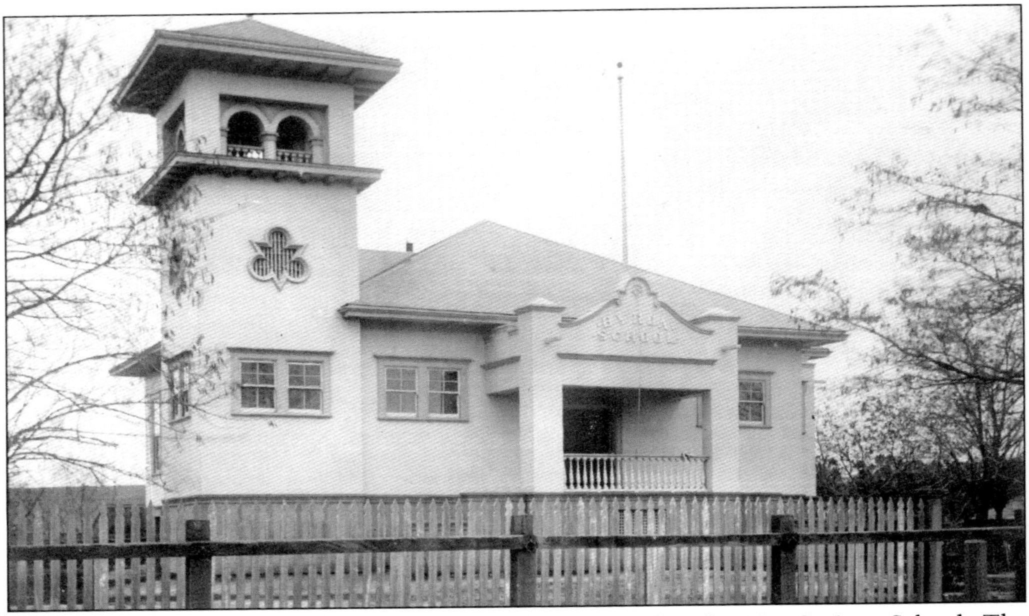

The Byron School was established in 1886 seven years after the Hot Springs School. The architecture is similar to the earlier school, but this building has a three-story bell tower to call children to class from far and wide.

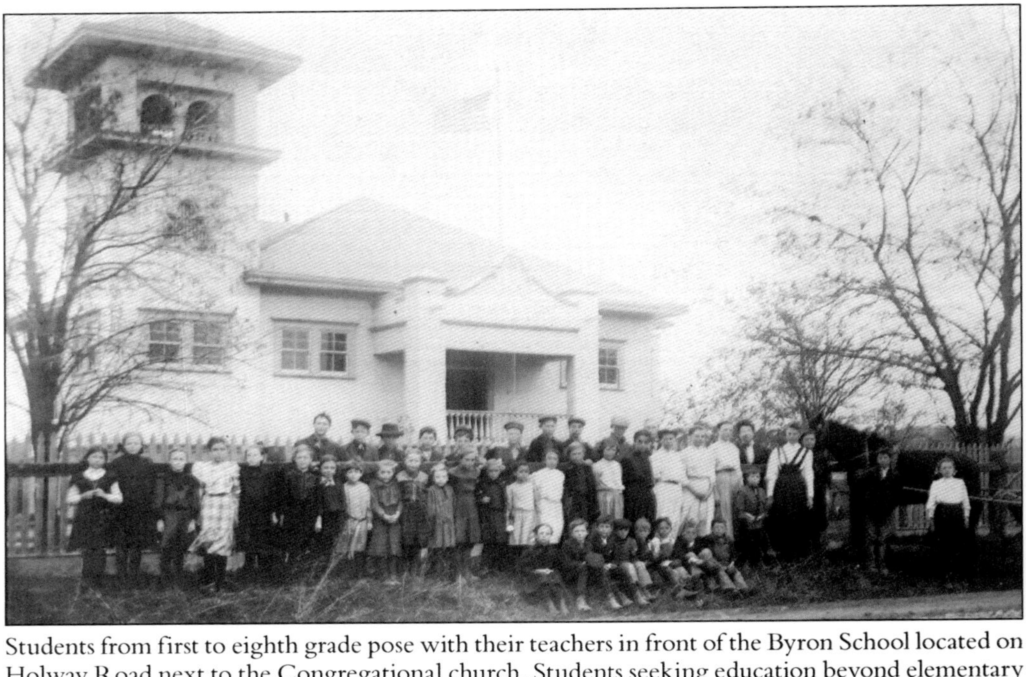

Students from first to eighth grade pose with their teachers in front of the Byron School located on Holway Road next to the Congregational church. Students seeking education beyond elementary reading, writing, and arithmetic would have to leave the community for the closest high school, located in Martinez until 1902 when Liberty Union High School was established.

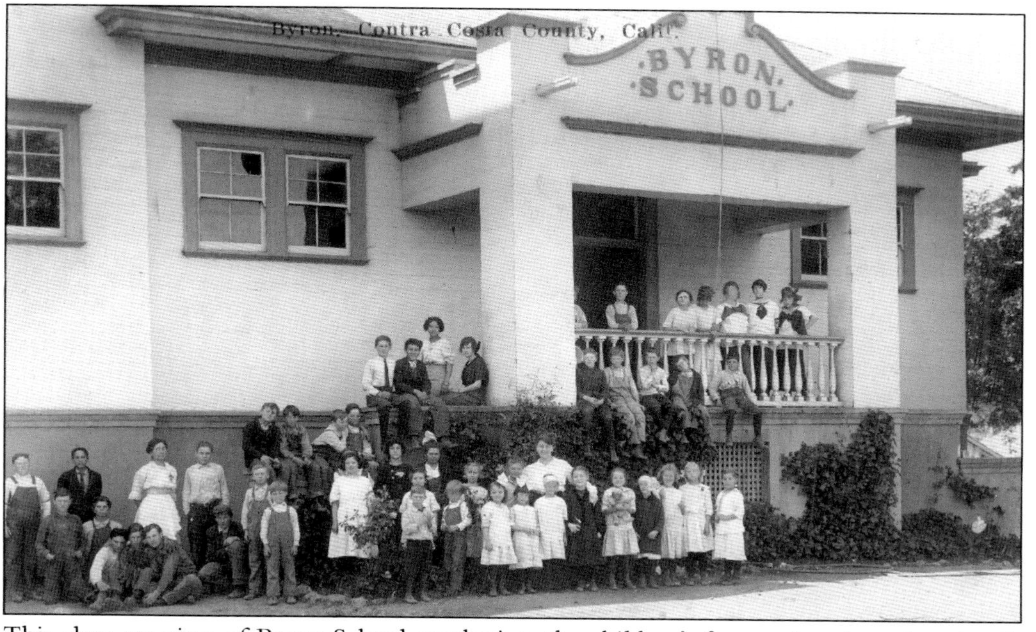

This close-up view of Byron School emphasizes the children's faces rather than the school's architecture, as was common in earlier school photographs. Some boys are wearing shirts and ties. Girls standing on the main entrance porch are dressed in middy blouses, a popular fashion in the 1920s.

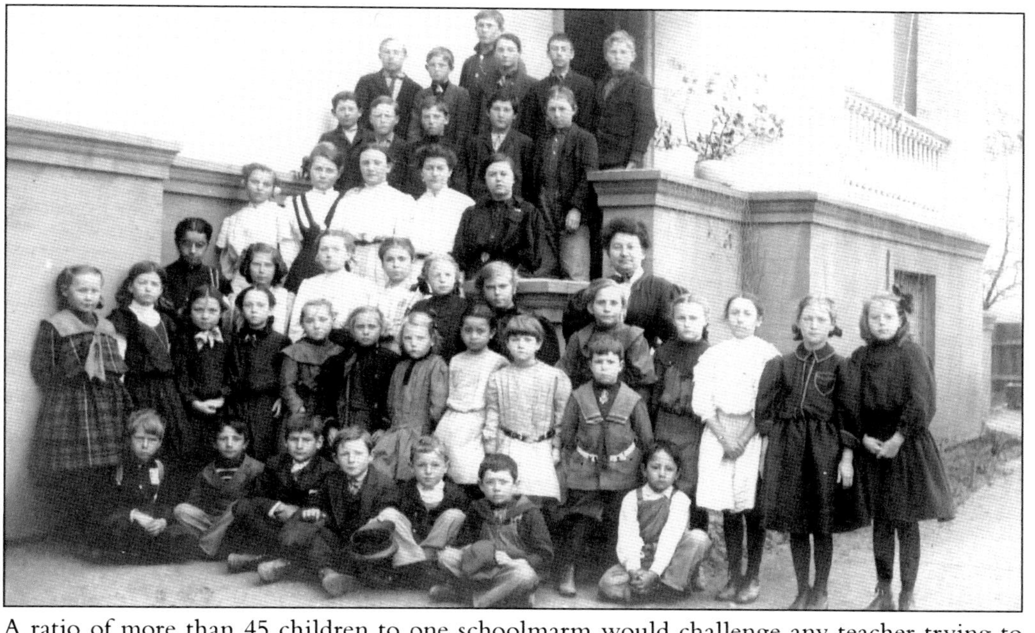

A ratio of more than 45 children to one schoolmarm would challenge any teacher trying to instill the golden rule and a little learning. Children and teachers wear clothing fashions of the early 20th century. Note the high collars and puffy sleeves of the women's blouses. Only the youngest boys wear bib overalls. Economic betterment and pride of community are clear in this school portrait.

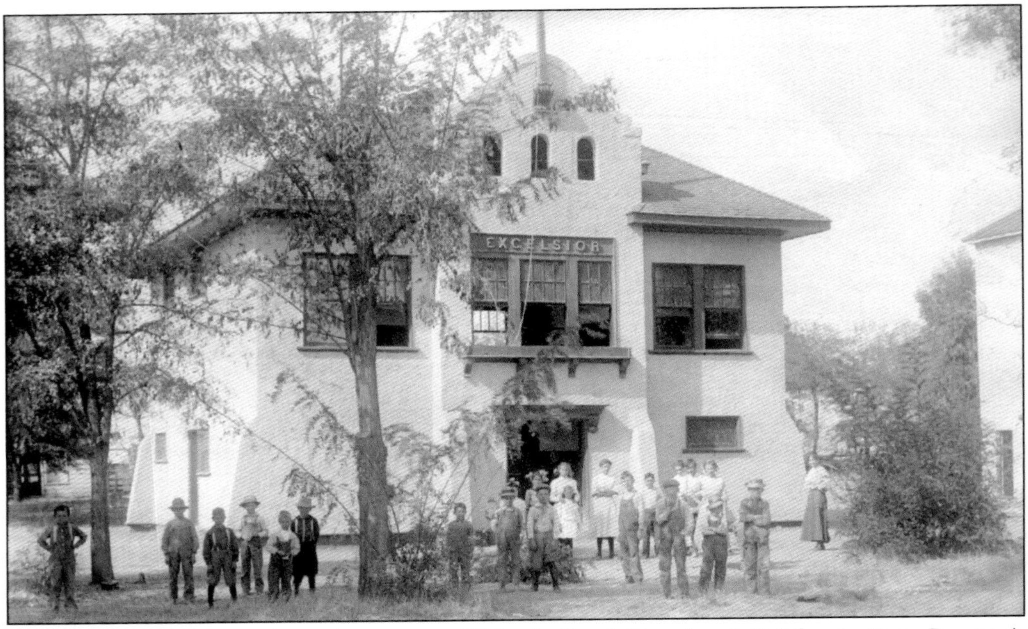

Excelsior School, located on the corner of Marsh Creek Road and California State Route 4, was one of the first schools established in east Contra Costa County. Elementary school classes were held in the school until 1946. Excelsior School consolidated with Byron Union School District the same year. The building exists today and has been converted to private use.

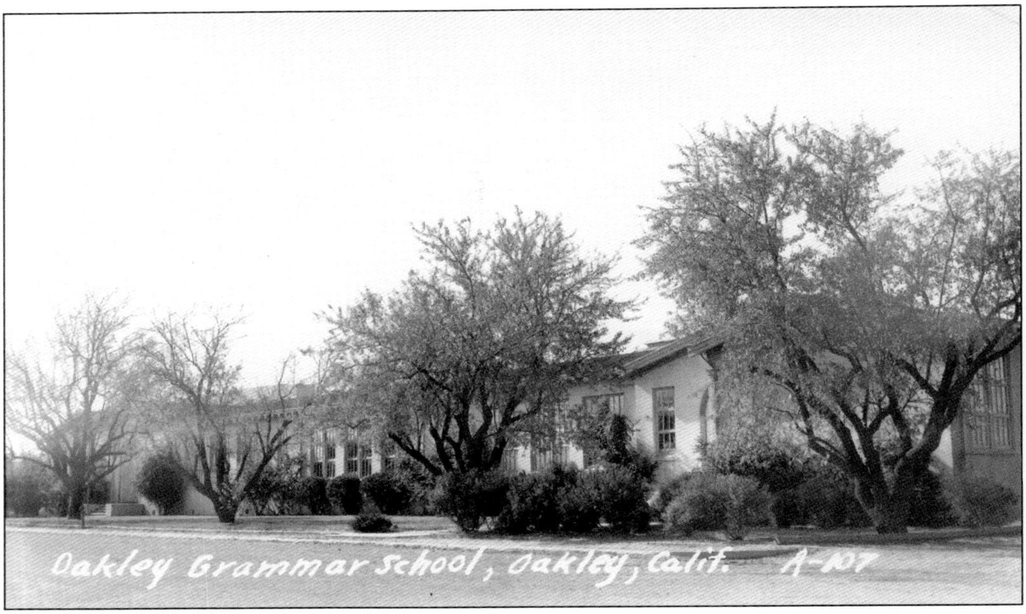

The new Oakley Grammar School, built in 1936, features the signature crop produced in the community: the almond tree. Students studied from kindergarten through eighth grade at this school before attending Liberty Union High School in Brentwood. Iron House, Sand Mound, Jersey Island, and Bradford School Districts united and became the Oakley School District that same year.

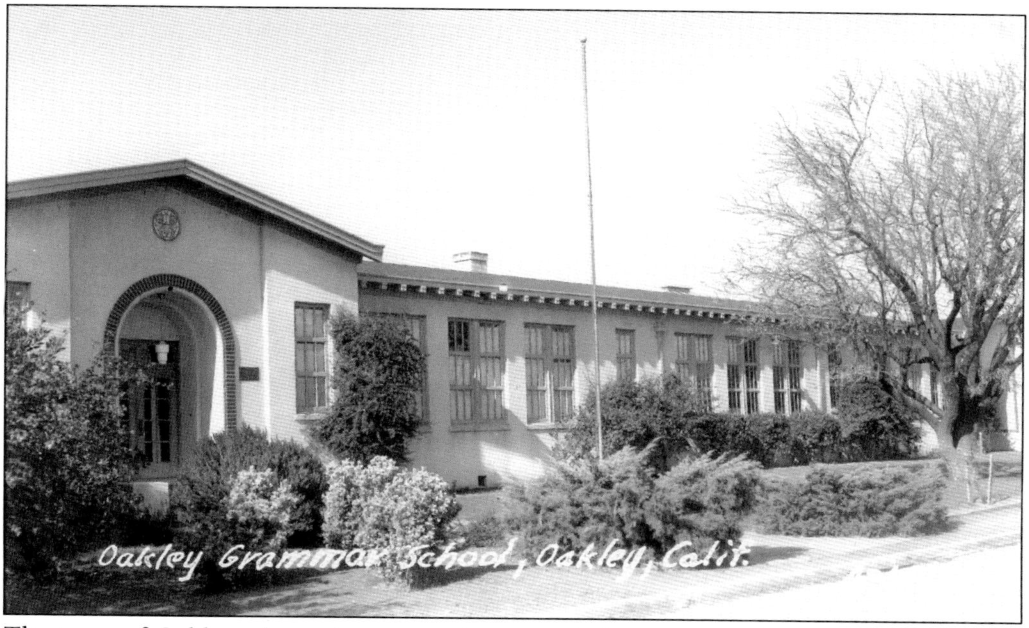

The town of Oakley educated a grade-school population second only in size to Brentwood in eastern Contra Costa County. Byron was the largest community in the area until the first decade of the 20th century when the Balfour Guthrie Investment Company's financial backing in the area caused the Brentwood population to dramatically increase.

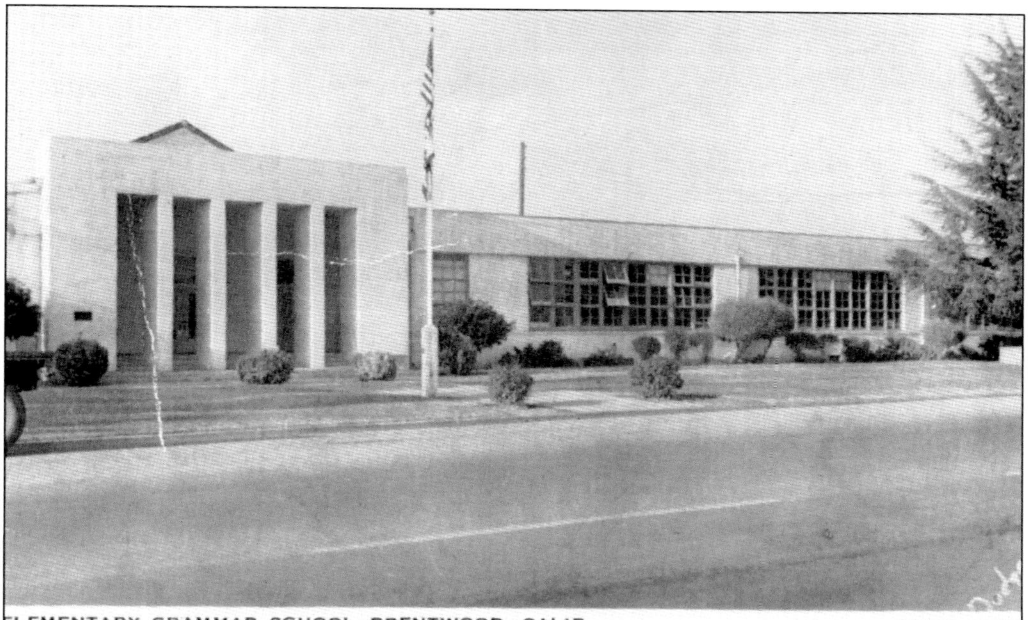

The original Brentwood Elementary School provided a child's education from kindergarten through the eighth grade until the 1950s. Edna Hill School, named in 1954 after a long-standing teacher, was built in the 1950s to accommodate grades six through eight. This building is now the home of Liberty Union Community/Adult Education.

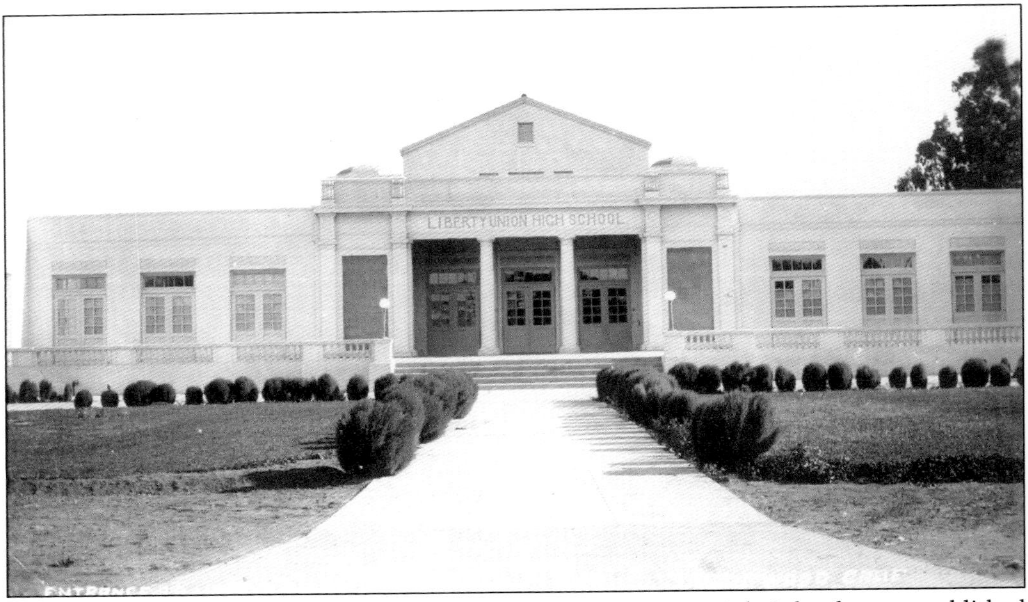

The first high school built in the community, Liberty Union High School, was established in 1902 and provided post-elementary education to students from Byron, Bethel Island, Knightsen, Oakley, and Brentwood. For the first time, students seeking academic and trade education didn't need to venture far away from Martinez for high school. This building was constructed in 1920 at a cost of $93,000.

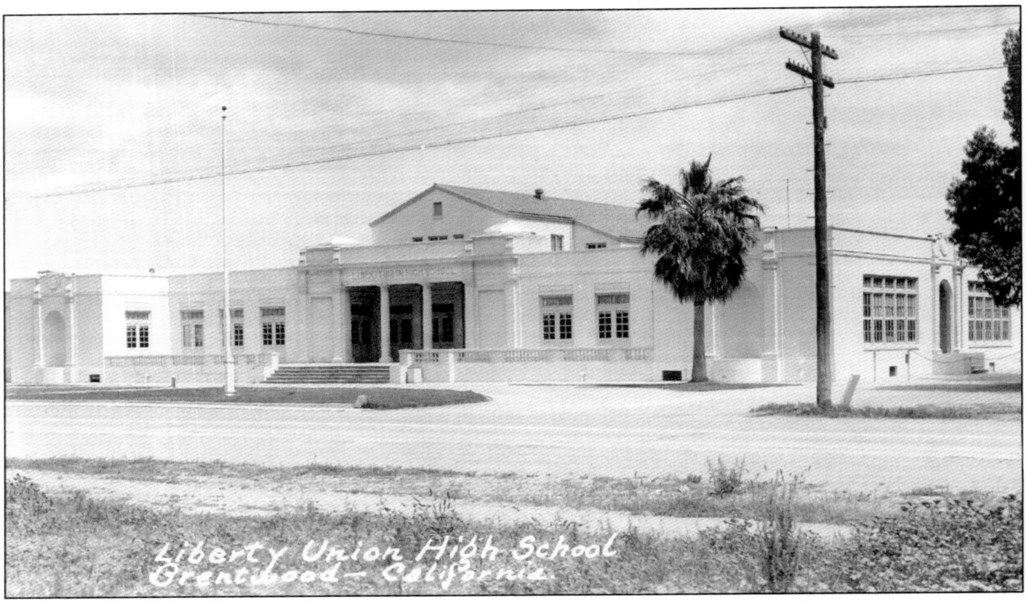

Graduating classes from Liberty Union High School increased to a high of 260 in the late 1960s. The flight of families to eastern Contra Costa County and the building boom during the 1990s and the first decade of the 21st century added four more high schools to the area to accommodate 6,400 students: Heritage, Freedom, Independence, and LaPaloma.

Seven

Recreation and Amusements

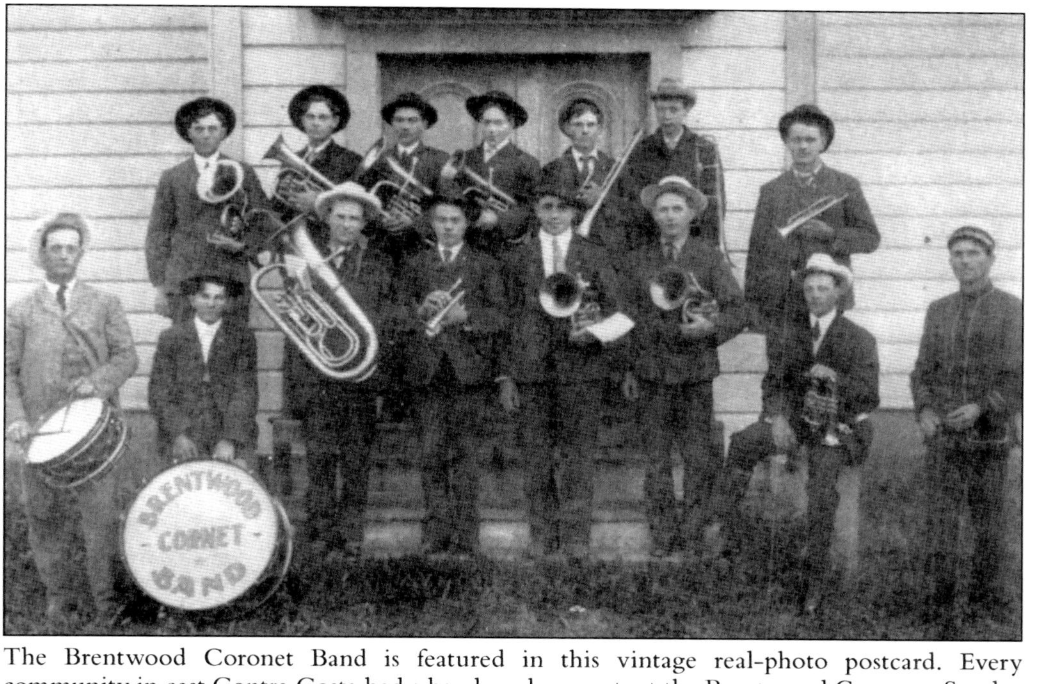

The Brentwood Coronet Band is featured in this vintage real-photo postcard. Every community in east Contra Costa had a band, and concerts at the Brentwood Grove on Sunday were common. The coronet was a popular instrument, but there are just as many trombones as coronets in this image.

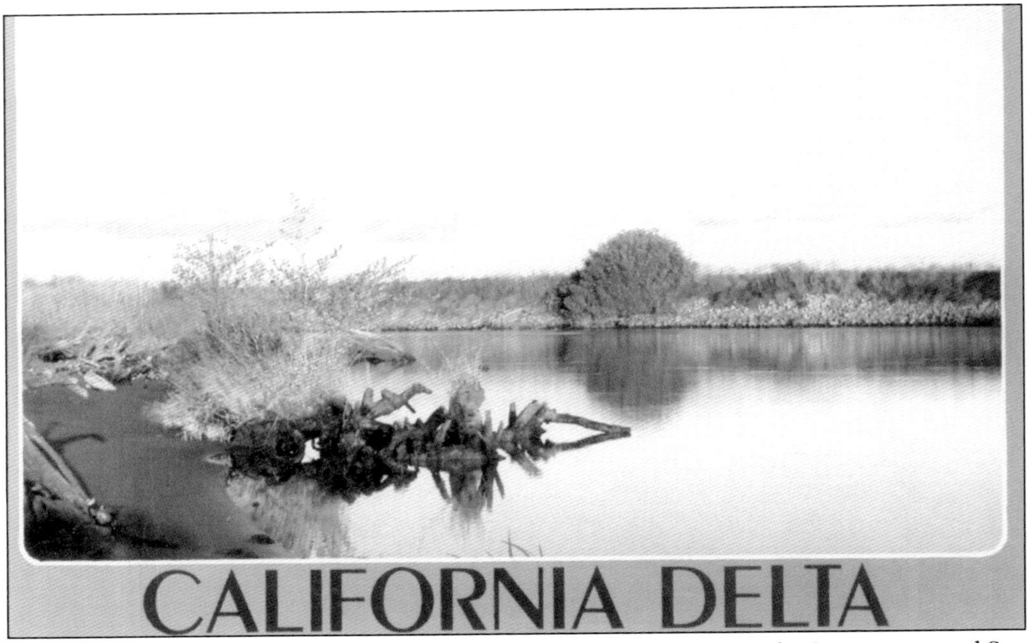

East Contra Costa is also called the delta county. It is the true entry to the Sacramento and San Joaquin River Delta for all Bay Area residents wanting to slip away for a few hours of fishing or lose themselves for a lifetime in its famed 1,000 miles of waterways.

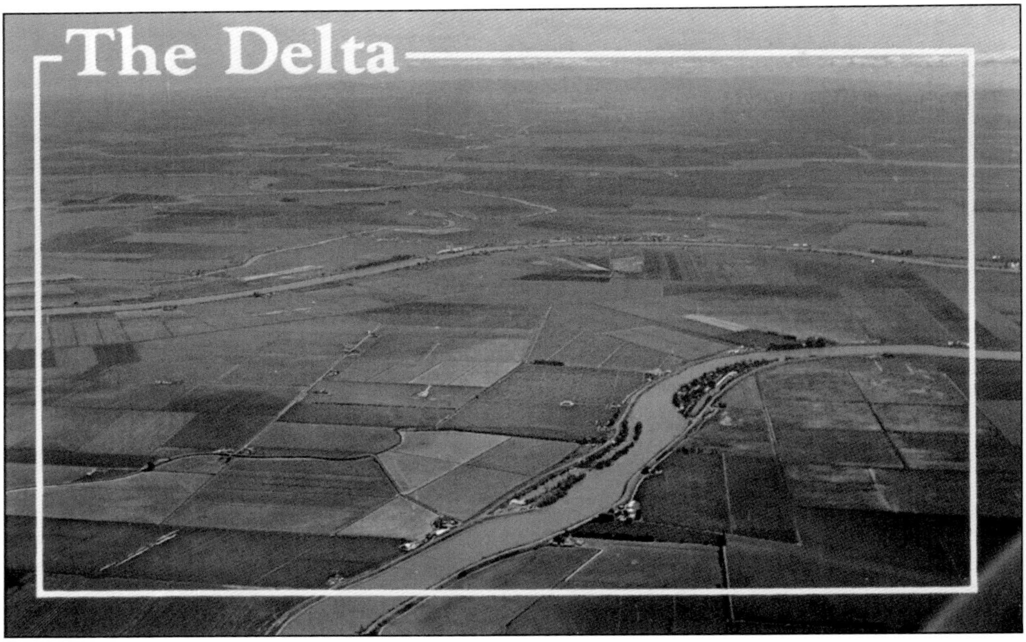

Local agriculture relies on delta waters but so does the commercial and recreational economy of the entire area. Some of the many recreations include seasonal striped bass derbies, water-skiing, wakeboarding, boating, sailing, bird shooting, wild game hunting, cabin cruising, and swimming. There is nothing finer than a day on the delta.

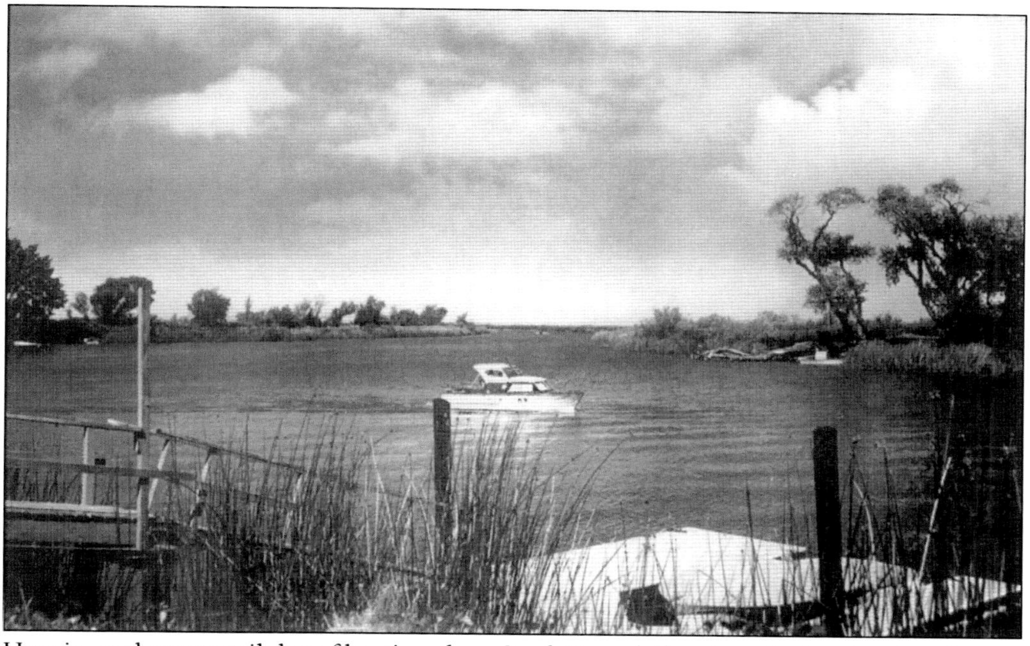

Here is another tranquil day of boating along Sand Mound Slough or Taylor Creek to Frank's Tract for good fishing. Then maybe cruise home via False River and Taylor Slough, returning to Bethel Island at dusk. This is the life.

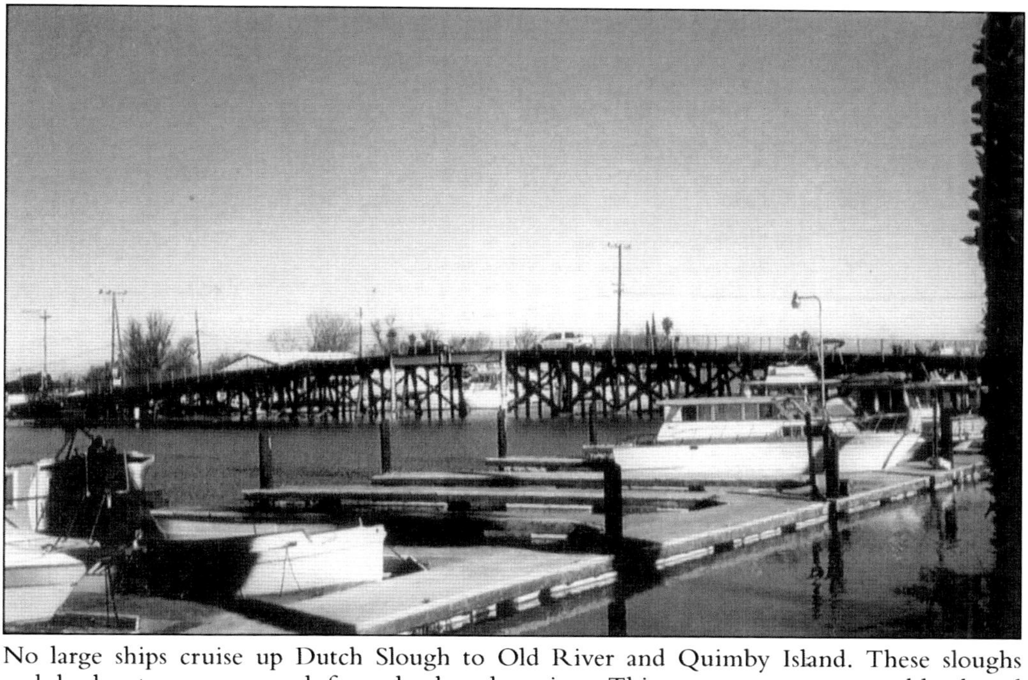

No large ships cruise up Dutch Slough to Old River and Quimby Island. These sloughs and backwaters are carved from land reclamation. This area was once marshland and wilderness. Levees changed all that, creating miles of interconnected channels leading to the San Joaquin River.

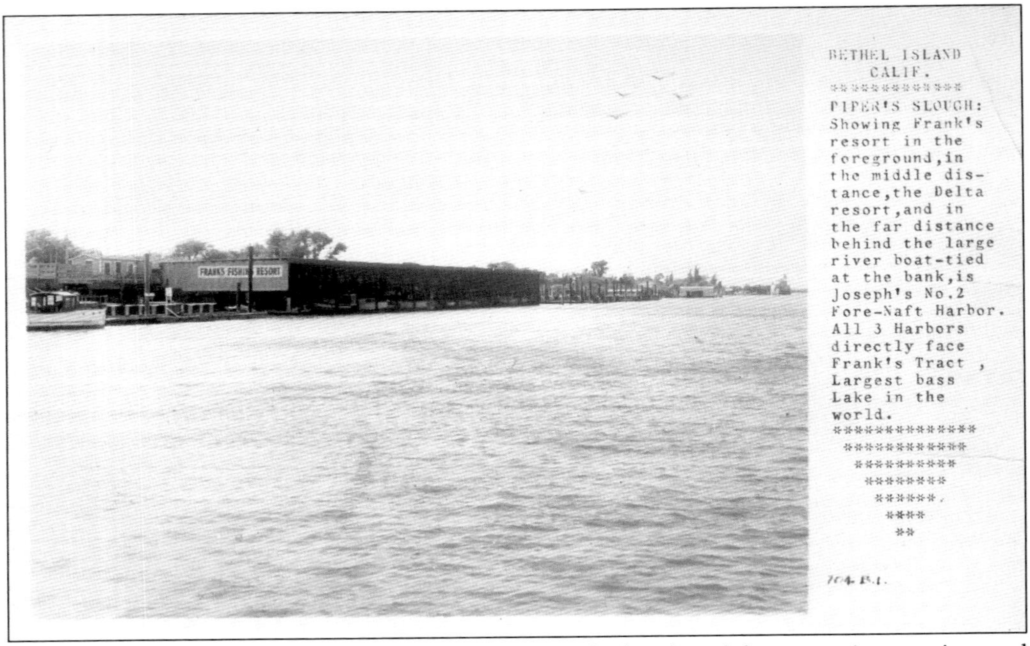

A mainstay of Bethel Island's fishing recreation is Piper's Slough and the convenient marinas and boat harbors dotting its banks. Together they provide access to many flooded delta land tracts. Big Break and Frank's Tract are just two large tracts of land once reclaimed from marshland and placed into productive agricultural use. The levees failed, and the land was abandoned.

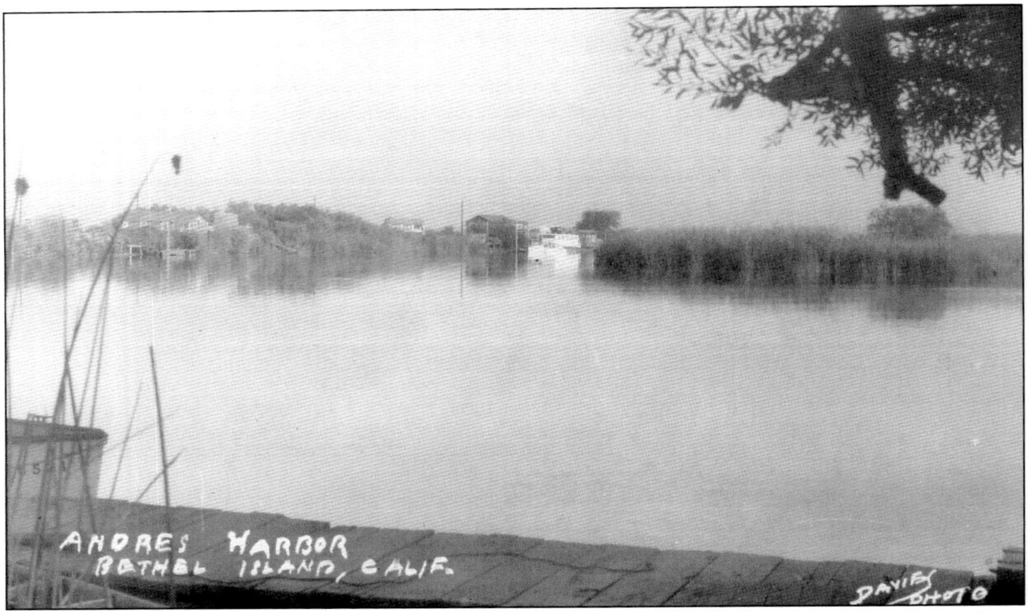

There are hundreds of little water encampments and personal island getaways throughout the Bethel Island area. Electricity and telephone service did not arrive on the island until the late 1940s. Most of these bungalows' owners lived happily without the conveniences of modern life.

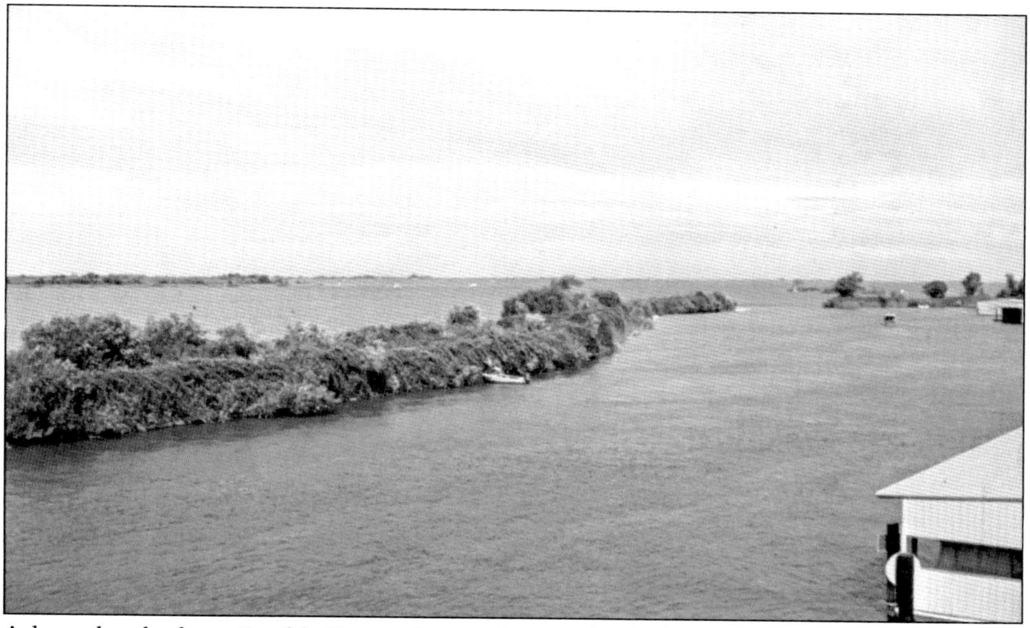

A levee break along Frank's Tract submerged an orchard, farms, and houses occupied until 1935. Water rushed in, creating a protected haven for striped bass. Who would have guessed at the time that this would become the largest bass lake in the United States?

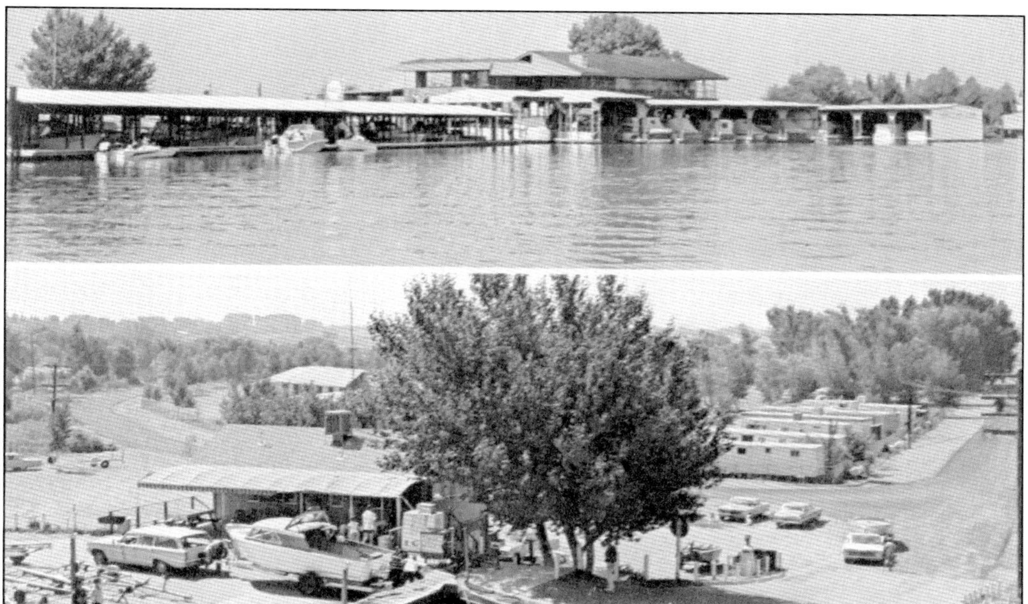

Recreational users discovered Bethel Island in the 1940s and 1950s. Many bought small, subdivided lots of land and built campsites or weekend cabins. Some lots sold for as little as $50. A boat launch ramp was always close by. Covered harbors soon followed.

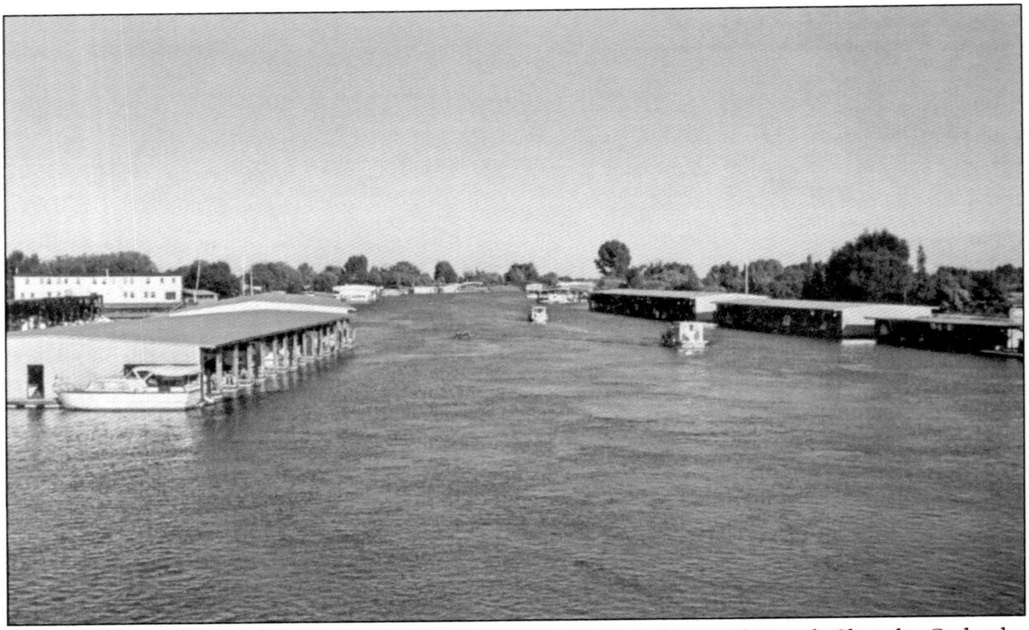

Main Street on Bethel Island is really paved with water and named Dutch Slough. Only the restaurants, the post office, and the real estate offices seem to be on dry land. Houseboats, fishing boats, and water-skiers all have a home here.

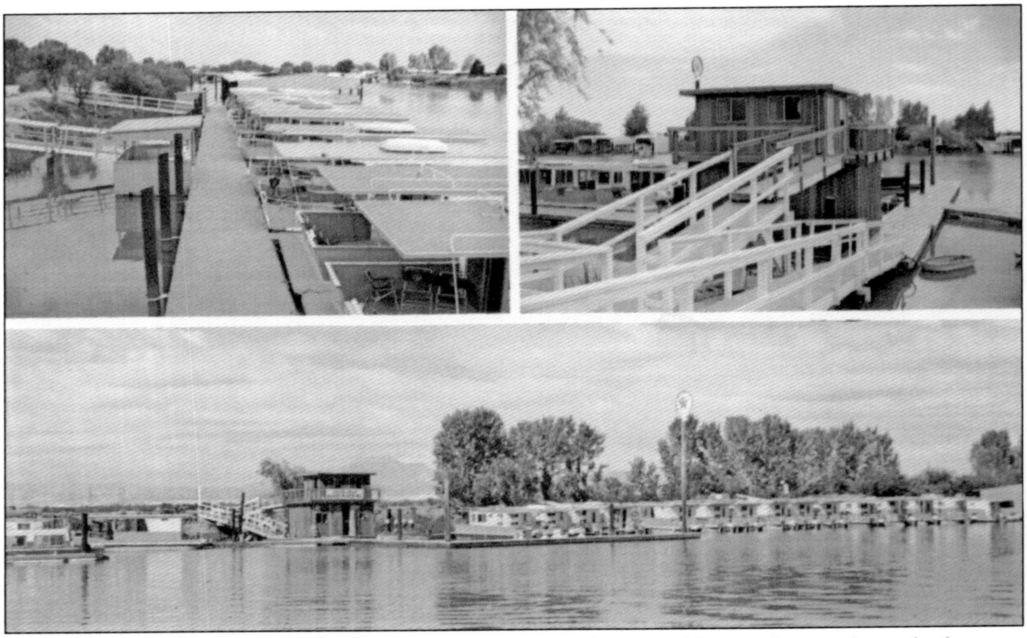

Houseboat rental is a large part of the river lifestyle. Take a weeklong sojourn along the byways to Rio Vista, Terminal Island, or Sacramento. Turn the tiller southeast and discover Old River and Clifton Court.

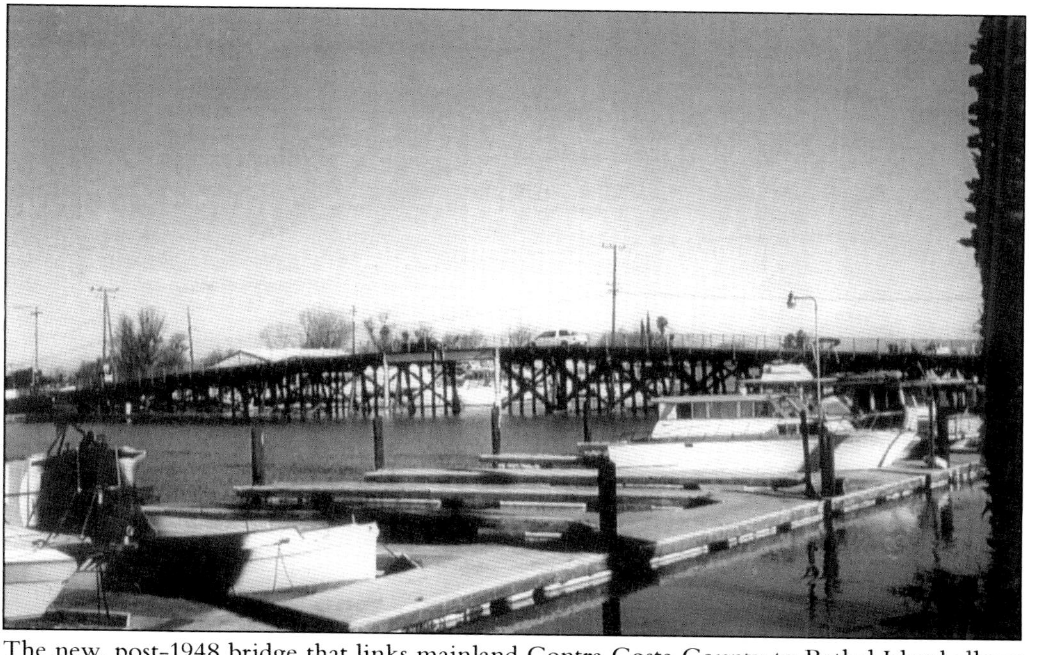

The new, post-1948 bridge that links mainland Contra Costa County to Bethel Island allows no room for error. The two-lane road connects to the island via land reclaimed from the delta by levees and pumps. The United States Swamp and Overflowed Land Act of 1850 allowed improvements and the purchase of property resulting in the creation of a new island in 1900.

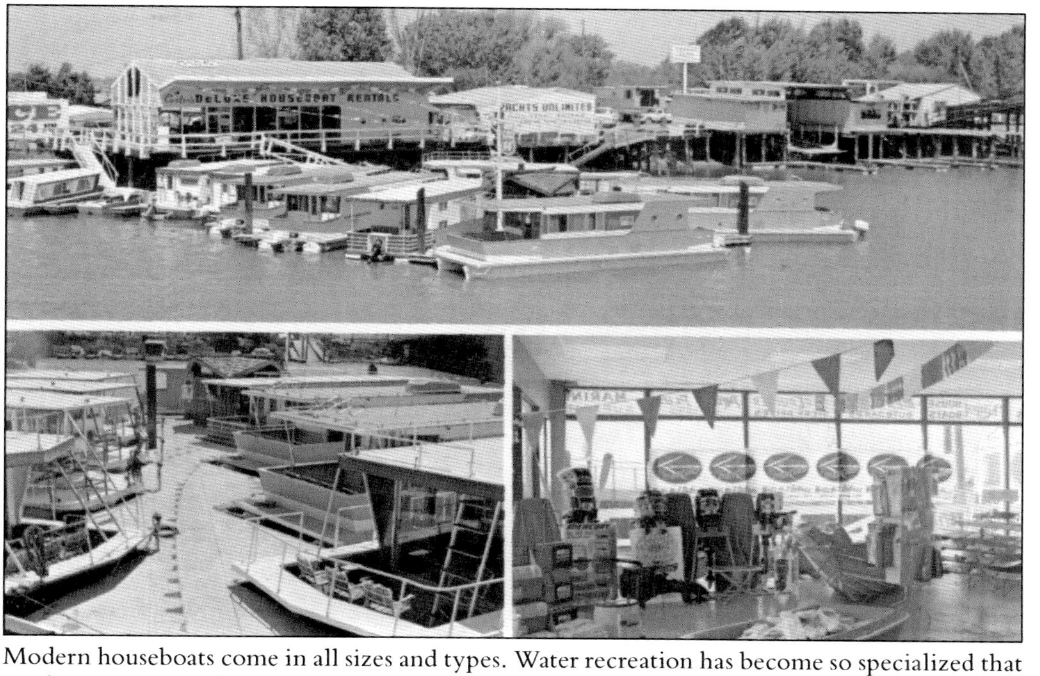

Modern houseboats come in all sizes and types. Water recreation has become so specialized that marinas now specialize in certain types of craft. All precautions are taken to ensure a safe and enjoyable boating experience.

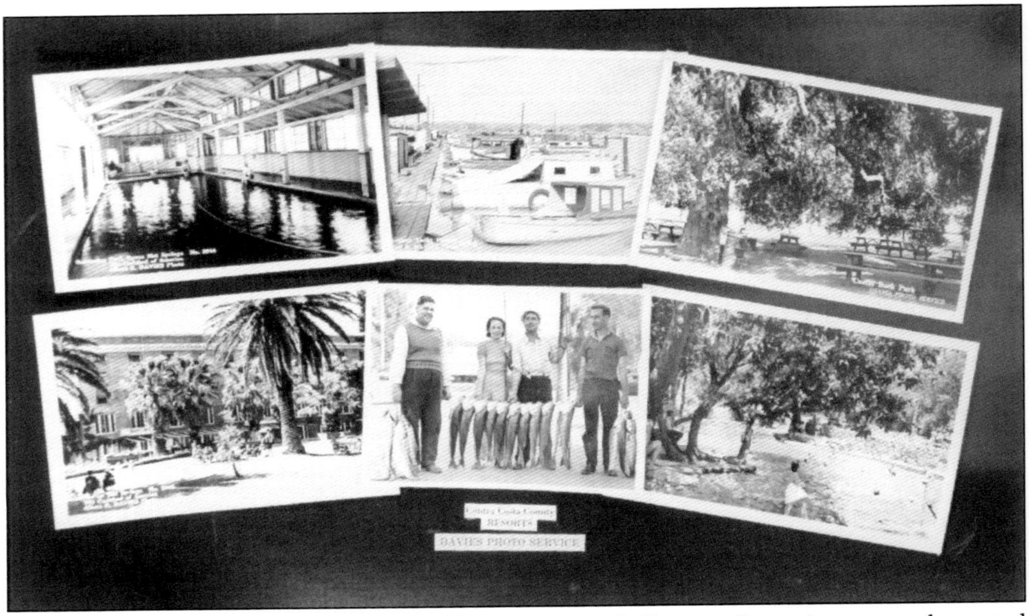

Davies Photo Service of Alamo, California, captured Contra Costa images and created postcards for most businesses and resorts in the county. This real-photo postcard shows all the recreational activities of east Contra Costa. The outdoor life includes boating, water sports, fishing, swimming, and picnicking.

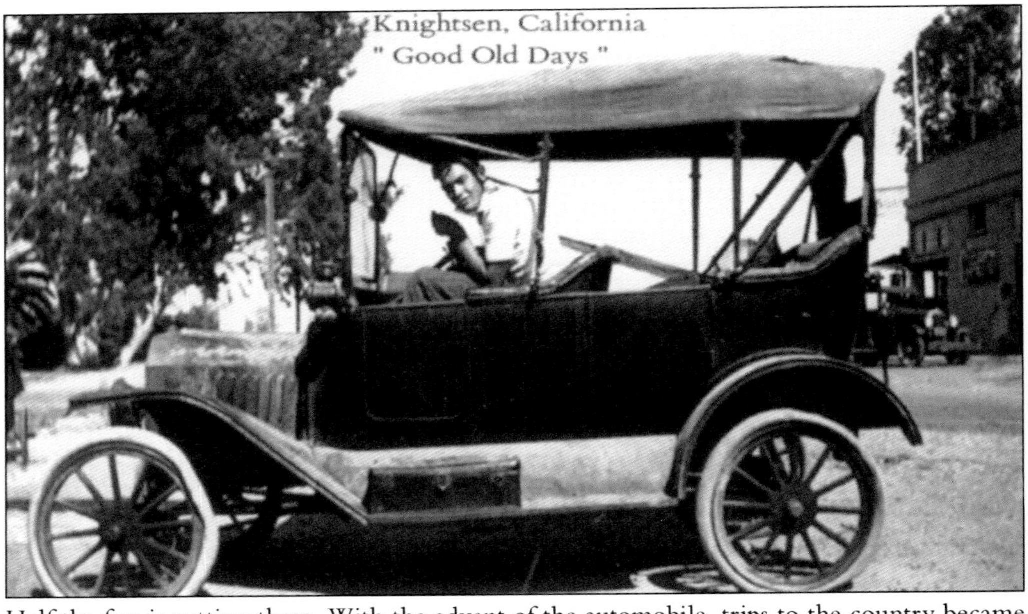

Half the fun is getting there. With the advent of the automobile, trips to the country became popular. Road trips to pastoral picnic grounds or visits to family still residing in rural areas became a pleasurable day's outing. Early postcards often incorporated cars in their advertisements. Stanley Duff poses in his "tin lizzy."

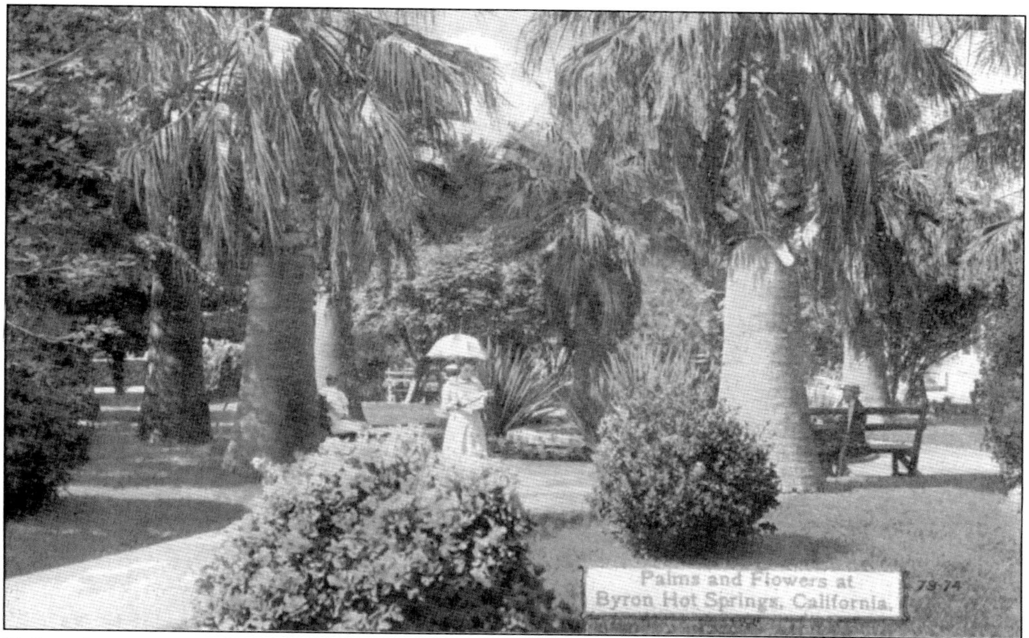

Enjoy the scenery of east Contra Costa County. Walking in exotic gardens was as popular in the first decade of the 20th century as it is today. The park setting of the Palm Court at the Byron Hot Springs attracted visitors as much as its mineral waters. Careful observation reveals the proprietor of the Byron Hot Springs, Lewis R. Mead, sitting on a bench to the right.

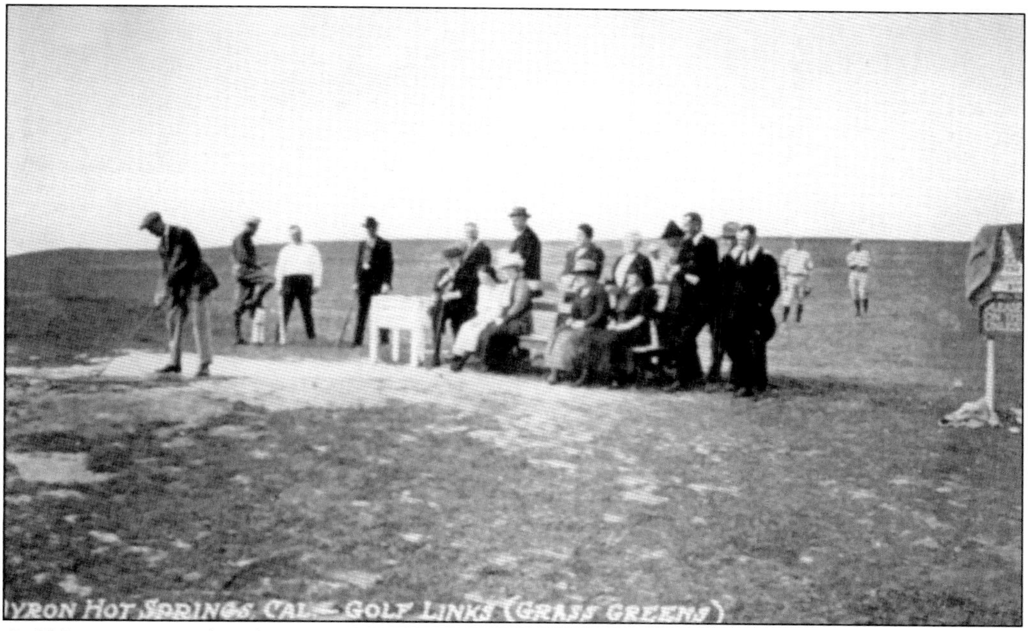

Golf became popular during the late 19th and early 20th century in the San Francisco Bay Area. The Hotel Del Monte had the first golf links in Northern California, but Byron Hot Springs was not far behind. The hot springs had two golf links at one time. This image of opening day in 1919 emphasizes grass greens on an otherwise rough golf course.

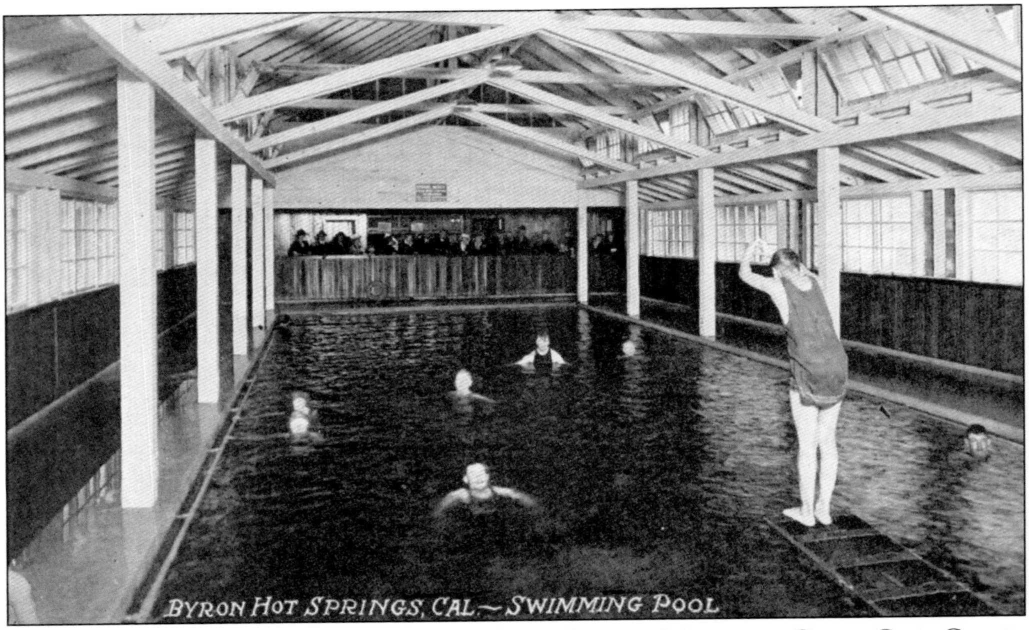

The only salt plunge, also known as a swimming tank or pool, in eastern Contra Costa County was this wooden-enclosed pool at the Byron Hot Springs. Many local children learned their first swimming lesson here. Men's and women's bathing suits could be rented. Children swam for free. Mineral water bubbled up from between open slats in the bottom.

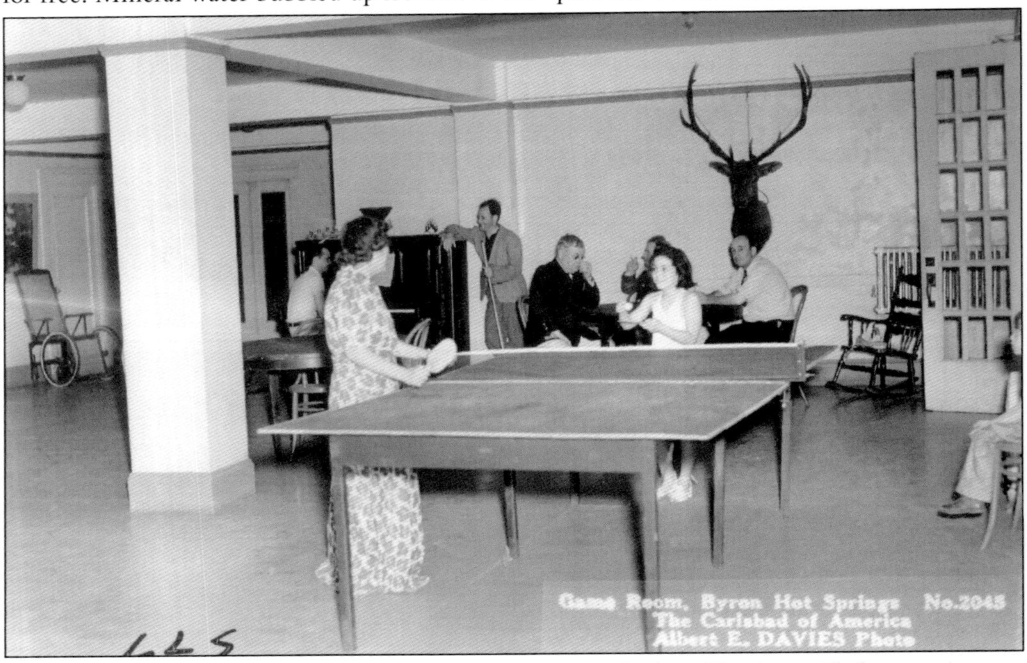

The game room on the lower floor of the 1914 Byron Hot Springs Hotel provided entertainment for all. A piano sits in one corner. Tables stand ready for a game of pedro or a ping-pong tournament. Note the wicker bath chair also known as an invalid wheelchair in the corner as a reminder of earlier health sanitarium years.

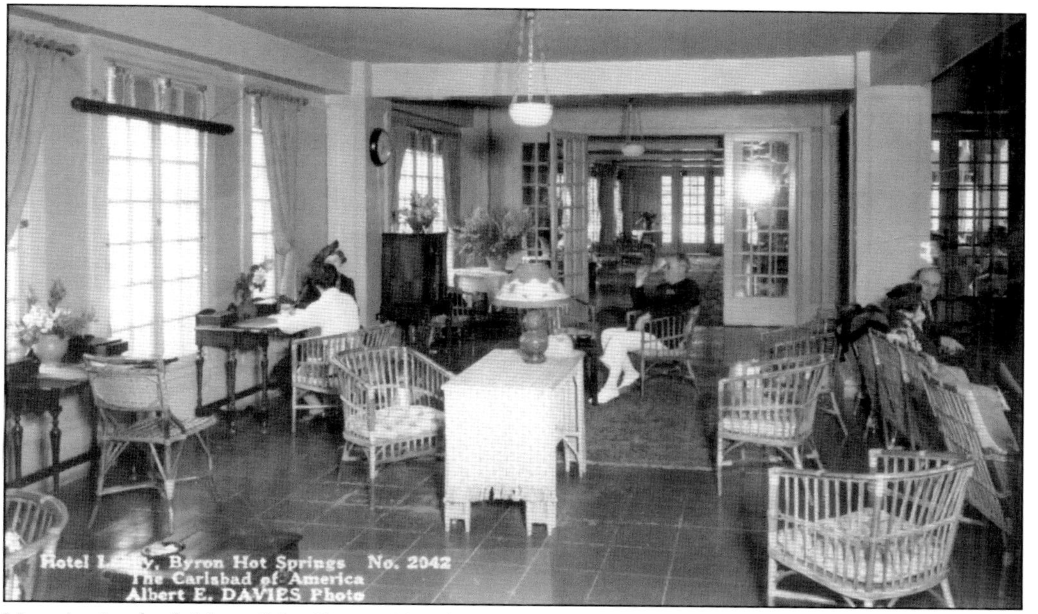

Upstairs in the lobby of the Byron Hot Springs Hotel, guests write postcards to their friends and family in 1935. The dining room is around the corner, set with white linen. All enjoy their stay. Within five years, the United States will enter World War II, and the continuous party at the springs of over 70 years will be over.

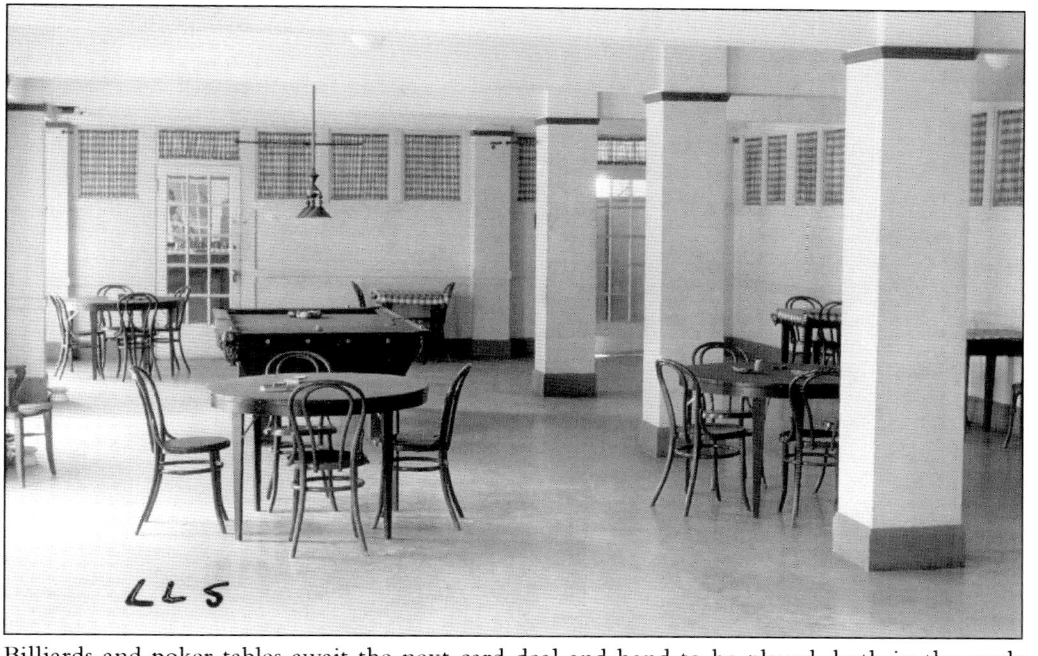

Billiards and poker tables await the next card deal and hand to be played, both in the cards and in politics. The San Francisco political bosses adjourned to the Byron Hot Springs for recreation. James "Sunny Jim" Rolph, San Francisco's mayor and a subsequent California governor, was a director of the Byron Hot Springs Corporation, as were other politically connected individuals.

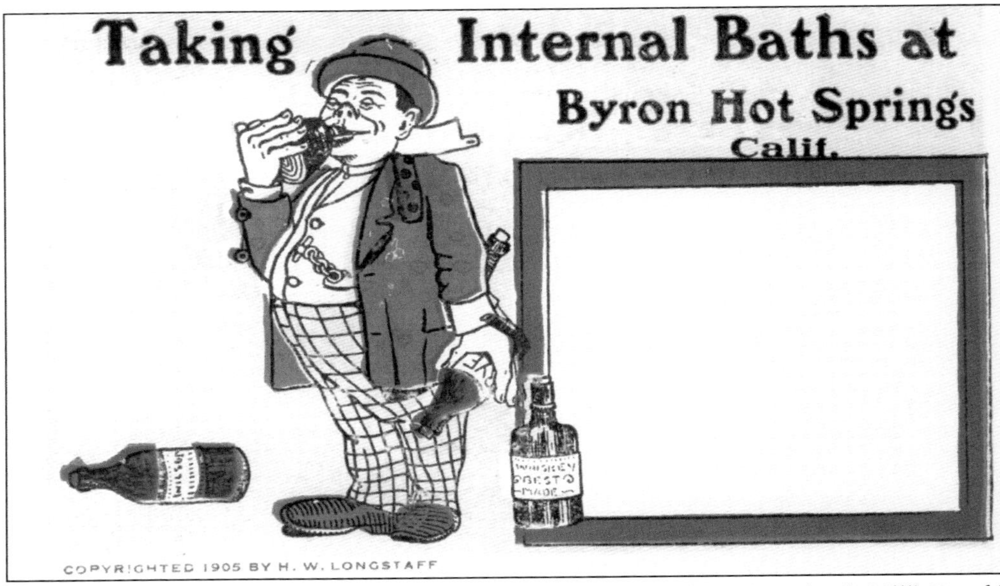

There are other recreations besides drinking the water. William "Cocktail Bill" Boothby began his career as San Francisco's premier mixologist at the Byron Hot Springs. Many went to the hot springs to recover from alcoholism. Others went there to drink. Bottles of Joseph Kennedy–brand whiskey found on the site suggest there was no Prohibition at the resort.

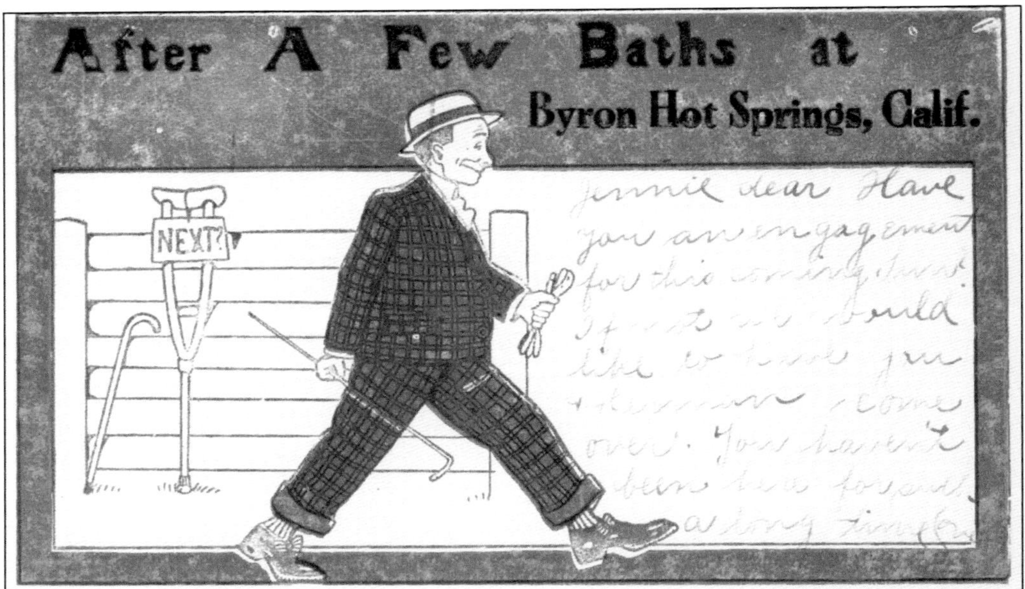

This popular cartoon postcard captured how many men felt after a few baths at the Byron Hot Springs. Gout was a common inflammation complaint caused by a decrease in uric acid metabolism, resulting in deposits of the acid and salts in the joints. The water from the hot springs did not cure it, but a week under a physician's care helped relieve the pain. Many people who were carried in on stretchers to the resort walked out on their own feet.

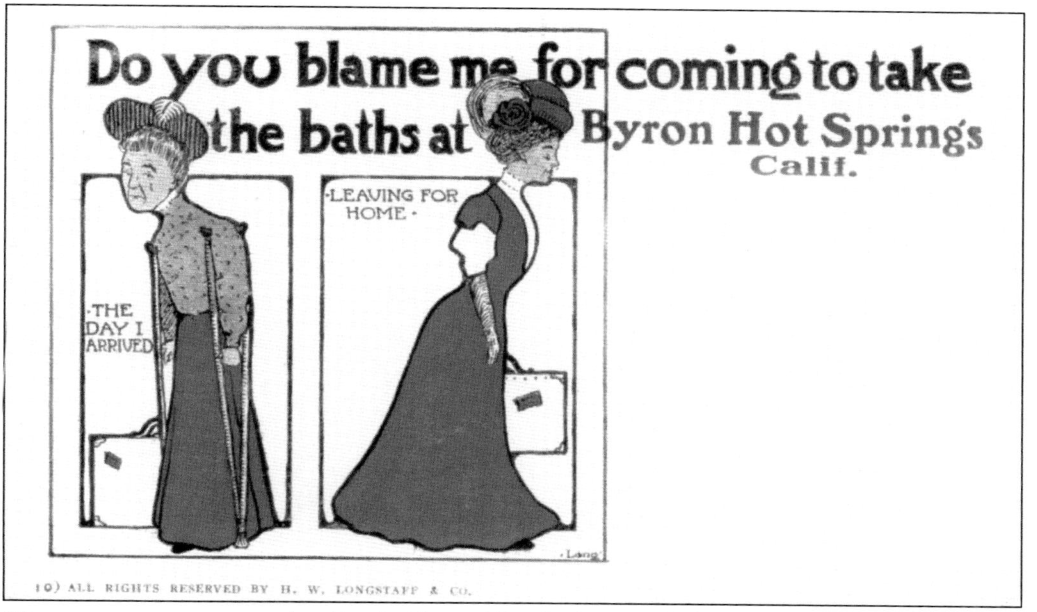

Women were a target market for the Byron Hot Springs with the arrival of Lewis R. Mead's second wife, Mae. The salt plunge became the "baths of beauty," emphasizing the benefits of water exercise and saltwater for the complexion. Meals were included in the room price.

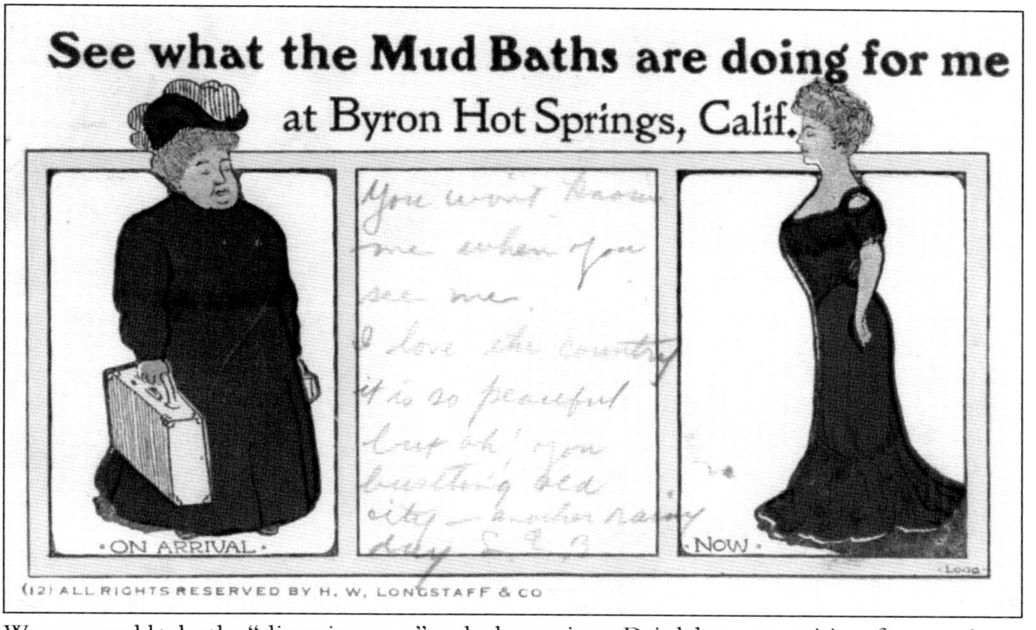

Women could take the "slimming cure" at the hot springs. Drink large quantities of magnesium-infused springwater and do not be surprised at the result. As this postcard reads, "You won't know me when you see me. I love the country, it is so peaceful but oh you bustling old city—another rainy day. [signed] L. A. B."

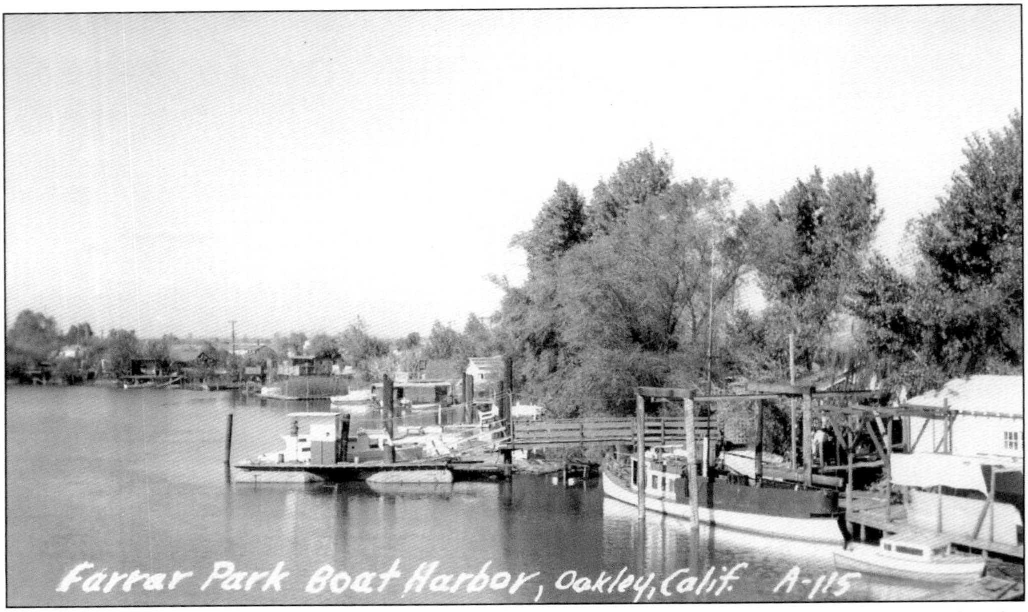

Farrar Park on Dutch Slough begins the story of Bethel Island development. Jack and Blanche Farrar came to Bethel Island in 1943. The Farrars made a life catering to others who enjoyed boating, swimming, and picnicking along Dutch Slough. Thanks to them, the island became known and settled by those who love recreation.

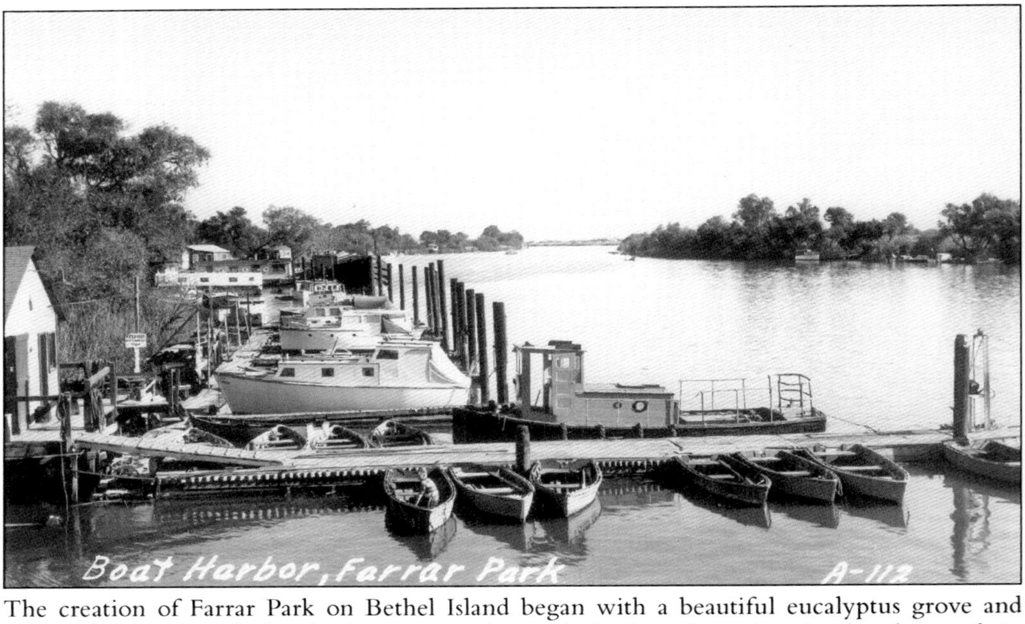

The creation of Farrar Park on Bethel Island began with a beautiful eucalyptus grove and picnic tables. Jack and Blanche Farrar opened a snack shack to the swimming beach crowd. In the late 1940s, it expanded to a marina, a boat harbor, a tent camp, a swimming area, and boat race site.

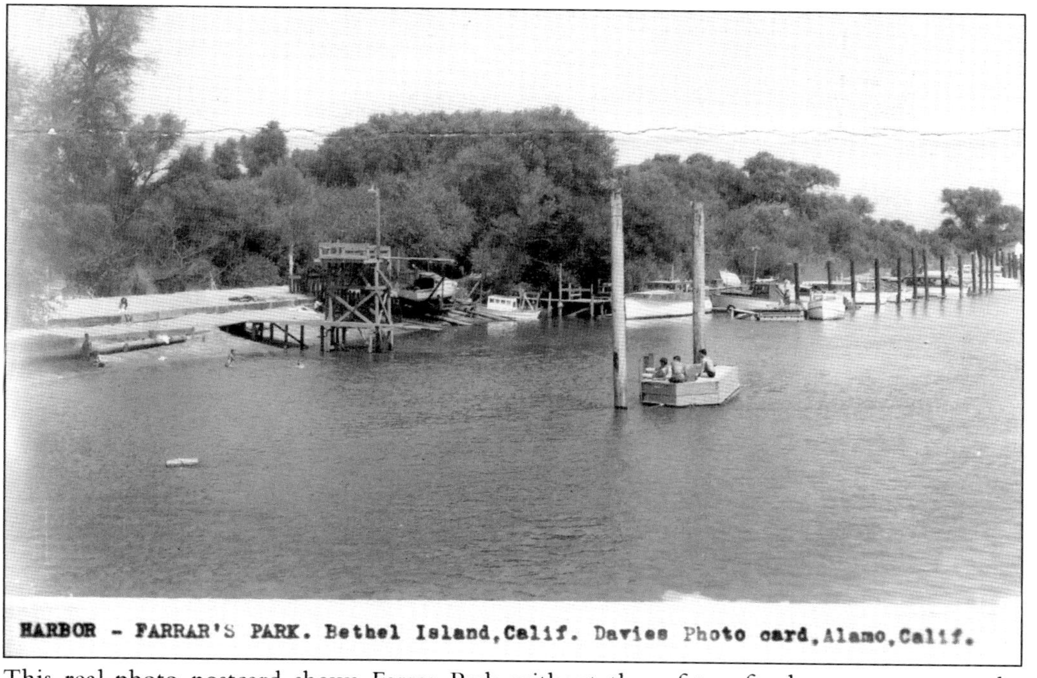

This real-photo postcard shows Farrar Park without the safety of a boom to protect the swimming area. A few brave swimmers venture out to the float secured mid-channel. Watch out for ski boats.

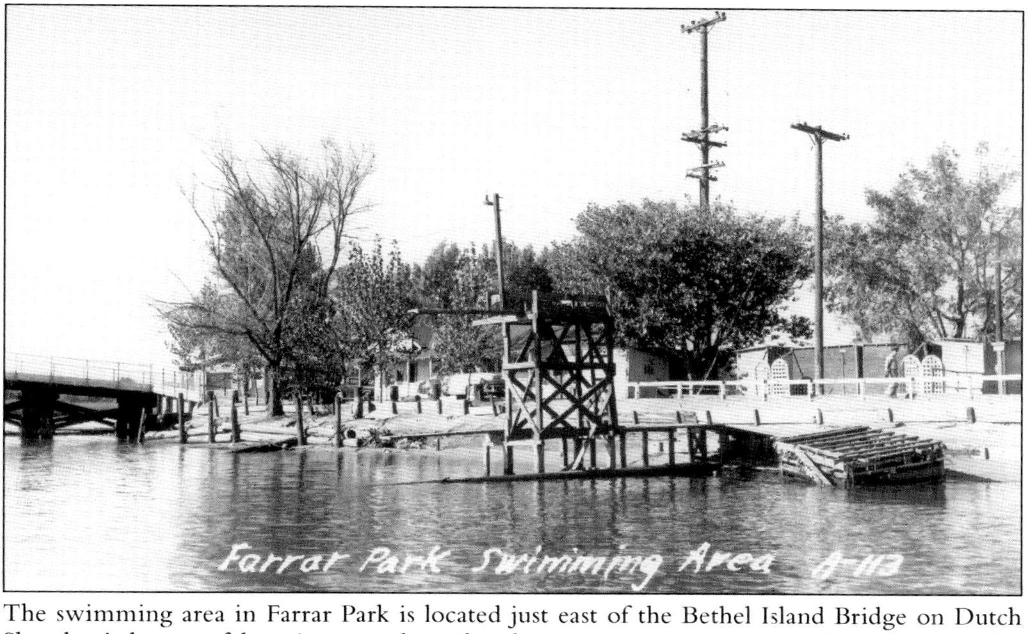

The swimming area in Farrar Park is located just east of the Bethel Island Bridge on Dutch Slough. A boom of logs is secured to the shore to protect swimmers from boat traffic. Sunbathing, floats, and a diving area soon followed. Delta waters are the perfect temperature.

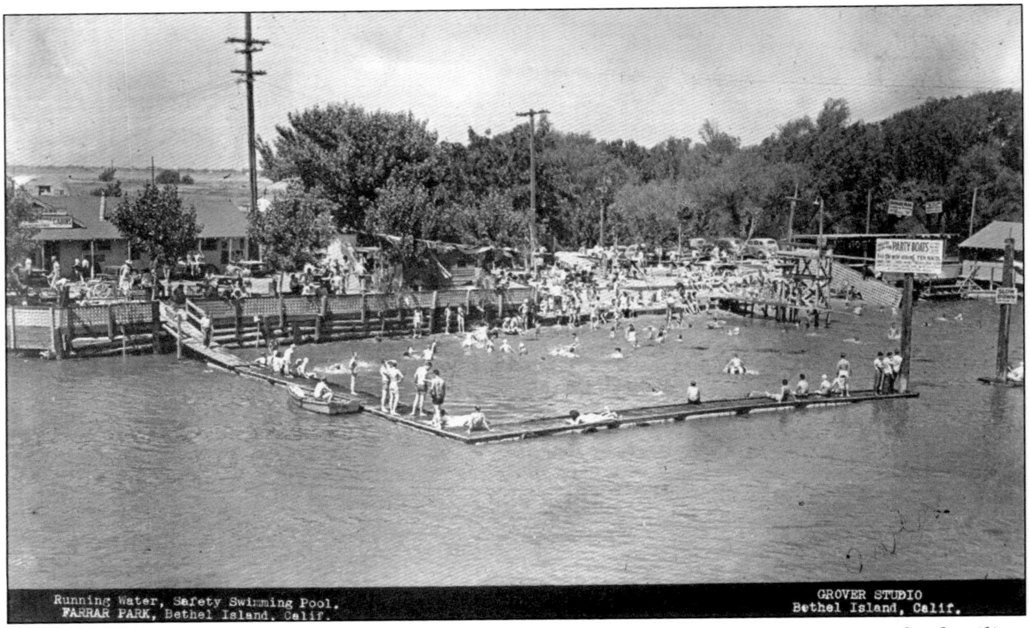

A safe and simple swimming area carved out of Dutch Slough soon became a mecca for families. A picnic area, a canteen selling food and beverages, and a campground soon followed. This image dates from the mid- to late 1940s.

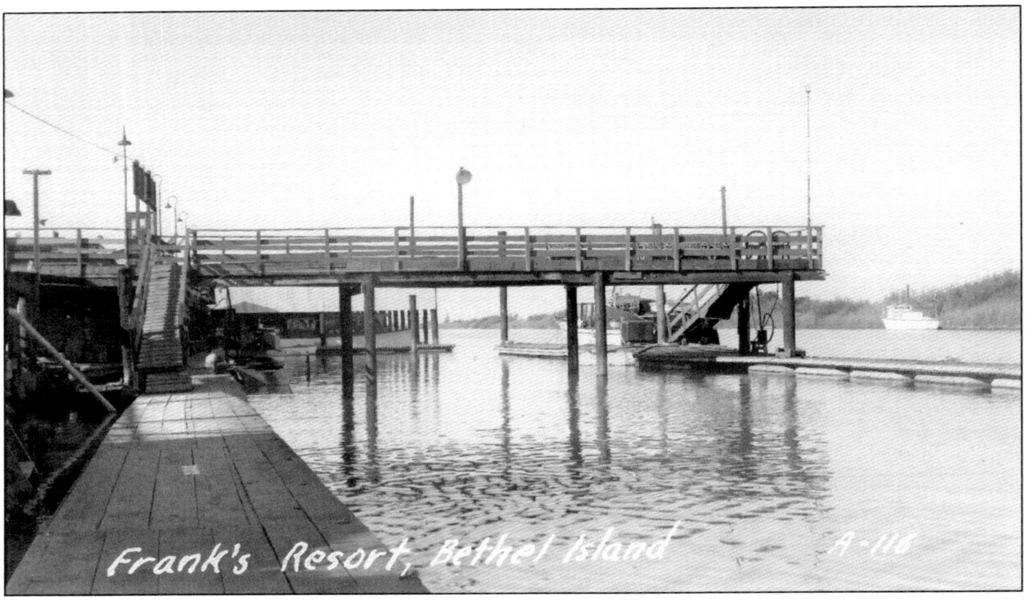

Frank's Resort provides swimming and fishing access to the large lake now known as Frank's Tract Lake State Reserve. It is famous for its striped bass and catfish fishing. Fred Frank of San Leandro owned Frank's Tract when the levee failed in 1935. Efforts to repair the levee and dredge the island were abandoned, creating an anglers' paradise.

Eight

Resort Life and Celebrity

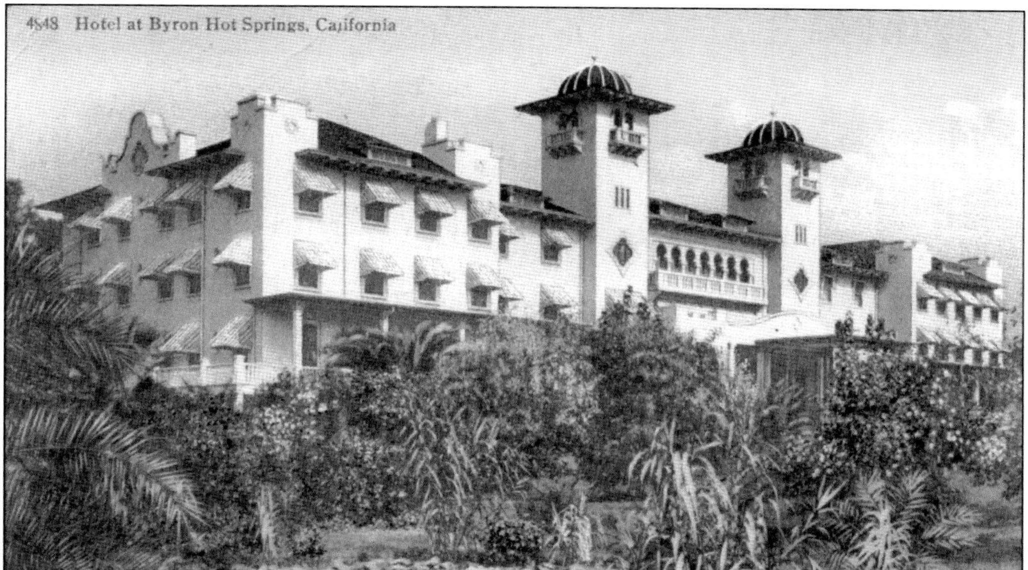

Byron Hot Springs provided height of pleasure and enjoyment since it opened in 1868. Its hotel, mineral waters, mud baths, gardens, cuisine, and hospitality drew visitors from California and the West for over 70 years. It transformed east Contra Costa County from a rural area to a health and recreation destination.

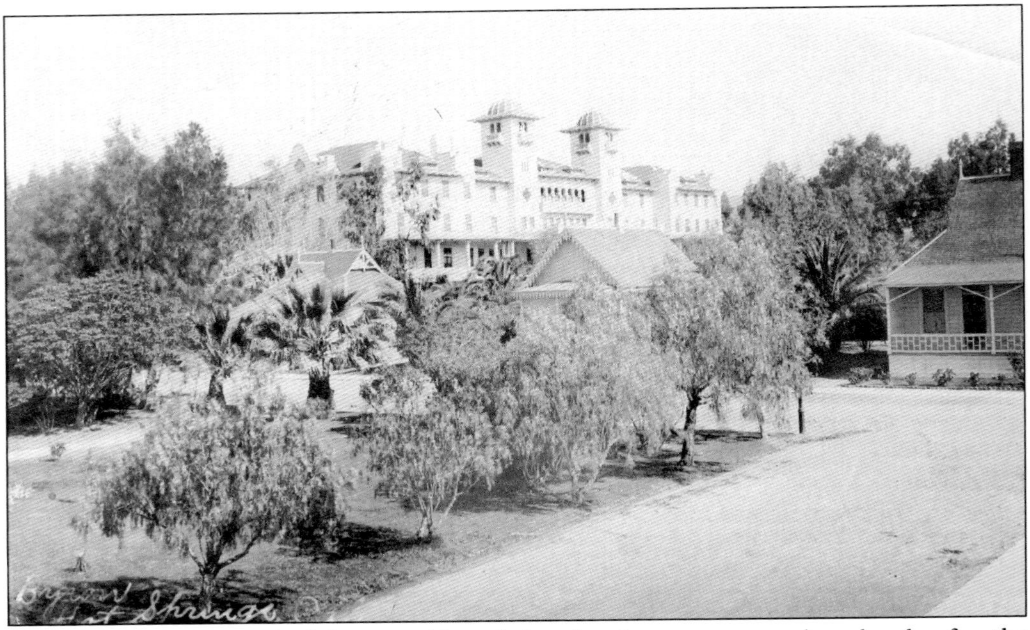

This real-photo postcard of the Moorish-style hotel and cottages was taken shortly after the hotel opened for guests in 1902. The Southern Pacific Railroad dropped guests at the hot springs depot eight times a day. A horse-drawn estate carriage, driven by Ed Crumland, met every train.

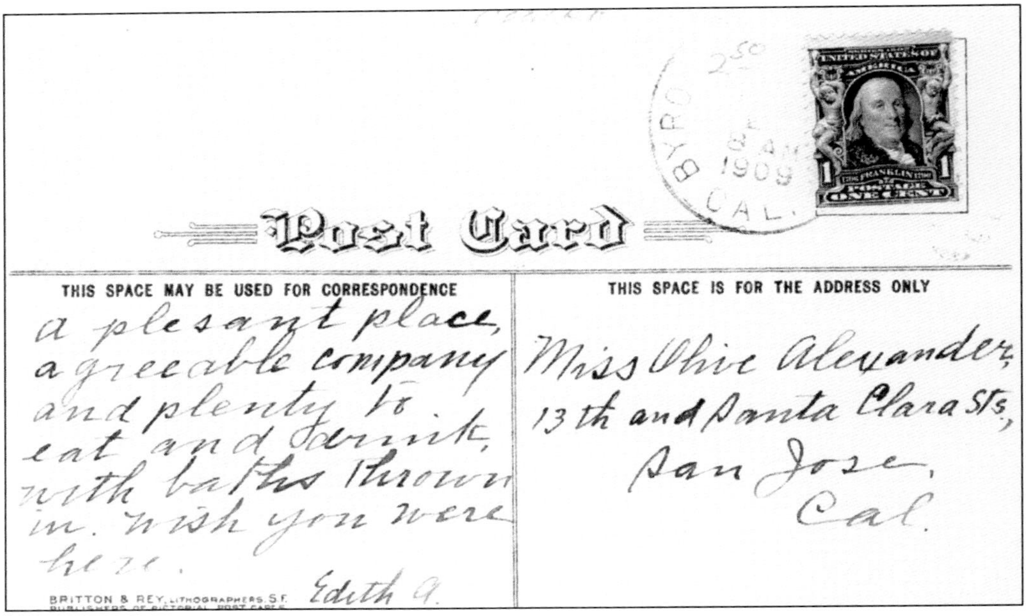

This postcard, *c.* 1909, reads, "A pleasant place, agreeable company, and plenty to eat and drink with baths thrown in. Wish you were here. Edith A." The postcard's printer, Britain and Rey Lithographers (active from 1851 to 1902), was the foremost West Coast printer of the age and was known for bird's-eye views and maps.

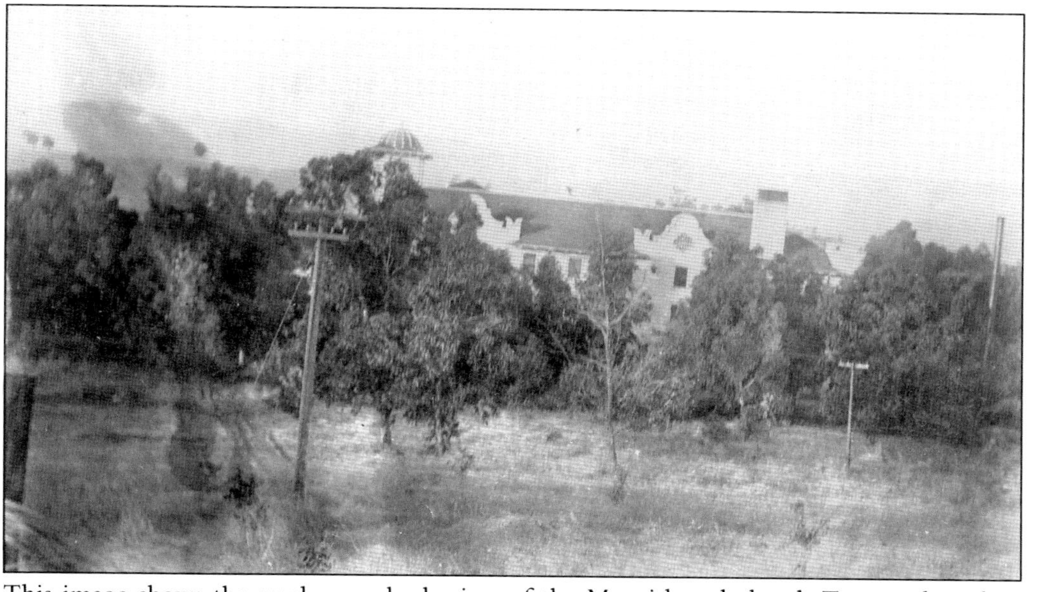

This image shows the rarely seen back view of the Moorish-style hotel. Trees and gardens surround the Byron Hot Springs. Outside of the man-made oasis are alkali flats heavy in mineral deposits. Native plants and grasses grow in contrast to the lush gardens planted in the trucked-in peat land.

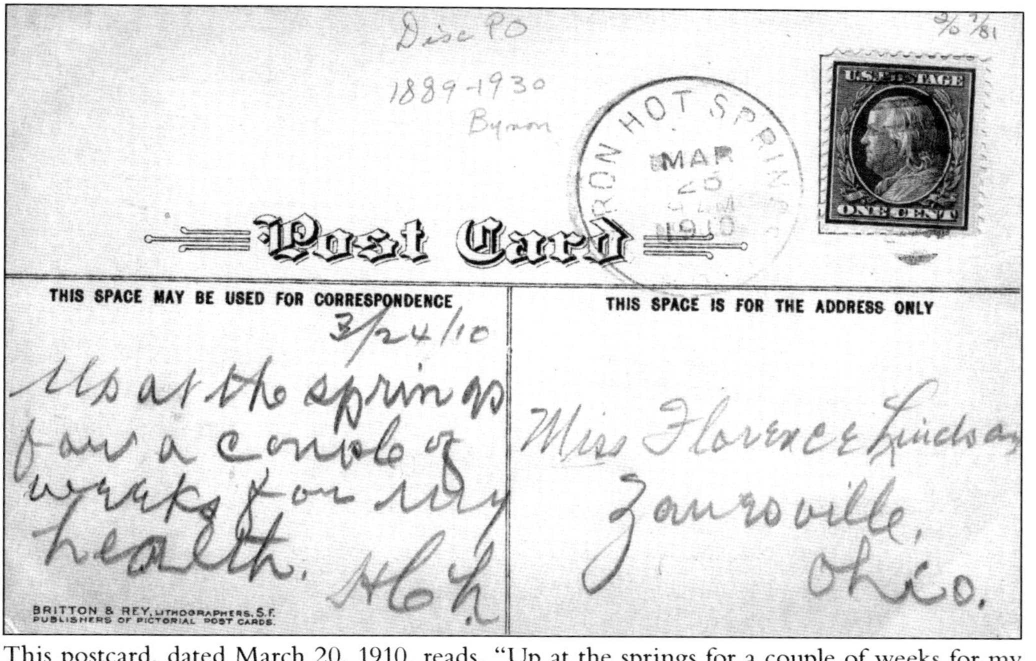

This postcard, dated March 20, 1910, reads, "Up at the springs for a couple of weeks for my health. H. C. H." One rested at Byron Hot Springs under a medical doctor's care in the years before modern life became too busy and contemporary medicine replaced sanitarium health with medication.

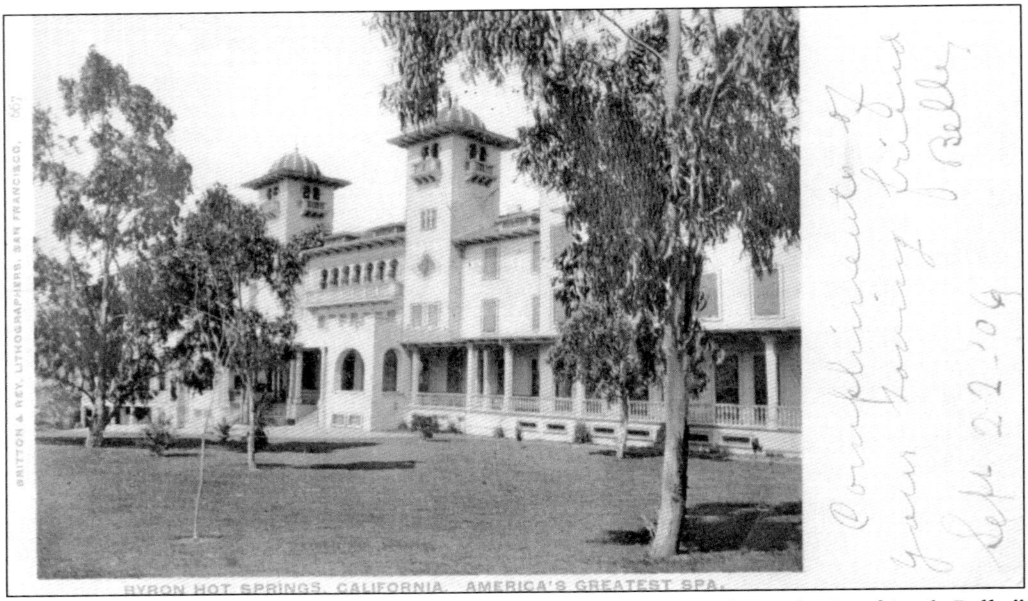

This postcard, dated September 22, 1906, reads, "Complements of your loving friend. Belle." The writer may well have needed a rest. The great San Francisco earthquake and fire was April 18 of that year. Life in San Francisco would never be the same. Byron provided a retreat.

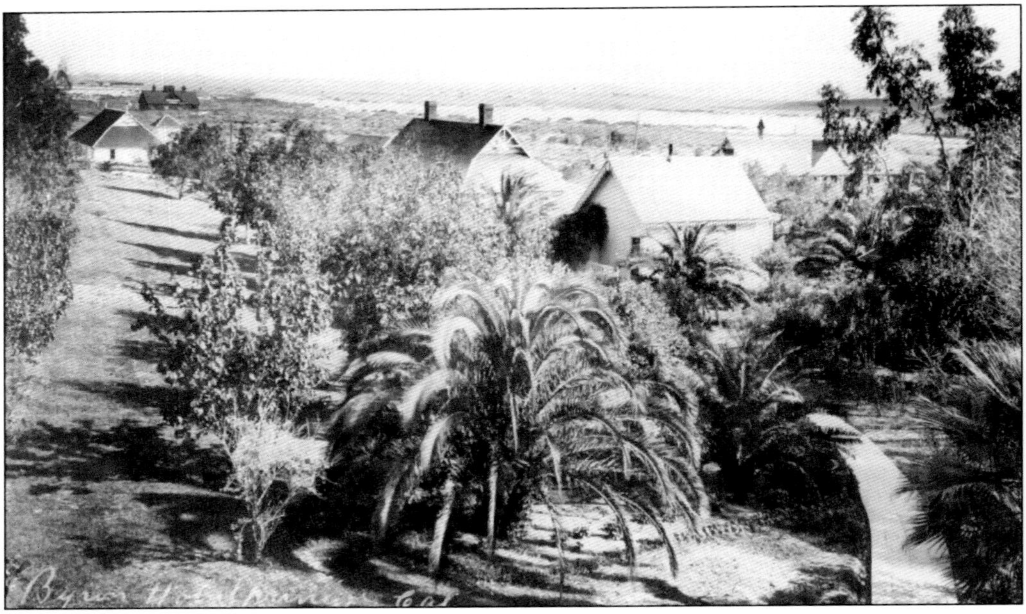

This real-photo postcard emphasizes the contrast between the hot springs' grounds and the surrounding terrain. The view of the Byron Hot Springs property is taken from the roof of the Moorish-style hotel. Alkali flats and sage are seen far to the east as the image looks toward the San Joaquin River. The salt plunge (swimming pool) is in the distance.

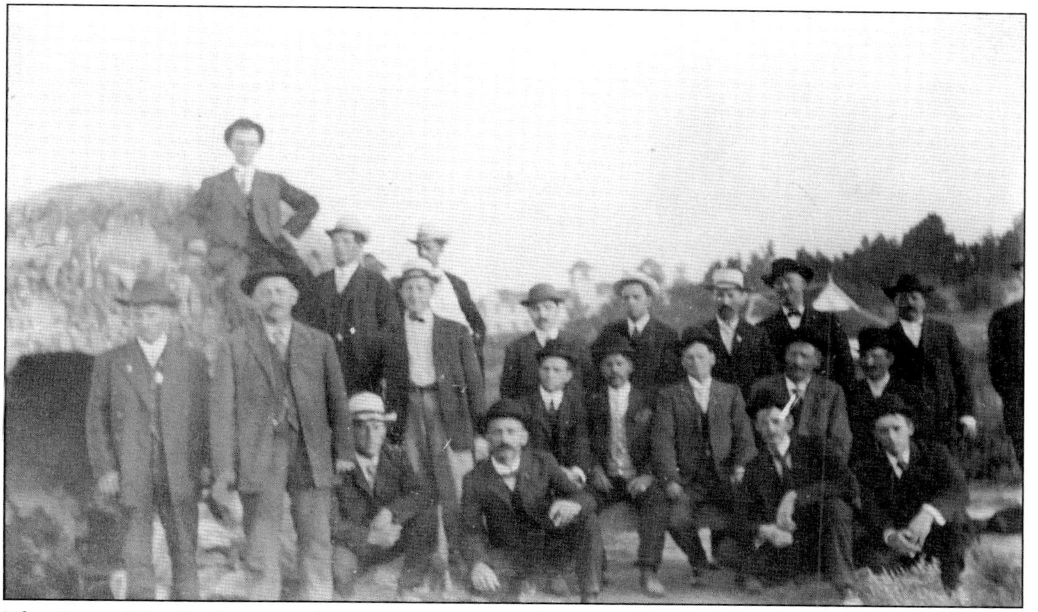

The Byron Hot Springs was in many ways a gentleman's resort, as the absence of women from this real-photo postcard suggests. The men stand next to the black sulfur springs, protected from the elements by a stone igloo. One drank the water from a communal dipper three or four times a day with a doctor's prescription. The water had a purgative effect.

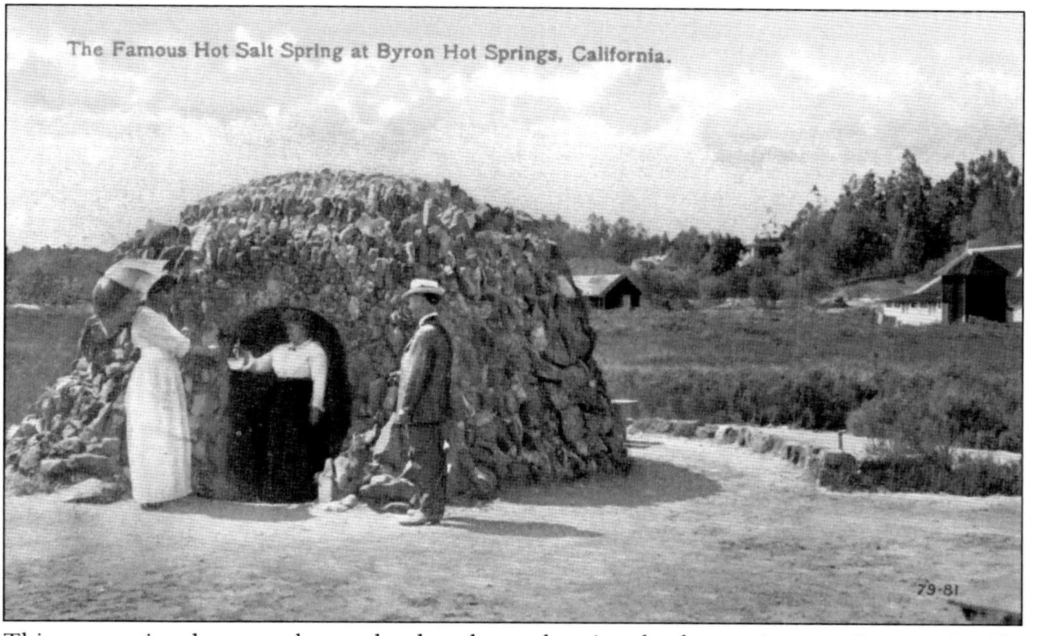

This promotional postcard was developed to advertise the hot springs to Panama-Pacific International Exhibition visitors. The man standing on the right is Dr. Lewis D. Mead, the resident physician at the hot springs. Dr. Mead was the only son of the hot springs' founder, Louis R. Mead.

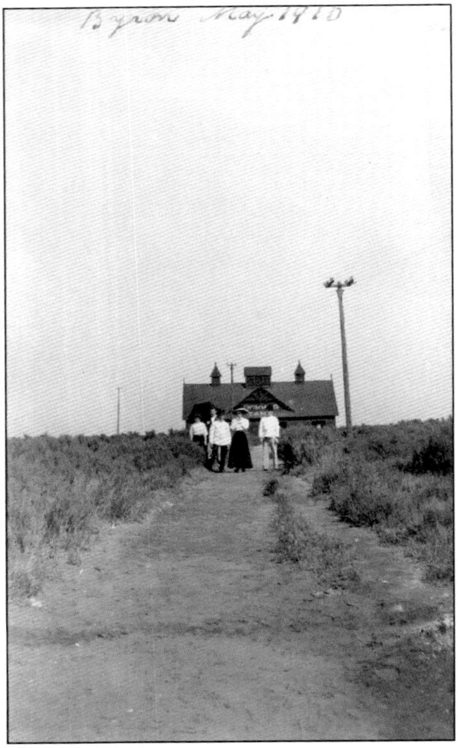

Employment outside of agriculture meant a job at the Byron Hot Springs. This 1910 real-photo postcard shows the hotel domestic staff posing in front of the swimming tank. Two men wear the white smocks denoting kitchen staff. The man in the back wears a black coat and white shirt, suggesting he is the maitre d' or a member of the waitstaff.

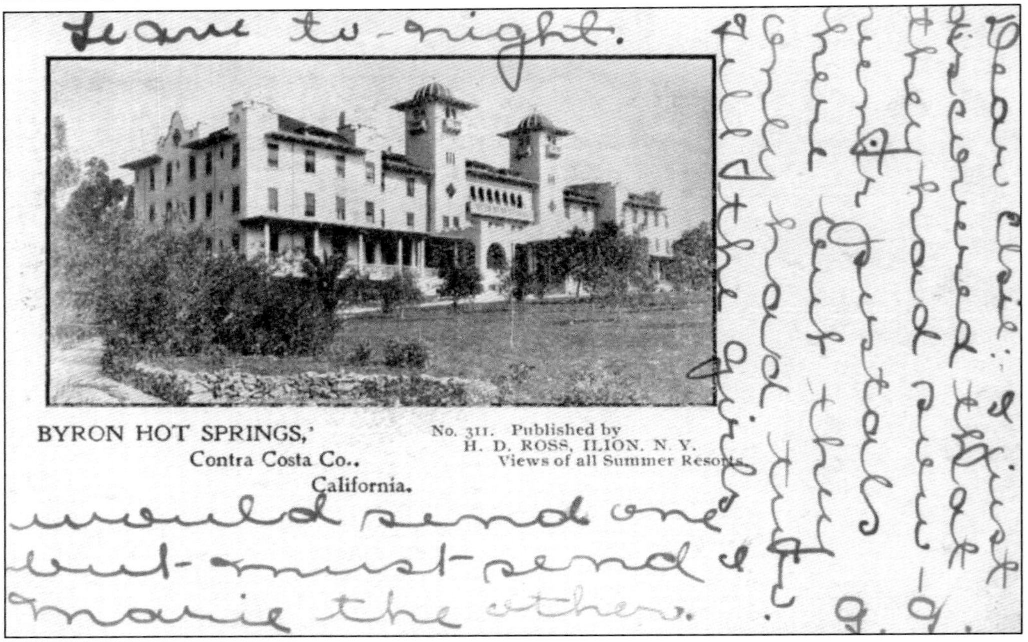

This postcard reads, "Dear Elsie. I just discovered that they had some new runir [*sic*] postals here but they only had two. Tell the girls I would send one but must send Marie the other to Leanne to night." Pictures used in vacation publications, such as *Views of All Summer Resorts*, published by H. D. Ross, provided new sources of postcard images.

Britain and Rey Lithographers once more provide one of the most romantic color images of this favorite hotel. A black-and-white reproduction does not do justice to the depth of color. Some postcards were hand colored. Note the early motorcars located at the gravel entrance area in front of the hotel.

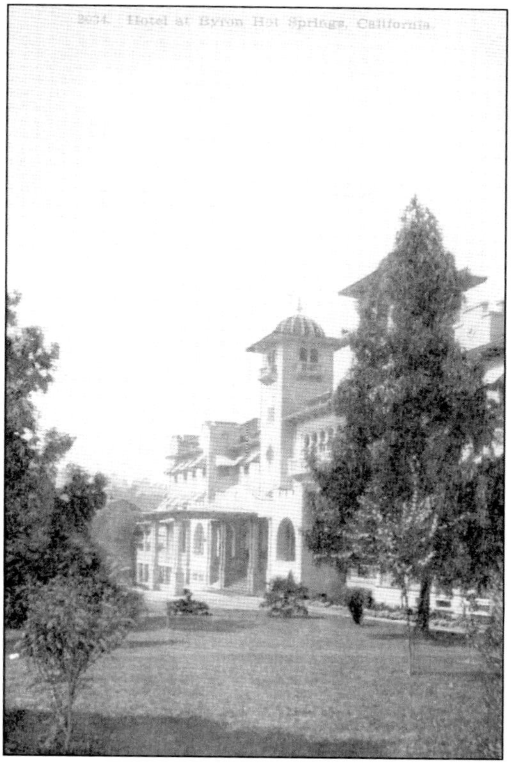

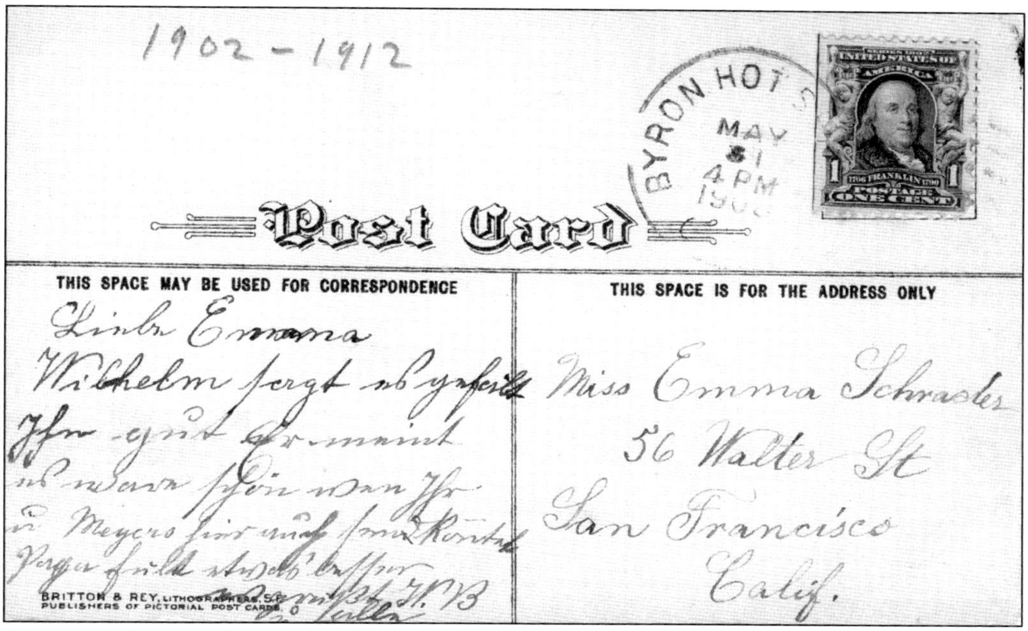

Guests of all nationalities enjoyed the Byron Hot Springs. This German American guest may have visited the European health spas popular in the late 19th century. Americans, especially San Franciscans, followed European fashion and trends fastidiously. The hot springs resort was created to parrot all things European in comfort, water treatments, and health treatments.

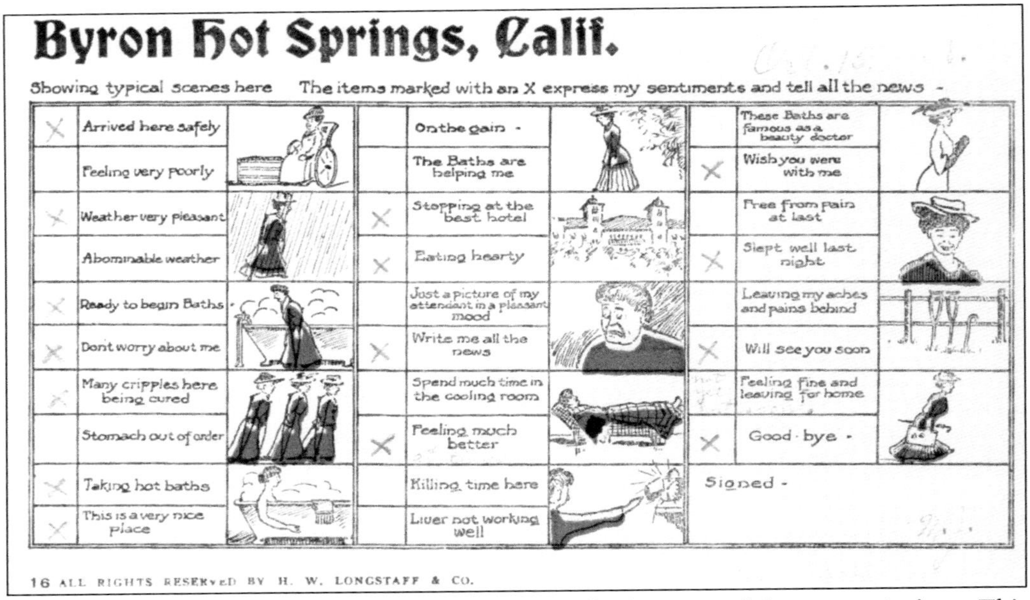

Humor postcards were popular, and printers took full advantage of the cartoonists' art. This trade postcard was printed for the national market with most of the illustrations standard. Some boxes are were left blank to allow cartoon inserts of a building or natural feature. The Moorish-style hotel is pictured in cartoon on the second line of the middle column to customize the postcard for the Byron Hot Springs.

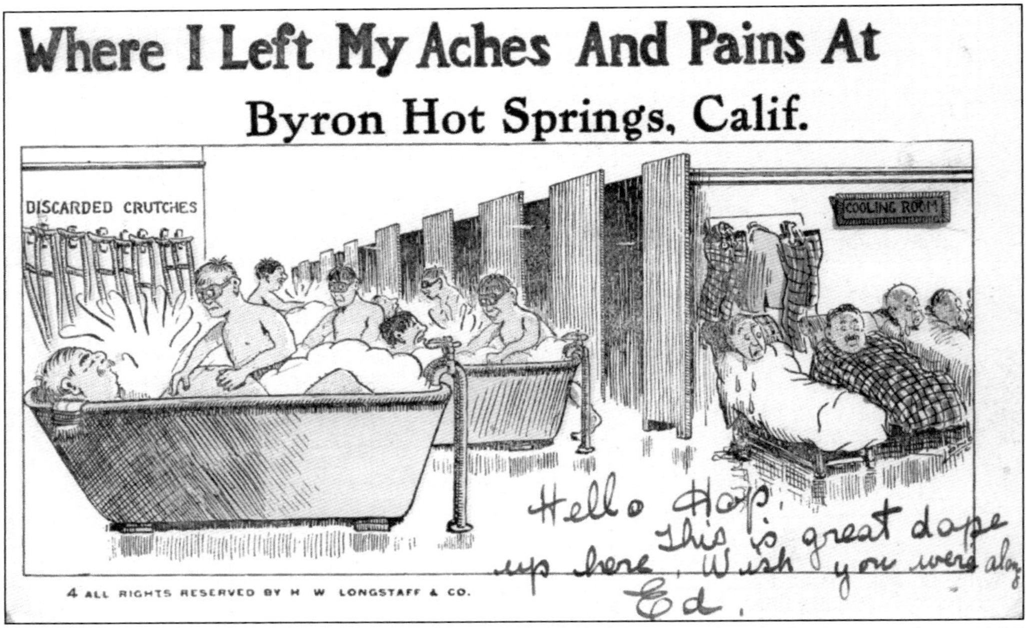

This postcard reads, "Hello Hays. This is great dope up here. Wish you had come along. Ed." Surely this card expresses a sentiment defined differently today. No doubt the "dope" referred to was liniment, hot salt, and peat mud baths that eased aches and pains away.

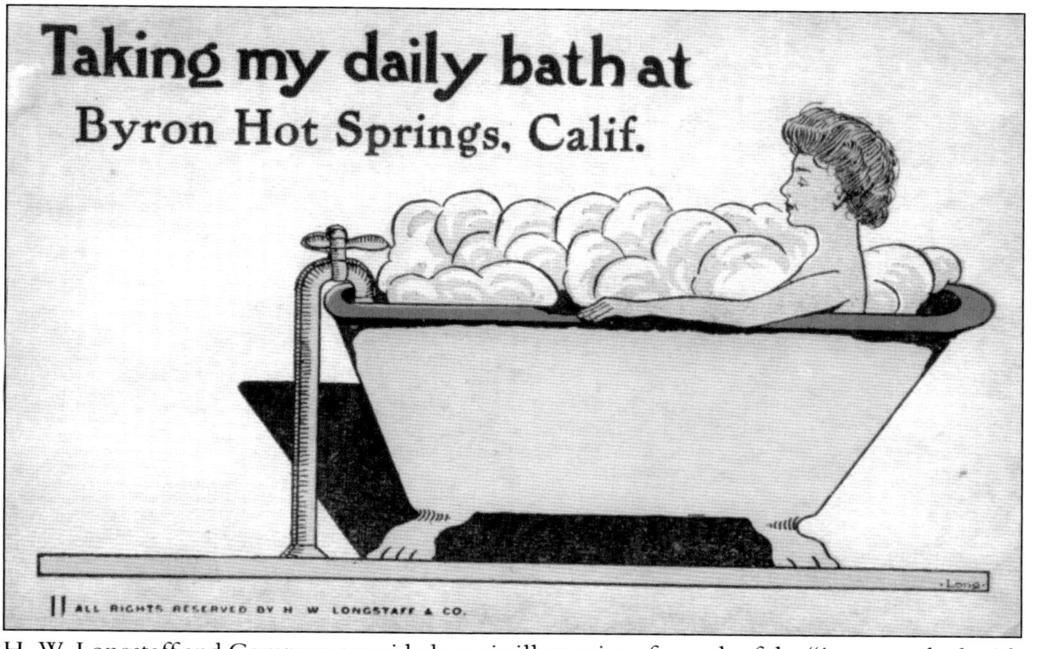

H. W. Longstaff and Company provided comic illustrations for each of the "items marked with a 'X'" card images. These standard trade cards were sold to spas and sanitariums throughout the United States. Each order was customized with the name of the resort.

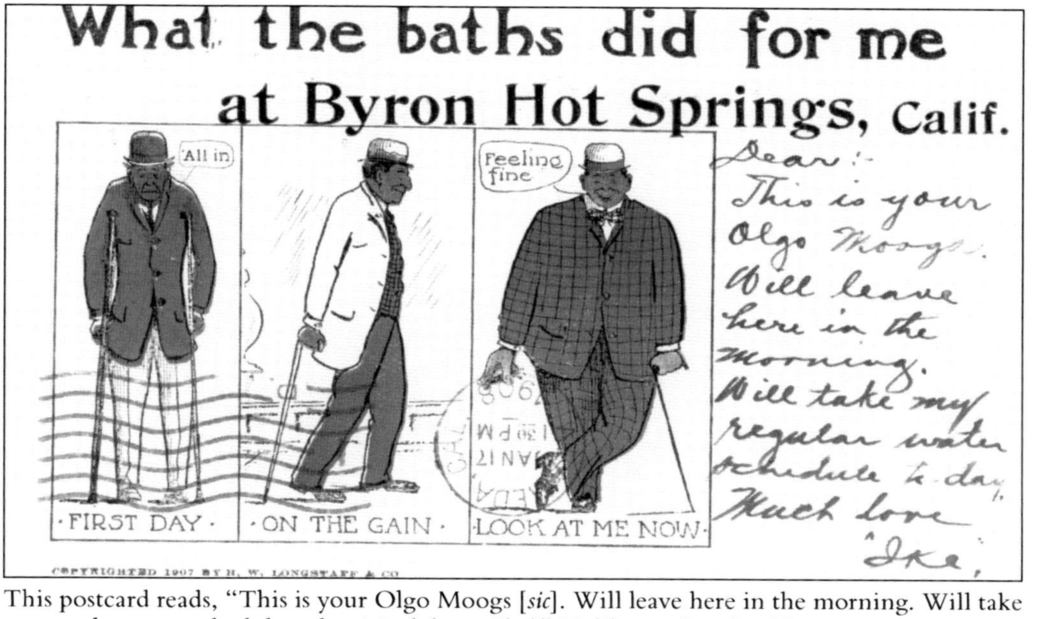

This postcard reads, "This is your Olgo Moogs [*sic*]. Will leave here in the morning. Will take my regular water schedule today. Much love. 'Ike'." Unlike modern health regimes, a corpulent physique indicated your health. Today this cartoon image would show the reverse—arrive at the spa fat and leave skinny.

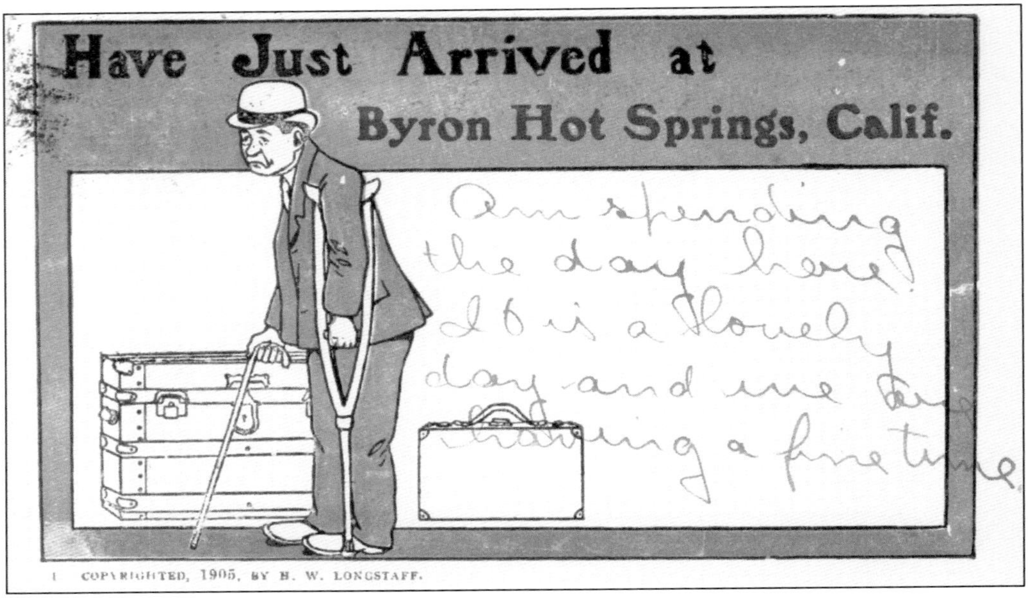

This postcard reads, "Am spending the day here. It is a lovely day here and we are having a fine time." Many invalids took the train from San Francisco to the "Home of Health" for the day. An early train arrived in Byron no later than 9:30 a.m., and after dinner at the hotel, the departure train would arrive once more at the Ferry Building by 9:30 p.m.

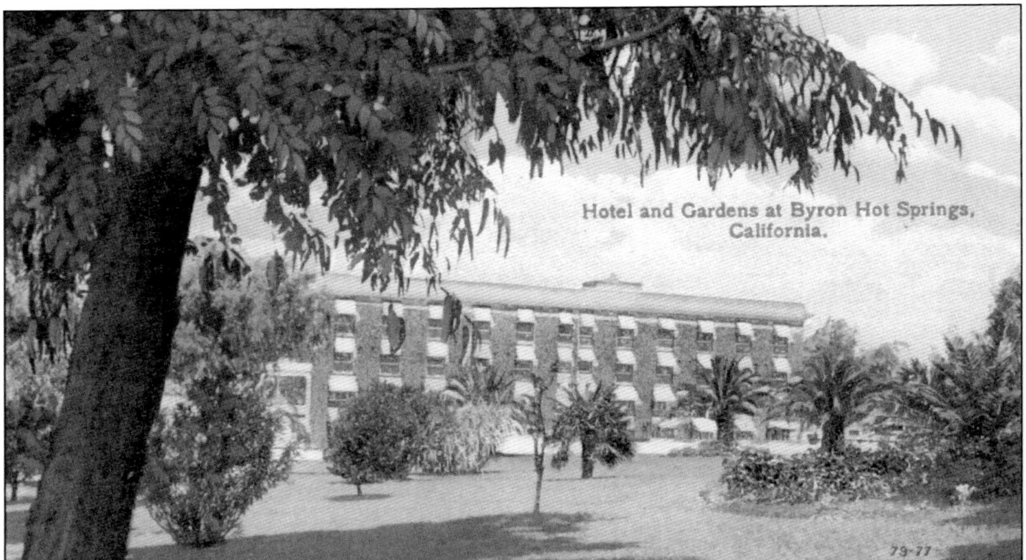

The third hotel on the Byron Hot Springs property opened in 1914 in time to serve an international clientele. Mrs. Lewis R. (Mae Sadler) Mead represented Contra Costa County on the Panama-Pacific International Exhibition Women's Board and served as its youngest hostess.

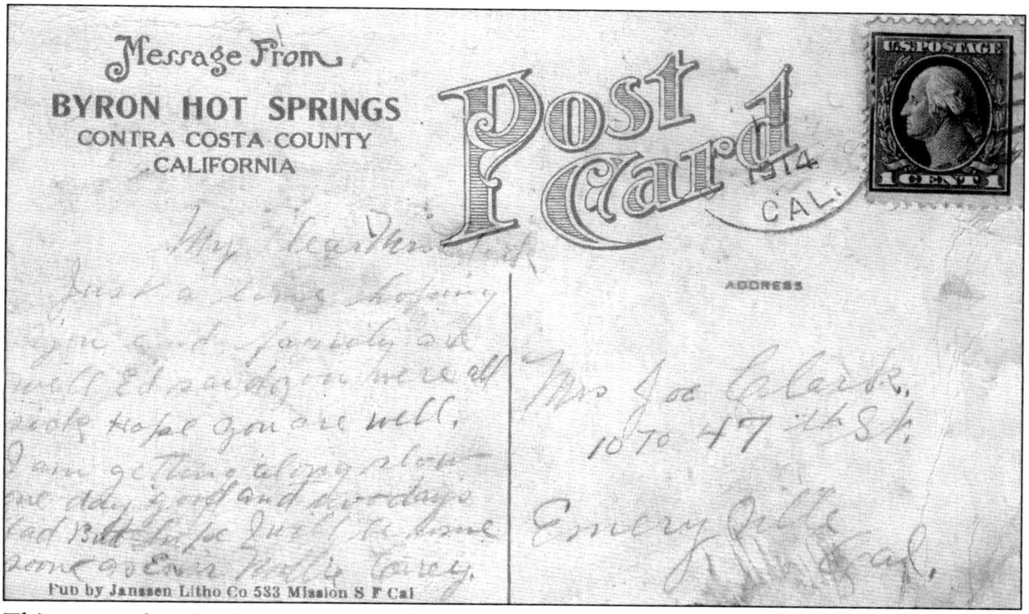

This postcard reads, "My dear Mrs. Clark. Just a line hoping you and family are well. Ed said you were all sick. Hope you are well. I am getting along slow one day good and two days bad. But hope I will be home soon as ever. Mollie Carey."

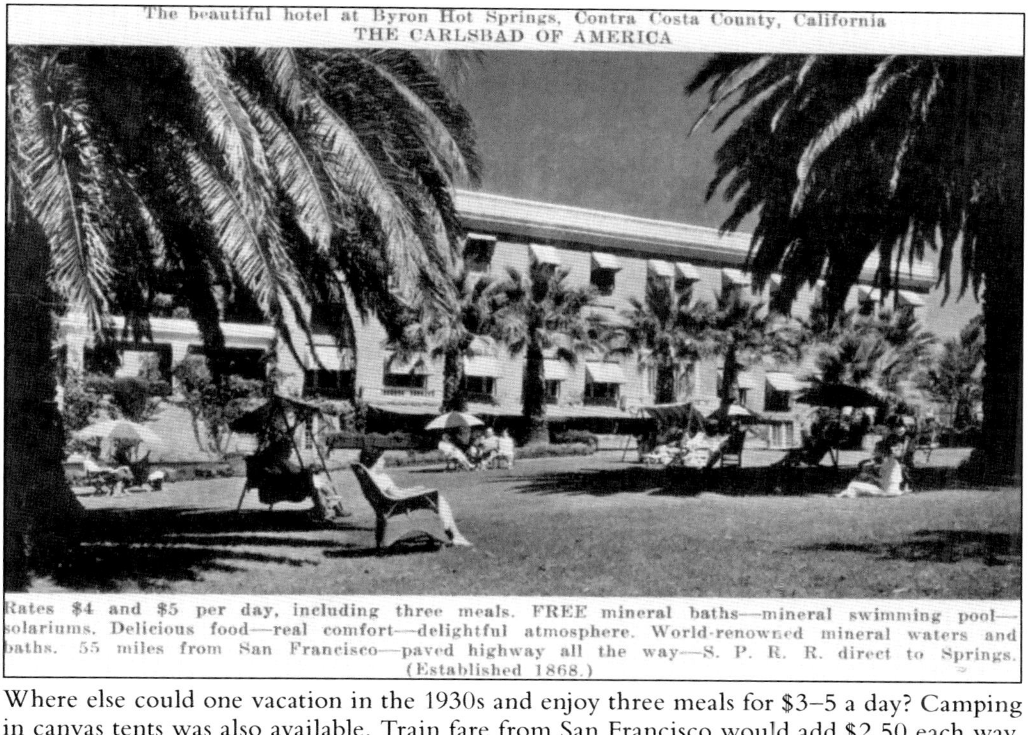

Where else could one vacation in the 1930s and enjoy three meals for $3–5 a day? Camping in canvas tents was also available. Train fare from San Francisco would add $2.50 each way. Travel from Los Angeles cost less than $15. In addition, the price included all the water a person could drink.

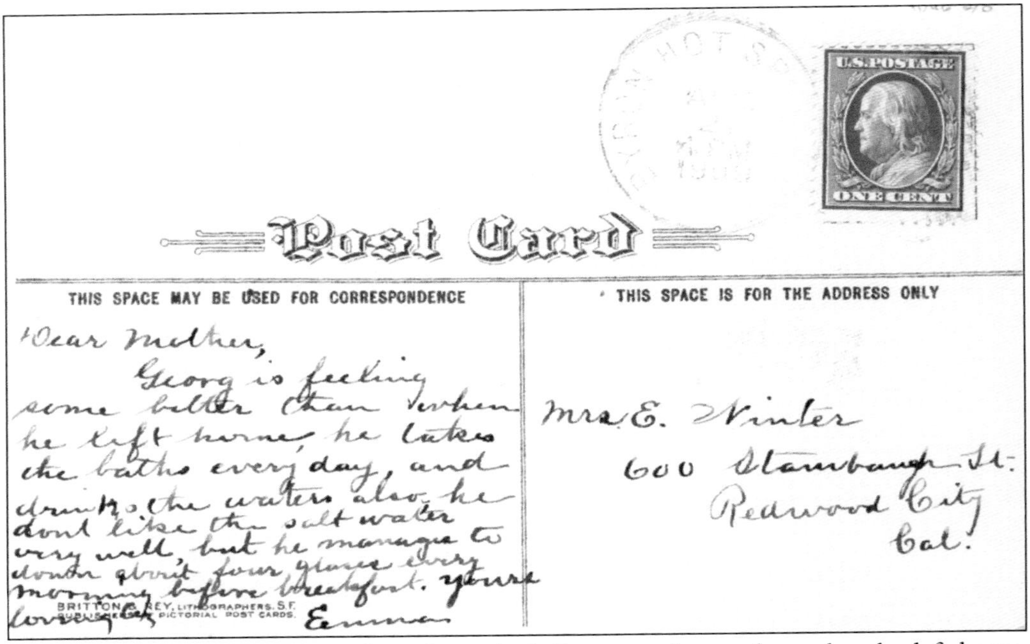
Post Card

THIS SPACE MAY BE USED FOR CORRESPONDENCE

Dear Mother,
Georg is feeling some better than when he left home, he takes the baths every day, and drinks the waters also. he dont like the salt water very well, but he manages to down about four glasses every morning before breakfast. yours lovingly
Emma

BRITTON & REY, LITHOGRAPHERS. S.F. PUBLISHERS OF PICTORIAL POST CARDS.

THIS SPACE IS FOR THE ADDRESS ONLY

Mrs. E. Winter
600 Stambaugh St.
Redwood City
Cal.

This postcard reads, "Dear Mother, Georg is feeling some better than when he left home, he takes the baths everyday, and drinks the waters also. He dont [*sic*] like the salt water very well, but he managers to down about four glasses every morning before breakfast. Yours lovingly. Emma."

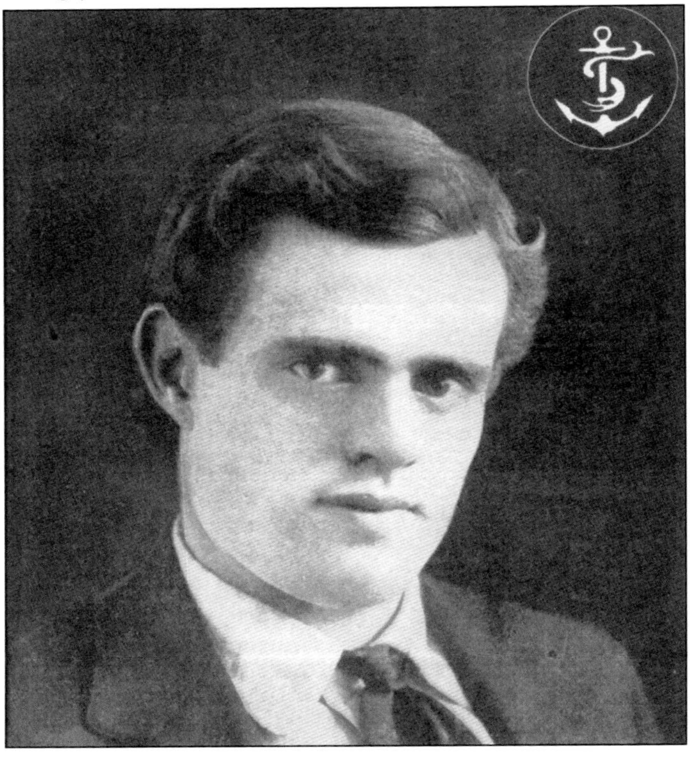

A frequent guest to the hotel bar was author Jack London. London grew up in the Amador Valley and enjoyed sailing his boat in the Sacramento and San Joaquin River Delta. He would tie up his boat at the point of Timber Landing and visit friends Captain Lent and Constable Jack Kelso of Byron.

Silent screen star Roscoe "Fatty" Arbuckle, shown here in cowboy attire, was a frequent guest at the Byron Hot Springs. His starring role in Panama-Pacific International Exhibition promotional films must have introduced him to Lewis and Mae Mead, owners of the Byron Hot Springs and prominent exhibition hosts.

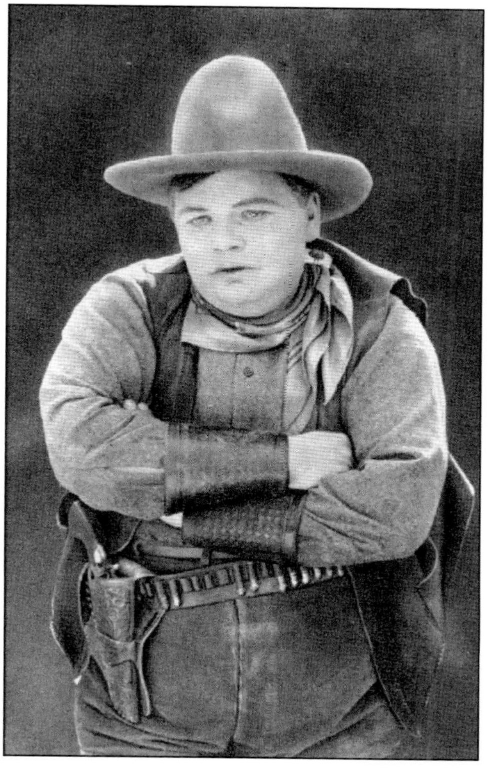

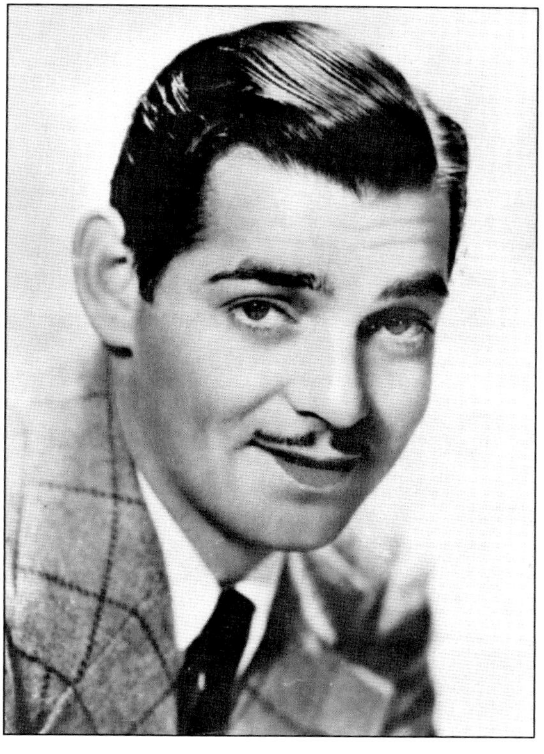

Clark Gable wooed the woman who would eventually become his wife, Kay Williams Spreckels, at the Byron Hot Springs prior to World War II. Spreckels divorced the heir to the Spreckels fortune and married Gable in 1955. Private cottages allowed for convenient assignations at a relatively remote location far away from prying eyes.

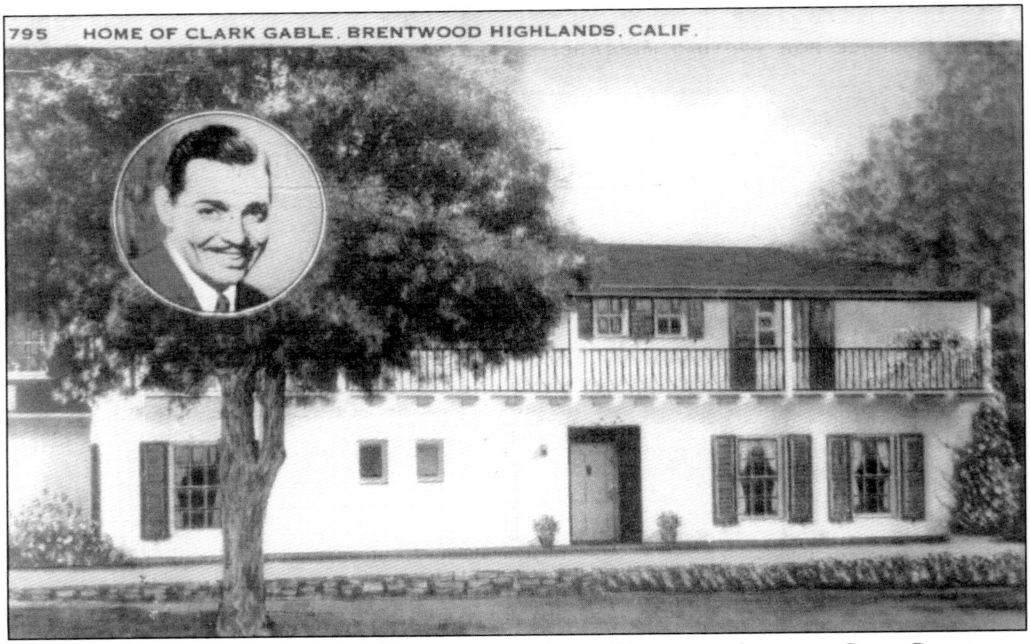

The Brentwood Heights District of West Los Angeles and Brentwood, Contra Costa County are 350 miles apart. Surprisingly, people can confuse the two communities every day. Clark Gable must have enjoyed the anonymity and the double entendre inherent in visiting "Brentwood." This image shows Gable's home in Los Angeles early in his Hollywood career.

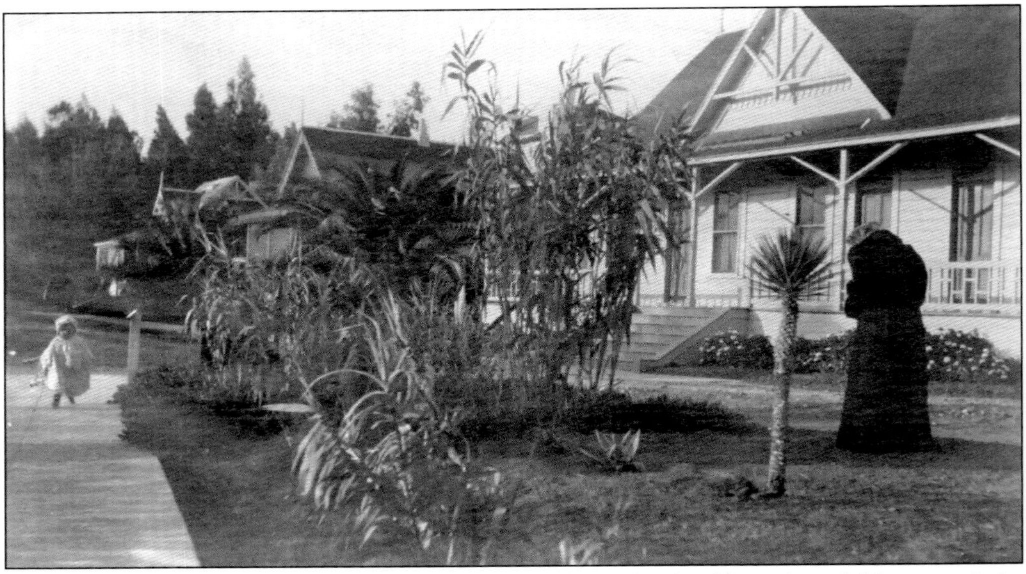

It may have been in a cottage just up the street from this building that Gable wooed the infamous Spreckels divorcée. Here a lightly clothed child plays in front of the sanitarium hospital building at the Byron Hot Springs under the watchful eye of an ailing woman warmly wrapped in a heavy coat.

Lefty O'Doul frequented the Byron Hot Springs for rest and recovery from his years as a pitcher and hitter for the San Francisco Seals and the New York Yankees. He attributed his ability to throw nine innings of baseball to the restorative properties of the Byron Hot Springs' peat mud baths.

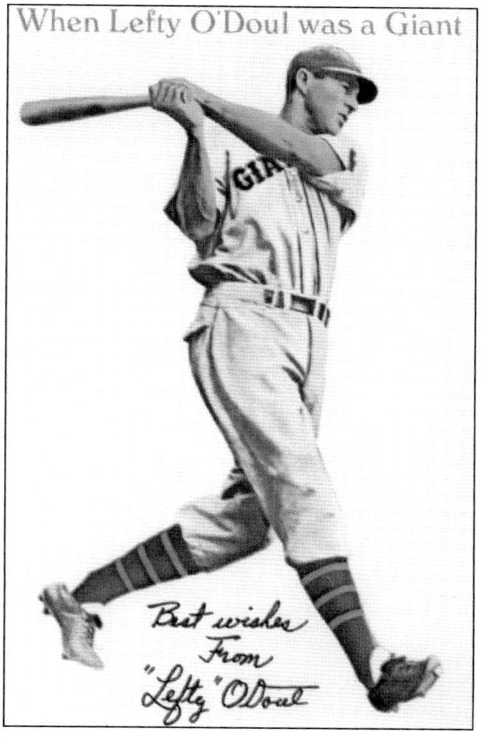

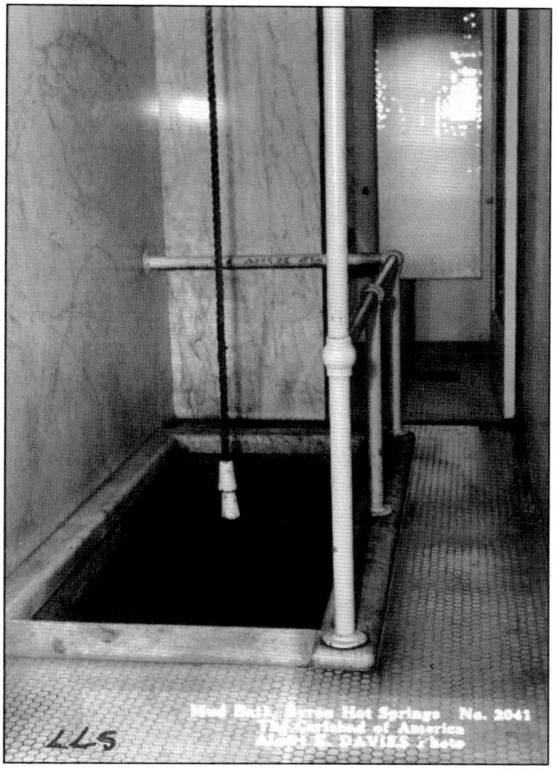

The Byron Hot Springs was the first to offer European-style mud baths in the West. Peat dirt was hauled in by wagon from the vast peat land east of the resort. Claw-footed bathtubs were filled with the peat earth, and mineral springwater was added. The mud was changed after every use. This image shows the hotel's marble-lined mud bath built in 1914.

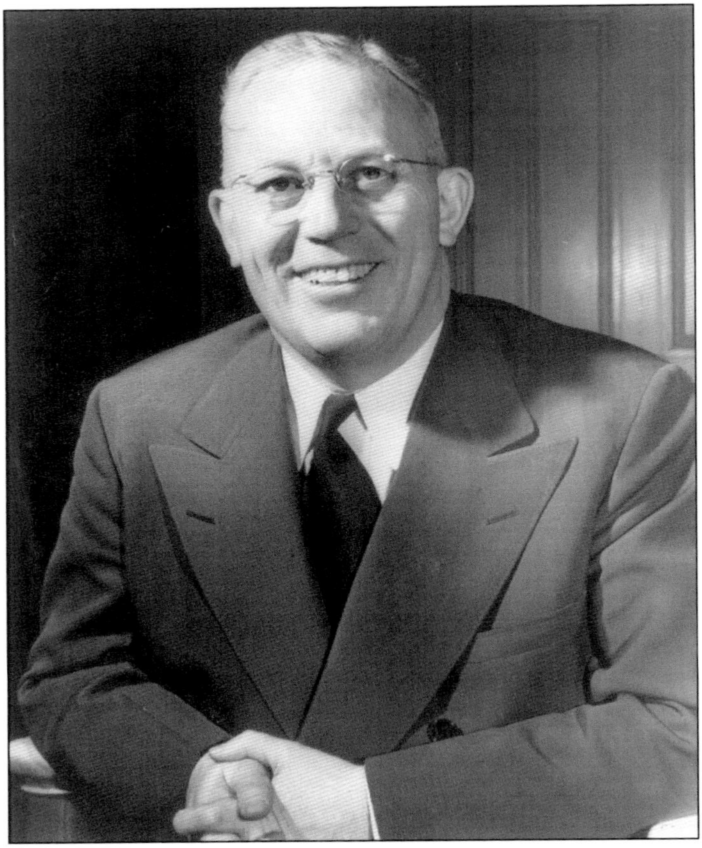

Earl Warren, chief justice of the U.S. Supreme Court, visited the Byron Hot Springs many times. He made his first visit when he was the district attorney for Alameda County.

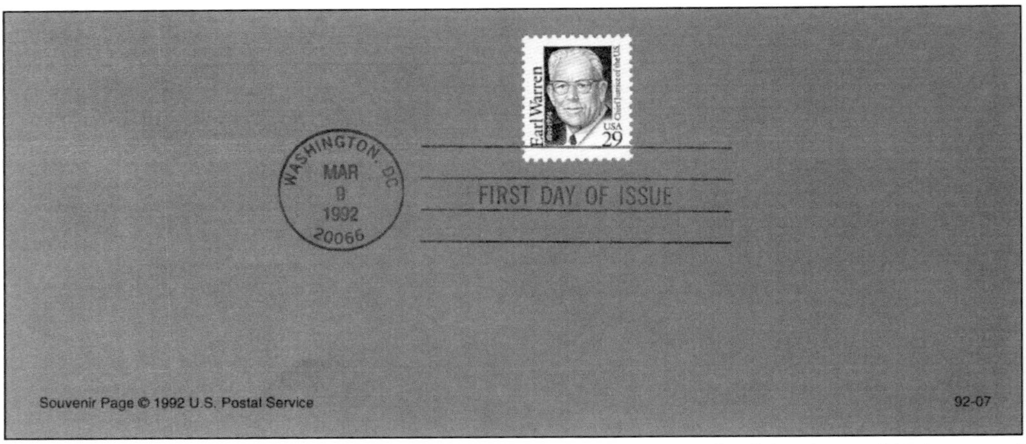

Philologists can make a stamp and first-day cover collection of celebrities, politicians, and notables who visited the Byron Hot Springs. The list of visitors included Charlie Chaplin, a silent screen star; Helen Wills Moody, an eight-time Wimbledon women's singles tennis champion and Byron resident; and Grover Cleveland, the 22nd and 24th president of the United States.

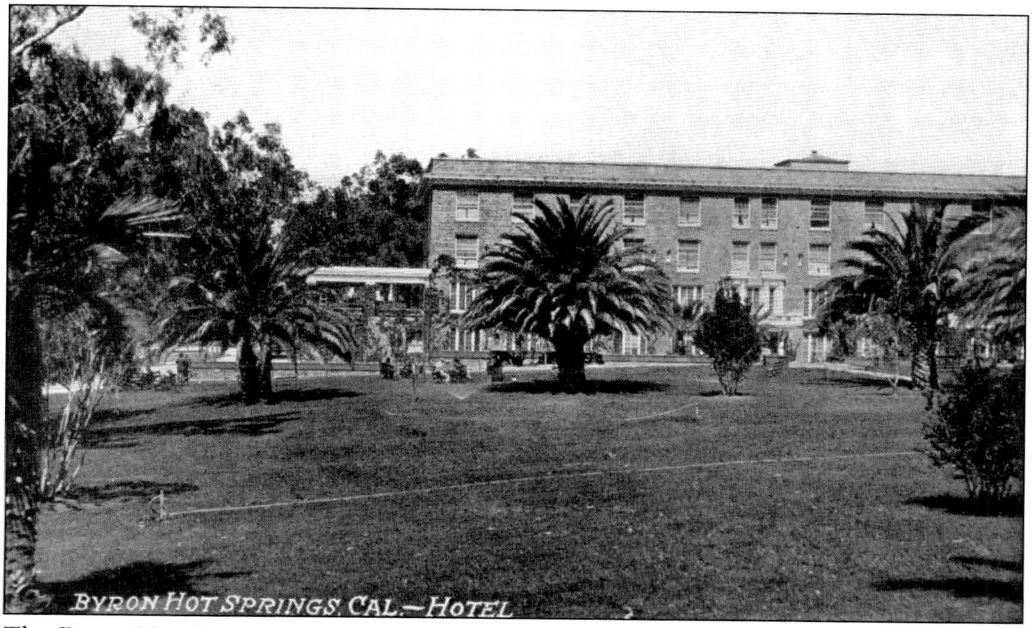

The Byron Hot Springs continued to operate through the 1930s until World War II. The Depression, declining numbers of visitors, war fears, and the declining popularity of health and wellness spas all foretold its closing. The resort became more and more a "locals" recreation.

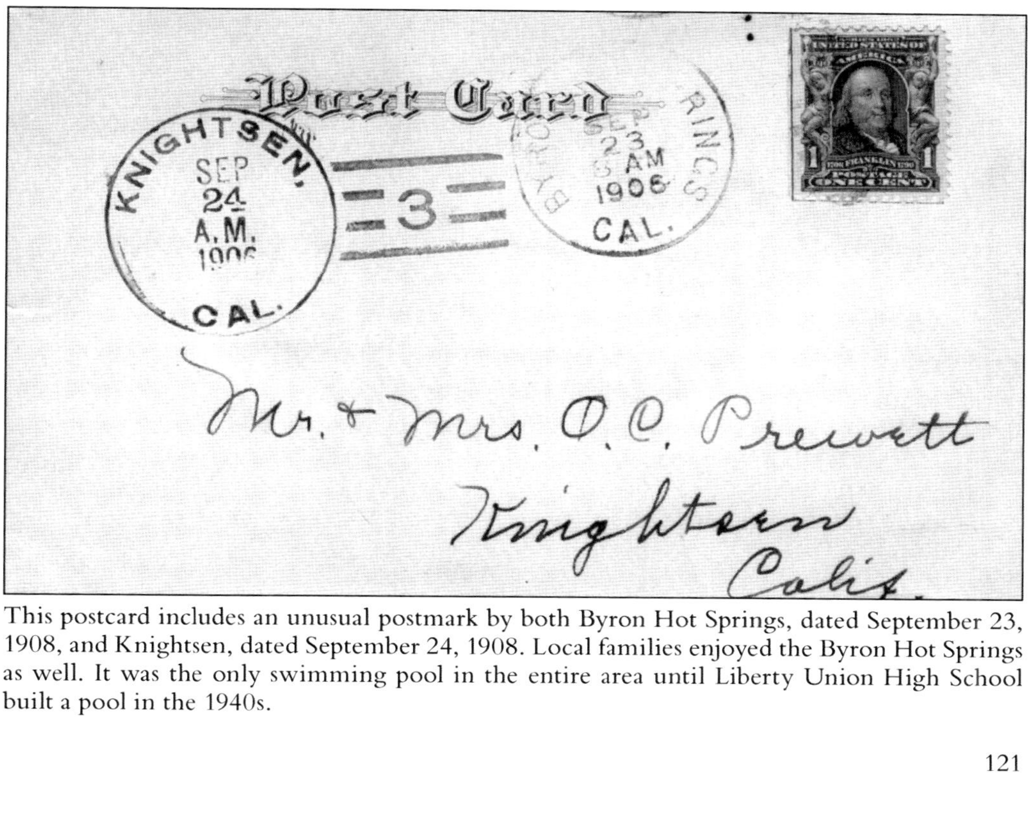

This postcard includes an unusual postmark by both Byron Hot Springs, dated September 23, 1908, and Knightsen, dated September 24, 1908. Local families enjoyed the Byron Hot Springs as well. It was the only swimming pool in the entire area until Liberty Union High School built a pool in the 1940s.

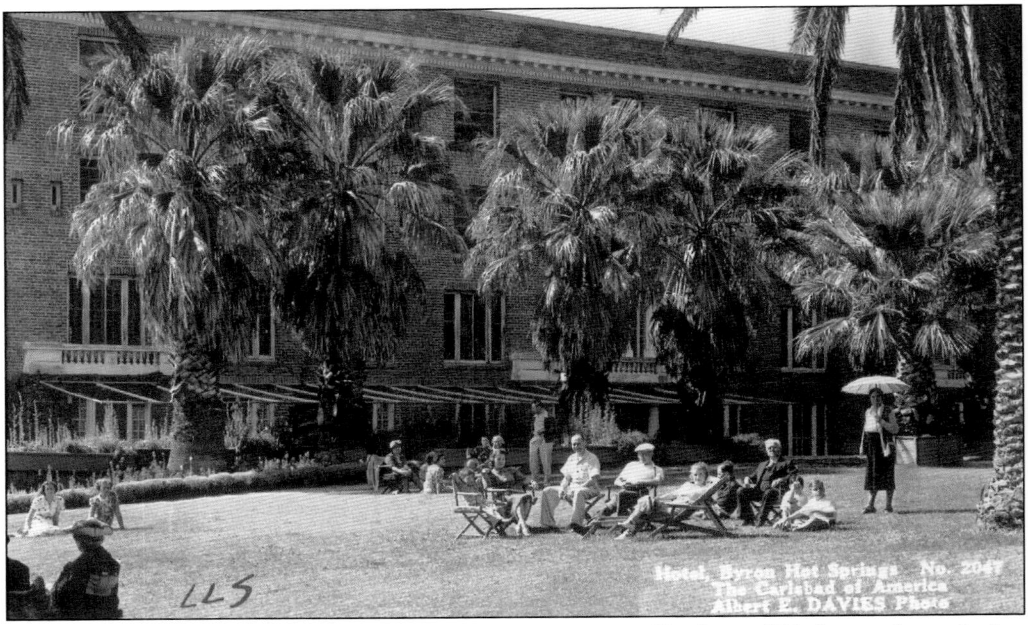

Sunbathing was a popular leisure activity. Byron can suffer from 107-degree heat during August. The hotel is not air-conditioned, but it has windows and fans. Brick and reinforced cement helps cool the rooms. Nevertheless, guests oblivious to the heat lounge on the grass, some with protective parasols and others bareheaded. No one wears a swimsuit in this image from the 1930s.

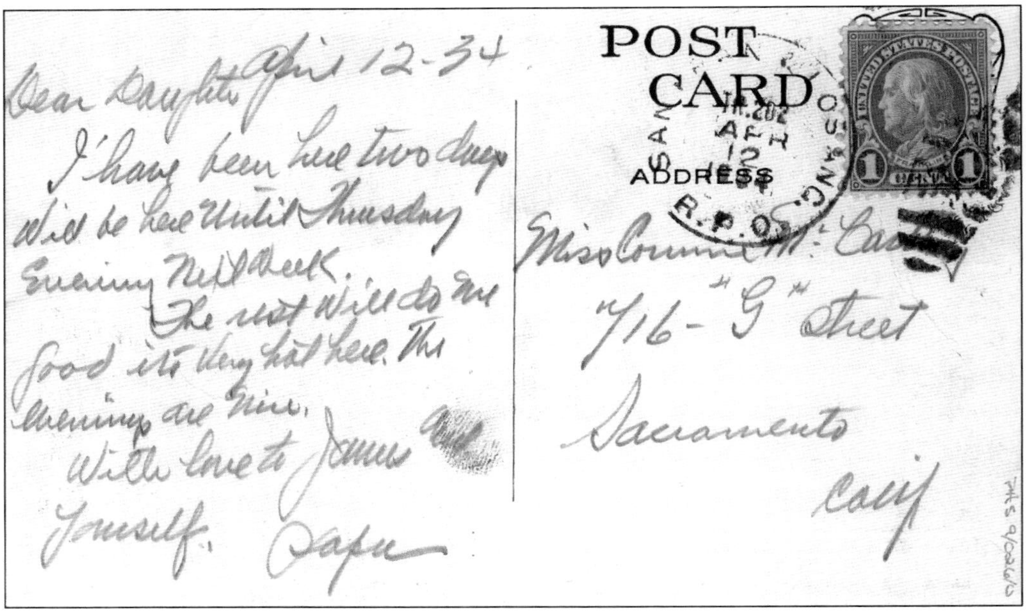

This postcard, dated April 12, 1934, reads, "Dear Daughter. I have been here two days. Will be here until Thursday evening next week. The rest will do me good. Its very hot here. The evenings are nice. With love to James and yourself. Papa."

As recently as mid 1960, local postcards featured the Byron Hot Springs Hotel. The property had been essentially closed to the public for over 40 years, yet its memory holds such a grip on the community that its halcyon days are reminisced in postcards. The family crest of the British poet Lord Byron and motto for the resort, "Crede Byron," hangs above the foyer entrance.

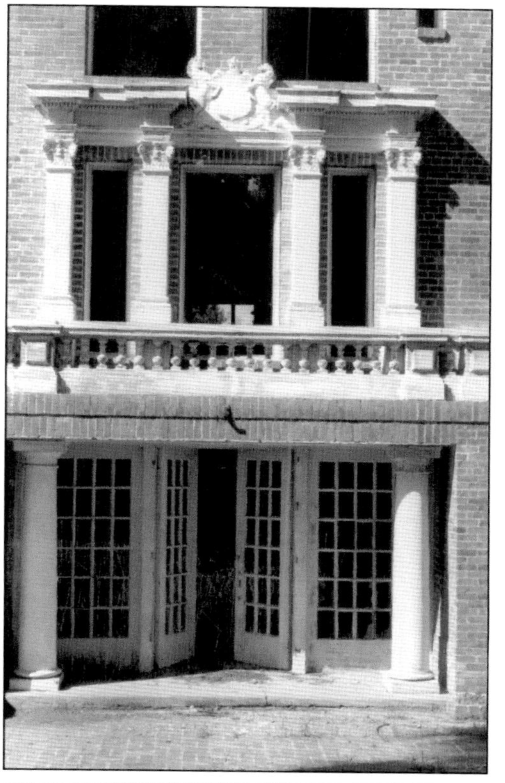

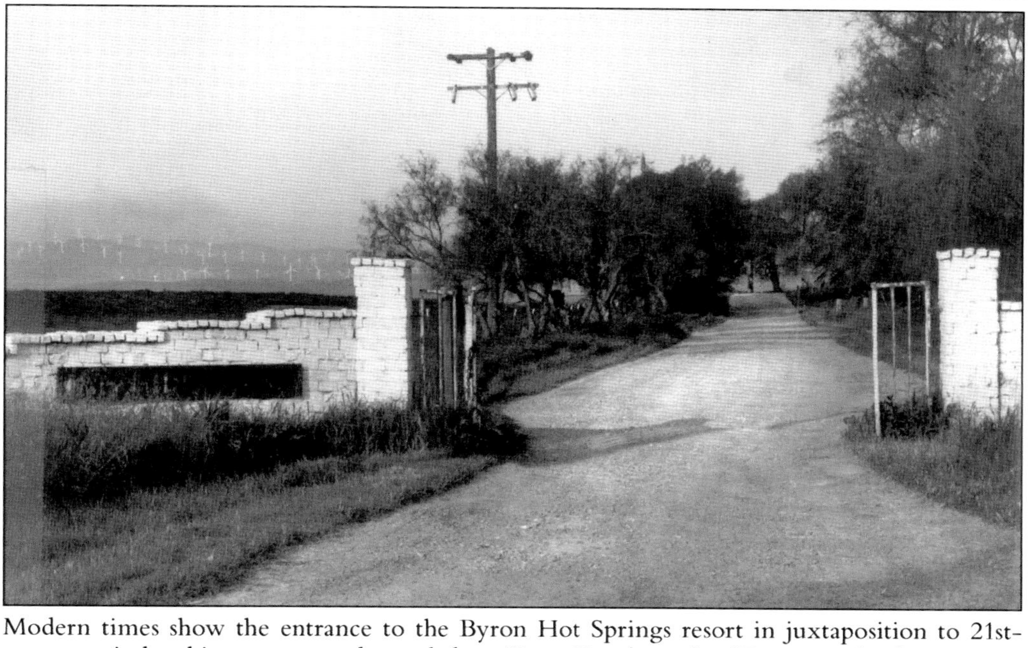

Modern times show the entrance to the Byron Hot Springs resort in juxtaposition to 21st-century wind turbine generators located along Vasco Road, south of Brentwood. The property gates are now closed, as plans are once more underway to rebuild and reopen the property to the public.

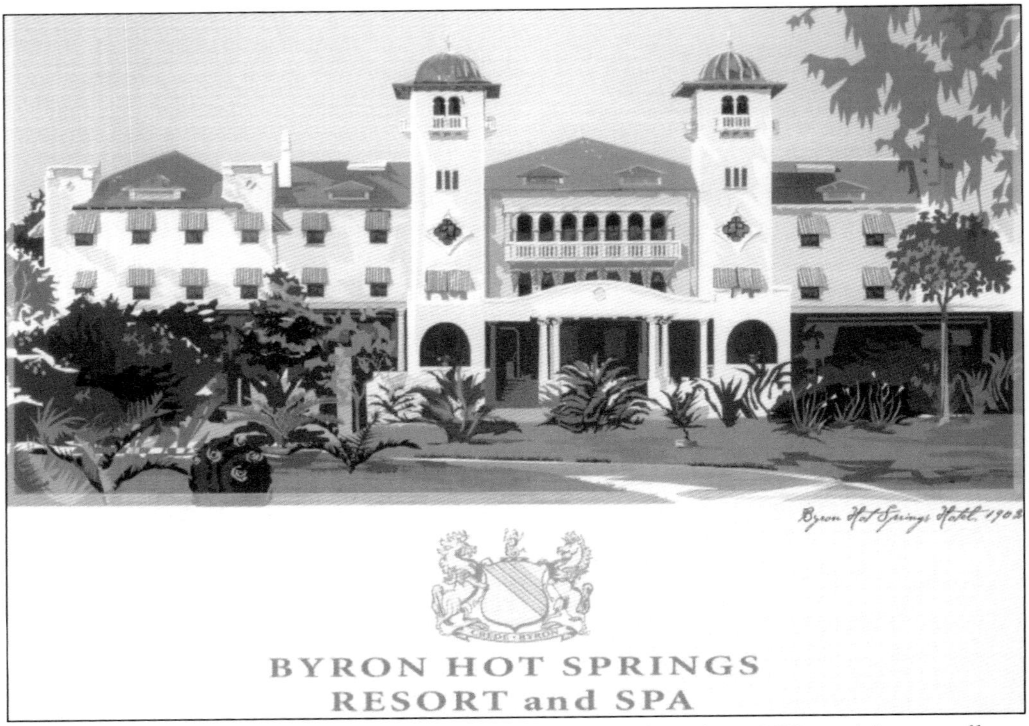

The current owners of the Byron Hot Springs, East Bay Associates LLP, envision a wellness conference center and new hotel on the property. The favorite Moorish-style hotel provides the inspiration for a new building located on the original site using all new materials. This card is part of the marketing materials for the proposed resort and spa.

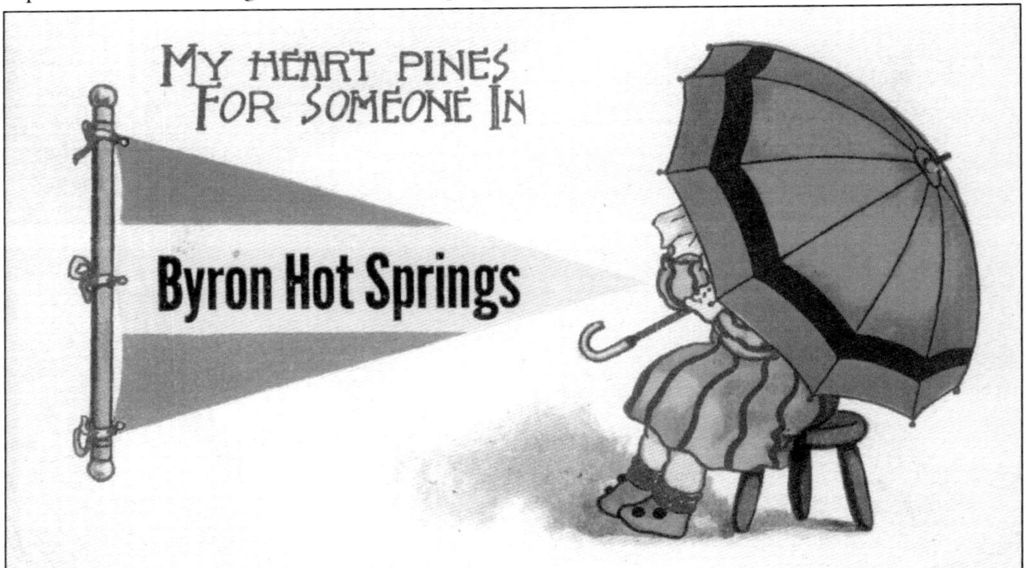

A child hides beneath an umbrella and dabs her nose with a handkerchief in this trade stock card. Nationwide distributors provided preprinted sentiments for local customizing. This pining child wishes for the restoration and reopening of the Byron Hot Springs.

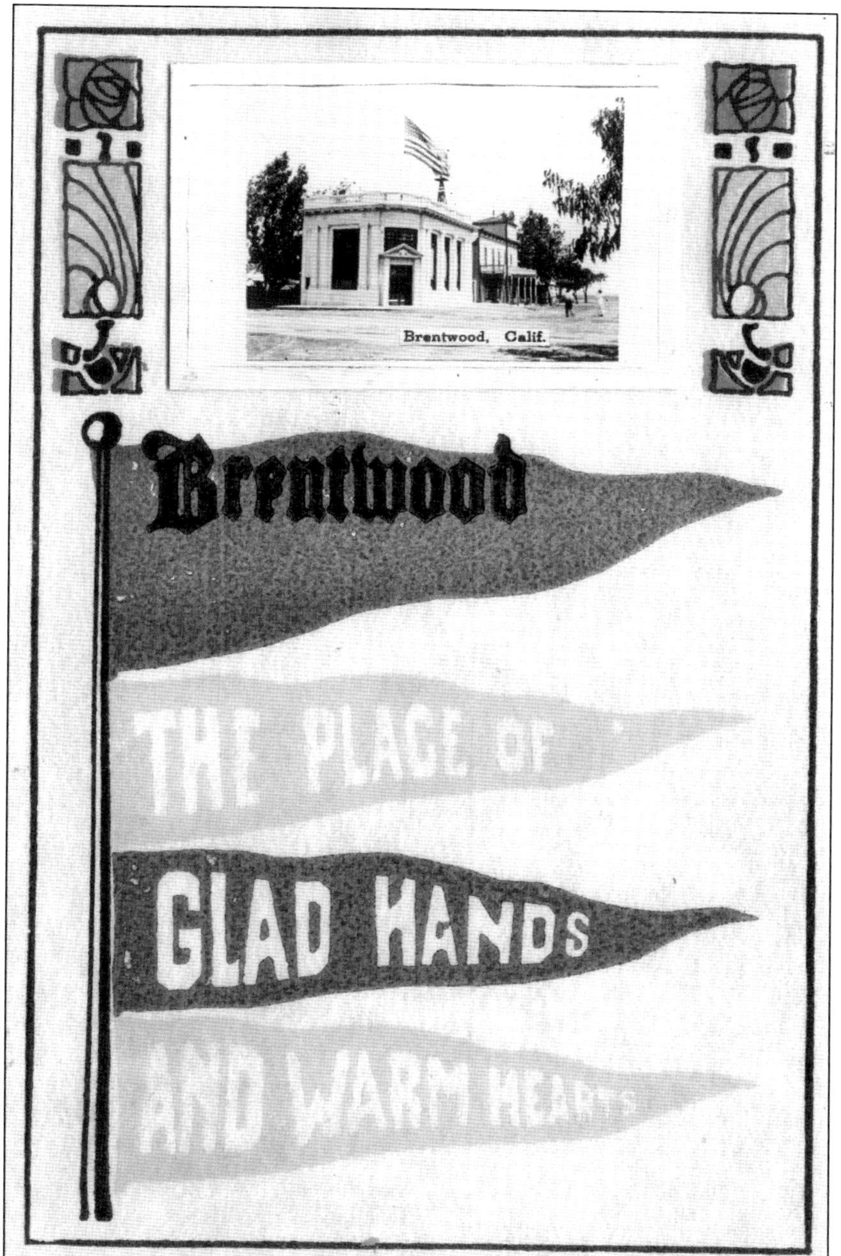

This postcard is silkscreen printed for the general trade with "Brentwood" offset printed later. It incorporates Craftsman design elements to the right and left of the image. Similar cards with this motto were produced during 1915 as Bay Area communities attempted to capitalize on the Panama-Pacific International Exposition taking place in San Francisco. Many were printed with "P.P.I.E.—1915" on the reverse. This card features a picture of the Bank of America, Brentwood, and is unique because of a silver, contact print being separately applied to the postcard stock. Brentwood and its sister communities of Byron, Bethel Island, Discovery Bay, Knightsen, and Oakley continue today as "The Place of Glad Hands and Warm Hearts."

Selected Reading

Bogdan, Robert, and Todd Weseloh. *Real Photo Postcard Guide: The People's Photography*. New York: University of Syracuse Press, 2006.

DeMartini, Carolyn. *The Brentwood Hospital: A Rural California Hospital and its Environs 1929–1931*. Concord, CA: Concord Graphics Arts, 1999.

Emerson, Katy. *Iron House School*. Lodi, CA: Abrahamson Printing, 1984.

Gromm, Robert D. *Historically Speaking on the Bethel Island Area: Stories and Pictures of Years Gone By*. Brentwood, CA: Black Diamond Print and Copy, 2005.

Hohlmayer, Earl. *Looking Back II: Tales of Old East Contra Costa County: An Illustrated History*. Antioch, CA: E & N Hohlmayer, 1996.

Jensen, Carol A., and the East Contra Costa Historical Society. *Byron Hot Springs*. Charleston, SC: Arcadia Publishing, 2006.

Leighton, Kathy. *Footprints in the Sand*. Ann Arbor, MI: Sheridan Books, Inc., 2001.

Leighton, Kathy, and Carol A. Jensen. *Betcha Didn't Know: Little Known Facts of East Contra Costa County*. San Francisco: Nomad Printing, 2004.

Slocum, W. A. *History of Contra Costa County California*. Martinez, CA: Contra Costa County Historical Society, 2000.

Tatam, Robert Daras. *Old Times in Contra Costa*. Pittsburg, CA: Highland Publishers, 1993.

www.byronhotsprings.com (Byron Hot Springs)

www.cocohistory.com (Contra Costa County Historical Society)

www.johnmarshhouse.com (John Marsh Historic Trust)

www.postcardcollector.com (*Postcard Collector* Magazine)

www.postcards.org (San Francisco Bay Area Postcard Club)

www.theschoolbell.com/history (East Contra Costa Historical Society, Historical Society and Museum)

INDEX TO COMMUNITIES

Bethel Island, 48, 49, 50(A), 63, 64, 71(B), 72(A), 91–95, 102(B), 103, 104
Brentwood, 9–16, 24(B), 25(A), 27, 28(A), 29(B), 30(B), 31, 33, 34, 37(B), 38–46, 47(A), 53(B), 54–58, 79(A), 81(B), 87(B), 88, 89, 125
Brentwood District of West Los Angeles, 79(B), 80, 118(A)
Byron, 28(B), 29(A), 32, 35, 36, 47(B), 59, 60(A), 75, 76, 77(A), 84, 85, 86(A)
Byron Hot Springs, 48(A), 60(B), 61, 62, 77(B), 78, 82, 83, 97–101, 105–115, 116(A), 118(B), 119(B), 121–124
Celebrities, 116(B), 117, 119(A), 120
Discovery Bay, 6
Knightsen, 50(B), 51, 66, 74, 96(B)
Oakley, 24(A), 25(B), 26, 30(A), 48(B), 65, 67(B), 72(B), 73, 86(B), 87(A), 102(A)

(A): Above
(B): Below